MODERN
MAURITIUS

MODERN MAURITIUS

The Politics of Decolonization

ADELE SMITH SIMMONS

Indiana University Press
Bloomington

To my parents, who helped me
understand and value pluralism

Manufactured in the United States of America

Library of Congress Cataloging in Publication Data

Simmons, Adele.
    Modern Mauritius.

    Bibliography: p.
    Includes index.
    1. Mauritius—Politics and government—To 1968.
2. Mauritius—Politics and government—1968-
3. Mauritius—Ethnic relations.   4. Decolonization—
Mauritius. I. Title.
DT469.M47S55   969'.82   81-47015
ISBN 0-253-38658-6   AACR2
1 2 3 4 5 86 85 84 83 82

CONTENTS

FOREWORD

As TENSION has mounted in the Middle East through the Soviet Union's occupation of Afghanistan, the war between Iraq and Iran, and the threat to the world's oil supply, the Western Indian Ocean and its scattered islands—Mauritius, the Seychelles, and the Malagasy Republic—have impinged on public consciousness as never before. Mauritius, in particular, has acquired a new significance because of plans for a new international airport and improved harbor facilities, potentially useful to the West or to the East should conflict erupt between the superpowers.

Long ignored as it moved uneasily toward independence in 1968, Mauritius was chiefly known in the past for its heterogeneous immigrant population, including a Hindu Indian majority, descendants of indentured labor brought to work in the sugar plantations after slavery was abolished by Britain in 1835, and Muslim, white, Chinese, and Creole minorities, of whom the latter briefly battled first Hindus and then Muslims between 1965 and 1968. The island was also known for its soaring birthrate, which John deJorre once called "a microcosm of the twentieth century global megabirth nightmare."

While, as the body of this book makes clear, Mauritius has been relatively successful since independence in coping with its communal strains, its overdependence on sugar exports, and even its phenomenal birthrate, the country acquired a new issue just before independence that has become more tense in recent years. Up to 1966, the British had administered the 17-square-mile atoll of Diego Garcia, lying between Ceylon and Mauritius, as a dependency of the latter. In that year, however, Britain ceded the United States fifty years of base rights over Diego Garcia, and moved the island's 1,200 inhabitants to Mauritius, where they have lived in penury ever since. Although compensated by a £3 million British grant (actually paid by the United States), the Mauritian government is now pressing for repatriation of these refugees to Diego Garcia. More far-reaching is the Mauritians' claim that the base agreement is invalid because they were not told the purpose for which the island would be used. Backed by the Organization of African Unity, they go still farther to demand the removal of all foreign bases from the Indian Ocean.

Diego Garcia is now the chief American air and naval base in the Western Indian Ocean and there is no chance of withdrawal, especially under present circumstances. The impact of the issue on internal Mauritian politics, however, is conceivably serious. Prime Minister Seewoosagur Ramgoolam, who pursues a mildly pro-Western policy, is now over 80, his Labour party, itself in disrepair, holds office with a slim majority only through its coalition with the right-wing *Parti Mauricien Social Democrate* and faces elections in 1981. He is challenged by the opposition neo-Marxist party, the *Mouvement Militant Mauricien* (MMM), whose objectives bear similarities to those of the left-wing, although so far pragmatic, regime of Albert René, who seized control of the Seychelles government in a coup in 1977. The MMM, supported by the trade unions and capitalizing on unemployment among the young and the professionals, presses for socialist policies at home, closer relations with the more radical regimes of the Seychelles and the Malagasy Republic, and a break in relations with South Africa (despite the value of its tourist trade). The MMM also urges Réunion with its strong Communist party to seize independence from France, and declares that if it wins in 1981 it will take back Diego Garcia, an unlikely possibility but a useful slogan.

Constant rumors that the Soviet Union is seeking bases on outlying islands of both Mauritius and the Seychelles have not been confirmed, but as tension increases in the region, so may the competition for such facilities in the Western Indian Ocean. These islands help to span the wide area between facilities on the East African coast recently acquired by the American government in Mombasa, Kenya, and Berbera, Somalia, and Diego Garcia itself. For these reasons, as well as for their general interest, Americans, in particular, and the West, in general, need to know much more about Mauritius and the other islands of the Western Indian Ocean, their history, their needs, and the economic and political forces moving them. This study, which provides the first full-scale account of Mauritius, comes, therefore, at a crucial period when we must all stretch our knowledge and insights to encompass new areas of increasing interest and importance to ourselves.

Gwendolen M. Carter
Indiana University

PREFACE

IN THE EARLY 1960s colonial powers as well as citizens of many colonial countries were struggling with different ways of recognizing the diversity of their populations. In some cases, such as Uganda and Nigeria, much of the problem lay in designing ways of ensuring that the interests of certain tribes did not dominate and ultimately destroy the politics of the country. In others, such as Guyana, the problem was finding a balance between the conflicting interests of people of different ethnic and religious backgrounds. And in still others, these differences were exaggerated by a sense that some of the people who felt entitled to power were newcomers whose legitimate interests in the past and future of the country were in doubt. My interest in the various ways of resolving these conflicts took me to Kenya, one country where each of these conditions existed. And my work in Kenya took me one step further, to the little-known and less-studied island of Mauritius, where ethnic and religious diversity is evident from the moment one first sets foot on the island. What interested me was a combination of the island's history—the fact that conflict had been resolved with minimal violence and that no one community had any special title to claim because all were immigrants—and its future. A sharp division about whether the island would be better off as an independent nation or as a colony had developed. Watching this conflict sharpen seemed a perfect way to pursue my own interests in ethnicity. The fact that little had been written about contemporary Mauritius added special appeal. Instead of adding my own interpretation to those of many scholars, I would be the first. Moreover, the archives were in excellent shape. It took only a few hours on the island to know that many people would help me in my effort to write about the island, and that Mauritius, with its tropical climate, extraordinary beaches, volcanic mountains, and daily double rainbows, would be a good place to settle.

ACKNOWLEDGMENTS

WHILE A NUMBER of scholars have done significant work on questions of ethnicity and on questions of decolonization, Mauritius figures all too rarely in these studies. Because of its small size and remote location, this laboratory has rarely been utilized by students of politics, history, and ethnicity. The scholars engaged in research on the island are few but special. Of these Donald Chesworth was particularly helpful to me as I sorted my way through the complexities of contemporary Mauritius. Burton Benedict's anthropological study of the Indians provides an outsider with important insight into that community.

During the years in which I was actively engaged in research, many, many Mauritians, government officials, politicians, professionals, and cane workers were of invaluable assistance. Because of the controversial nature of this book, it would not be appropriate to name those Mauritians who helped me. They know who they are, and I take this opportunity to thank them for the time they spent with me, for their perspectives on events and political relationships within Mauritius, for making available to me their personal papers, and for rescuing from the cockroaches the records of the Labour party. I can only hope that these extremely valuable documents are now stored safely, so that future scholars will also have access to them. There are two Mauritians who are now dead whose contributions to this work were of special importance, Dr. J. M. Cure, founder of the Labour party, and Mr. Jules Koenig, founder of the *Parti Mauricien*. For any scholar of Mauritius, Madelaine and Hugette Li Tio Fane are the best guides to Mauritius's written resources: the Library of the Sugar

Research Institute, and the Mauritius Archives—among the best a student of colonial history could want.

Mauritian hospitality became apparent to me upon my first visit to the island. To those who helped make my many visits easier and more pleasant I add a special thanks. Not only did they tell me about their island, they introduced me to the traditions of their own ethnic and religious groups. In few other places can one travel such cultural differences in such a short space. It is an easy walk from the noise of Mah-Jongg in the Chinese section of Port Louis to the French race track. But en route one passes Hindu chipati's for sale and a mosque as well as a church which draws the Creole community. But the best understanding of the cultures came when I visited the homes of Mauritians and joined them in their customs—chatting with Hindu women in the kitchen; drinking with their husbands in the living room (what after all were men to do with a western woman?); going on stag hunts; spending days at a campement by the sea, sailing and waterskiing with the French, talking and eating with the Indians, watching Chinese children diligently complete their homework. An outsider has access to Mauritius that eludes Mauritians themselves—in my case tea in a two-room house where a family with six children struggled to make ends meet would often be followed by dinner in a fourteen-room embassy residence or a minister's home.

I was fortunate to be able to interview three Mauritian governors: Sir Hilary Blood, Sir Robert Scott, and Sir John Rennie. The colonial officer most involved with Mauritius during the struggle to find new and viable forms of government, Robert Newton, also helped me to understand the emotions of the time.

I am grateful for the lasting friendships that developed during the years I was working on this manuscript, and for the support, criticism, and counsel provided by several colleagues. George Bennett read and criticized the early chapters. Robert Rotberg and Martin Kilson helped me to place the Mauritian experience in a broader context of other plural societies and recently independent nations, and they encouraged me throughout the process of revising my initial manuscript. Finally, Gwendolen Carter conspired with my husband and several friends to remind me that it could and should be finished. The final drafts were helped by Cynthia Lang's editorial pen and made legible by Mildred Kalmus and Dorothy Anderson, who typed them.

MODERN
MAURITIUS

1. Mauritius
and Mauritians

Day dawned on January 12, 1867, bright and clear, and the sun
rose brilliantly in a cloudless sky, as we hove in sight of Mauritius.
On nearing the land, the fields of waving canes, topes of cocoas,
and groves of Casuarinas, gave a pleasing impression of the place,
but when approaching Port Louis Harbour the beauty of the view is
unsurpassed, and no easy task to describe. (Nicholas Pike, United
States Consul to Mauritius, 1867)[1]

ONLY 720 square miles—barely a pinprick on most maps—Mauritius
is 500 miles east of Madagascar in the Indian Ocean. Nicholas Pike,
making his first landfall on the island, may have found describing the
beauty of the view "no easy task," but he shared with other early
voyagers an enthusiastic first impression.[2] Given the sailing conditions of the 1800s, the sailors' delight may have been partly due to
relief at ending a long sea voyage. Yet even today Mauritius is strik-
ing, with its vast white beaches, its rugged volcanic mountains, and
its large plateau some thirteen thousand feet above sea level, which is
green between December and June while the sugarcane is growing
and ripening.

Four centuries ago the island was uninhabited. Today it is one of
the world's most densely populated countries. Nearly nine hundred
thousand people are packed together in a space smaller than the state
of Rhode Island. Port Louis, the capital (population 140,000), is not
an impressive city. Except for the seven-story Anglo-American Building, the Louis XVI Government House, and a few wooden houses,
the city is shabby, buildings and roads are in a poor state of repair,
and every block, it seems, has a quota of stray dogs. But the city is

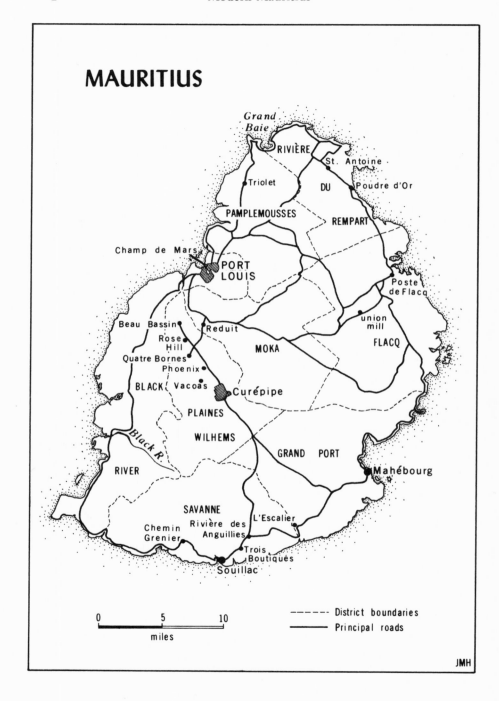

MAURITIUS

Grand Baie

RIVIÈRE

St. Antoine

Triolet

DU

Poudre d'Or

PAMPLEMOUSSES

REMPART

Champ de Mars

PORT LOUIS

Poste de Flacq

Beau Bassin

Reduit

union mill

Rose Hill

FLACQ

Quatre Bornes

MOKA

Phoenix

BLACK

Vacoas

Curépipe

PLAINES

WILHEMS

Black R.

GRAND PORT

RIVER

Mahébourg

SAVANNE

Rivière des Anguillies

L'Escalier

Chemin Grenier

Trois Boutiques

Souillac

| 0 | 5 | 10 |

miles

- - - - - District boundaries
───── Principal roads

JMH

alive: cars, carts, and people of all sizes and races push each other down the streets. Franco-Mauritians, Hindus, Muslims, Creoles, both light skinned and dark, and Chinese elbow each other as they go about the business of the day, mixing in the traffic in a way that even now they would never think of doing socially. A babble of tongues fills the air. Even the newspapers are printed half in French and half in English. Port Louis is a lively city, at least during the day. Quite suddenly, in the evening, the city closes down, and only in the Chinese section—a center for prostitution, opium, and gandhia (the local marijuana)—is there any activity after dark.

Narrow, winding roads link Port Louis with the island's other towns: Curépipe and Rose Hill, Mahébourg, and smaller villages such as Poste de Flacq, Poudre d'Or, and Souillac. Most of the villages on the plateau are Indian, with a Chinese shopkeeper or two (just as in East Africa, where the villages are African with an Indian shopkeeper running the *duca*). The Franco-Mauritians live in the towns, or on large sugar plantations, the Chinese mostly in the towns, and the Creoles in Port Louis, in towns in the center of the island—Beau Bassin, Quatre Bornes, Vacoas—or in fishing villages along the coast. People commute surprisingly long distances to work, considering that this is a small island and not a large American megalopolis. They often ride buses for nearly three-quarters of an hour to travel from home to jobs in another part of the island. The climate is warm, and usually sunny. In tropical fashion, sudden rain storms punctuate the afternoon, and clear quickly, finishing—frequently—in double rainbows.

A political history of Mauritius reveals how all these people came to the island and struggled with one another, through settlement, colonization under the British, and finally independence, to establish and maintain a place within the social, political, and economic order of the island.* The island's history is of course its own. But at the same time, a study of Mauritius has relevance beyond the island because the problems of Mauritius are similar to those of other new nations, particularly small nations with plural societies. Familiar patterns appear. Planters import slaves. Multiracial groups become more European than the Europeans they emulate. New ethnic groups arrive, seen first as even lower in the pecking order, then feared as

---

*A brief chronology is presented in Appendix A.

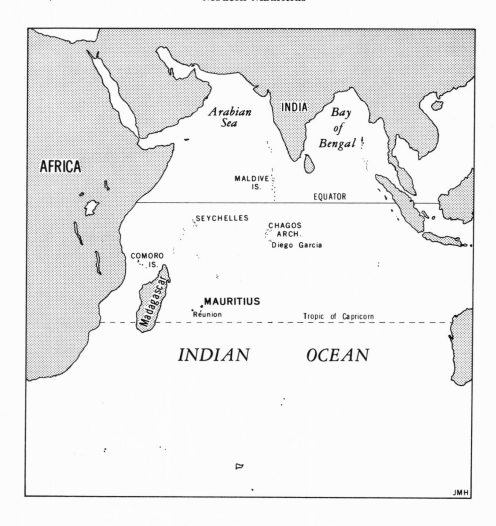

possible usurpers of land and jobs. Sons of old families stay blind to the changes around them. New groups gain strength and develop a voice, to be met with the standard arsenal of paternalism and defense before the entrenched recognize that accommodation is essential for survival. Society is divided vertically, by communal allegiances, and horizontally, by socioeconomic ones, and which will prove stronger varies over the years.

A study of the island's history in the years between 1936, when the largest and poorest population groups in Mauritius organized to express their grievances, and 1968, when Mauritius became independent, clearly shows the forces that shape the conflict between class and community.[3] What happened over the years on this very small island can be viewed as a microcosm for the larger story of colonialism and independence.

The People

Today's Mauritians have their origins on three continents: Europe, Asia, and Africa. It is a puzzle that this fertile and extraordinarily beautiful island had no inhabitants until the eighteenth century, and explanations are elusive. Since Mauritius appears on seventh-century Arab charts, we can assume that Arab traders did land there to collect food and fuel. The Portuguese also stopped in Mauritius en route from Cape Town to Goa. But it was the Dutch who in 1598 claimed the island and named it after their ruler, Prince Maurice van Nassau. Two Dutch settlements failed because of lack of food and inefficient administration, and in 1710 they abandoned Mauritius to pirates. When the first French settlers came in the eighteenth century, the island was uninhabited.

The Mauritian population today is composed of four ethnic groups and four major religious groups: the Franco-Mauritians and Creoles, who are Catholic; the Indian community, Muslim and Hindu; and the small Chinese community, either Buddhist or Catholic. All Mauritians are immigrants; the Franco-Mauritians, Hindus, Muslims, and Chinese have some cultural ties to their original homelands. The Creoles, descended from slaves brought to Mauritius from East Africa, have no such ties. Somewhat like the Coloureds of South Africa, descended from the now-vanished race of Hottentots and from

white settlers who did not choose to claim them, the Creoles have no
country to call their own except the island where they live.

The largest ethnic group on the island (68 percent) is Indo-
Mauritian; most of these people are descended from indentured
laborers who came to the island between 1832 and 1885. Three-
quarters of the Indo-Mauritians are Hindu; nearly all the rest are
Muslim, with a sprinkling of Christians. Muslims have their own
religious and educational institutions as well as their own political
organization, and have traditionally held different types of jobs from
those of the Hindus. They consider themselves, and are considered
by others, as a separate community, so that the term "Indian" usually
means all Indo-Mauritians who are not Muslim.

POPULATION BY ETHNIC GROUP
(in thousands)

Ethnic Group	1972 Totals	Percent of Total
General	236.9	28.7
Hindu	428.2	51.8
Muslim	137.1	16.6
Chinese	24.0	2.9
Total	826.2	100.0

The Chinese today comprise approximately 3 percent of the total
population. Over half are Catholic, and nearly one-quarter are
Buddhists. Two-thirds live in Port Louis; the rest are shopkeepers in
the villages. Mainly from the Hukka region of China, the Chinese are
the island's retail traders, and nearly every village, however remote,
has a Chinese "boutique."[4] Until recently there had been considerable turnover within the community as traders came to Mauritius,
made money, and then went back to China. In turn, their relatives or
friends came to take over the island business, so that most of the
older Chinese were born in China. The younger generation, however, is forced by circumstance to think of Mauritius as a permanent
home. Because of their small numbers, the Chinese cannot be a
strong political force and must depend upon the good intentions of
the government for their survival.

The "general population," a term that became popular after the
1948 election, refers to the remaining Mauritians, those of European

URBAN POPULATION = 43 percent

City/District	1979
Port Louis	146,101
Beau-Bassin/Rose Hill	86,192
Curépipe	56,205
Quatre Bornes	55,366
Vacoas/Phoenix	53,687
Urban Total	397,551

or African descent or any Mauritian of mixed origins. Most of them are Catholic. Most of the Europeans, only 2 percent of the total population, have French ancestors. A very few are British. The Creoles, the largest group within the general population, are for the most part descendants of slaves who were brought to the island by the French.[5]

Until recently, the small but powerful Franco-Mauritian elite was at the top of the Mauritian hierarchy. Next came the light-skinned Creole professional and middle class; although some were entitled to many of the privileges of the white minority, they were never integrated socially. At the bottom were the dark-skinned Creoles and the Indian laborers. To a large extent, the stratifications in society derive from the hierarchical organization of the sugar industry. Just as the waving fields of sugarcane dominate the plateau, sugar—the crop, the industry, the employer—dominates the economic, political, and social patterns of the island.

Sugarcane Economy

Mauritius is a sugar island; the fortunes of Mauritians are tied directly to the vagaries of the weather and the world sugar price. Until the opening of the Suez Canal in 1869, Mauritius did benefit from being strategically located on the major trade route from Europe to India. But even before 1869, and certainly since, sugar was and continues to be the island's main source of income. Early settlers experimented with coffee, indigo, and cotton, but soon found the climate best suited for growing sugarcane. Rains in the hot season, between December and April, precede a much drier period during which the plants produce sucrose. Today, 93 percent of the arable land on the island is planted with sugar, 85 percent of its export income comes from sugar, and nearly one-third of the labor force works in the sugar industry, producing between six and seven hundred thousand tons* of sugar for export.

Revenues from sugar sales gave Mauritians a per capita income of $680 in 1976, well above that of India and Egypt. But this figure is deceptive. Already, planters are using the latest varieties of cane and cultivating all the available land, so without further technological development there is little chance of a substantial increase in production. More important, sugar prices are not stable. World prices increased immediately following the island's independence in 1968, but are once again low. As demonstrated in the mid-1960s, low prices can have a serious impact on the island's economy. (Mauritius currently sells 70 percent of its crop at prices negotiated with the Common Market, which helps ensure price stability in view of the fluctuations in the world price.)

In addition to price fluctuations, planters are preoccupied with cyclones and drought. Sugar can withstand the rains and winds of Indian Ocean cyclones better than can any other tropical crop, but it is not indestructible. Between 1912 and 1952, every three or four years the island suffered a cyclone that destroyed nearly a fifth of the crop; droughts, which plague the island about every ten years, accounted for another loss of an average of one-sixth of the crop.[6] Although sugar is crucial to Mauritius, Mauritian sugar is not crucial to the world market. Since Mauritius does not rank among the top ten world sugar producers, fluctuations in its crop do not affect the world price; a small crop in Mauritius will not reduce supply enough to cause an offsetting rise in world prices. A cyclone and drought insurance fund, established by the government in 1962, now reduces the risks of loss.

Over half the one hundred thousand arpents† planted in sugar are owned by twenty-one large estates with factories. Much of the rest of the crop is produced by small owner-planters on plots of less than five arpents. There is a marked difference in yields per acre between the miller-planters, the owner-planters, and the tenant planters.[7] Millers produce nearly twice as much sugar per arpent as do small tenant

---

*Tons are metric tons unless otherwise stated.
†One arpent is 1.043 acres.

planters, partly because when lands were originally distributed to small planters, estate owners chose to lease or sell their less productive plots.[8] But the major reason for the difference in productivity is that the small planters do not use the best techniques. Many also work for wages at other jobs and have less time to care for their own crops.

The sugar industry employs nearly one-third of Mauritius's labor force, but until recently employment in sugar has been seasonal: during the five months of intercrop (September–January) only a minimum force is needed for weeding, ground clearing, and planting. As a result, until 1965 legislation required estates to provide employment during intercrop, over one-fifth of those employed in sugar usually had no job for half the year.[9]

Mauritius's dependence on sugar has often been deplored, particularly by outside observers. While pointing out that the island was extremely well adapted for sugar production, the report of a 1909 royal commission added:

> We cannot but regard this position of affairs as unfortunate . . . this excessive concentration of its resources upon one industry exposed it to serious difficulties and even dangers. It makes the Colony entirely dependent upon the world price of sugar, over which it has no control; it prevents any chance of depression in one local industry being balanced by the prosperity of others, and it caused the finances of the Government to be almost entirely dependent upon a single fluctuating and uncertain factor. Accordingly we find that when the sugar industry is depressed the whole community, with very few exceptions, suffers. The depression soon seriously affects the revenue, while, at the same time, it leads to additional demands on the public purse.[10]

More recently, Brian Hopkin, from the British Ministry of Overseas Development, has described the "mesmeric effect of the tradition of putting land under cane."[11] Jacques Koenig, executive-secretary of the Mauritius Chamber of Agriculture, found that attempts to diversify have met with planter opposition. Sugar has been the source of the island's revenue for so long that Mauritians have been unwilling to experiment with other crops, particularly when the price of sugar is high.

Mauritius has recently begun to use foreign exchange earned from sugar to diversify the economy and to promote labor-intensive projects and local manufacture of products to reduce imports. Tea, potatoes, tobacco, and fiber are all being grown on the island now, but these minor agricultural industries employ fewer than eight thousand people. The problem grows, because neither sugar nor government (the island's second largest employer) will be able to absorb the thousands who join the labor force annually; the government already employs more than sixteen thousand relief workers.

In addition to diversifying agriculture, the government hopes to encourage investment in light industry and tourism by reviewing tariff and income tax ordinances to provide incentives. Tourism now contributes a mere 3 percent of the gross national product, but clearly the island's beaches and spectacular coral reefs can attract increasing numbers of people in search of sun. With wages one-fourth of those in Hong Kong and Singapore, Mauritius has attracted some small-scale, labor-intensive industries to its Export Processing Zone, enabling investors to process for export products such as wigs, transistor radios, and textiles in the duty-free area.

At the time of independence, when sugar prices were low and the population was growing at a steady rate, Mauritius's future looked bleak. A spirit of cooperation generated by independence, a rise in sugar prices, and a dramatic decline in the rate of population increase generated a brief period of genuine optimism. But although statistics may demonstrate that Mauritius, with a growth rate of 4 percent, has done well economically since independence, the real income of the average laborer has been declining. Redistribution of income is a problem the government has not yet fully considered, but obviously any scheme will have to take into account the impact on the sugar industry, which for over one hundred and fifty years has been the backbone of the Mauritian economy. The chances of any significant change in the island's dependence on sugar are minimal.

Communities and Politics

In the past thirty years the correspondence between occupational status and community has been diminishing, but generalizations still apply. Statistics largely bear out the image of the Indian as predominantly rural, working as a cane cutter or owning a small plot of land. According to the 1952 census, which is representative of the period discussed in this book, over 90 percent of the agricultural laborers, farm managers, and gardeners were Indian. Similarly, 75 to 80 percent of the skilled laborers and artisans were Creole, as were 68 percent of the dockers and teachers, all characteristically urban occupations. Sixty-one percent of the owners and 82 percent of the shop assistants in the mixed retail business were Chinese. The remainder of the retailers, listed in the census as Indo-Mauritian, are assumed to be Muslim.[12]

Each community is itself divided by class; each has some doctors and lawyers, as well as poorer members (although it is safe to say that even the poorest Franco-Mauritians have a higher standard of living than most Indian laborers). There are more Franco-Mauritian and Creole than Indo-Mauritian doctors, lawyers, and teachers, certainly. But even so, the Indians tend to use Indian doctors, and the Creoles use Creole doctors, reinforcing communal divisions. And socially, as well as professionally, a Mauritian's life is usually confined to people from the same community and similar economic and educational backgrounds.

Differences in religion and in language act to reinforce occupational and ethnic divisions. Both the Indian and the Chinese communities have preserved their own languages; 74 percent of the Indians usually speak Hindi or another Indian language. Forty percent of the Chinese community speaks a Chinese language at home. Half of Mauritius's population, including the Creole community, uses Creole, a patois based on French. In addition, the *lingua franca* among communities is Creole, but few people take pride in it.[13] The choice of a European language is fairly telling, reflecting as it does certain historic alignments. The Indians tend to prefer English and the Creoles prefer French. At the same time, most Indians acknowledge an intellectual debt to British philosophers and writers, while most Creoles turn to the French, with whom they have identified since emancipation.

Mauritius became an independent ministate in 1968. The independence celebrations were the culmination of three decades of active political maneuvering—a period of rising nationalism marked by sharp class and communal divisions in the multiracial population of the island. In no other plural society was the question of legitimacy so confused, for there were no original Mauritians who could claim that the land had been theirs before the Europeans came, and no single population group that had sufficient numbers to dominate. And yet, in few other plural societies have the communities been able to resolve their differences with as little violence.

The shifts in the relative power of each community that occurred between 1936 and 1967 caused anxiety and anguish. It was not easy for those accustomed to power to concede their absolute position, nor for those who had been at the bottom of the social hierarchy for a century to use their newly gained power wisely. Tensions were high, as the Europeanized Creoles and the Franco-Mauritians were passed over and political power moved into the hands of the numerically larger Indian community. Most recently, however, Mauritians have come to accept that they will be living permanently in a society where communal divisions are important. Assurances that each community will be represented in the Legislative Assembly are written into the constitution. Although the Franco-Mauritians still control the largest proportion of the island's economic resources, each community dominates a different sector of the economy. And as the Indians' share of the economy grows, so too does their interest in continuing political stability.

In many plural societies that have also been colonies—Malaysia, Ceylon, and Kenya, for example—the question of which ethnic or religious group would ultimately rule was not an issue. But in Mauritius the question of which community would have what Max Weber called "title to rule" following independence was crucial. The balance of power had been more or less stable for nearly a century, and the impending transfer of political power fostered the growth of intense communal politics.

The issue was not whether one group could maintain its customs and religion, nor was there a single, common oppressor to bring unity to the indigenous population. The basis for conflict was clear: that group which held political power at the time of independence would probably hold that power for decades thereafter. The sharpest divisions, then, occurred over those issues that affected access to political power—the electoral system and the elections themselves. The stakes were high. In the end, political power was transferred from the British colonial administrators and the Franco-Mauritian oligarchy to an Indian-dominated alliance, but it was not always clear which community or communities would ultimately dominate the political life of the island.

Each communal group was deeply affected by the qualifications for franchise, the size and shape of the electoral constituencies, the process of registration, the reservation of communal seats, the environment at the polls, and the quality of the census on which the distribution of seats was based. The extent to which these issues were settled in Parliament and in constitutional conferences, and the degree to which the elections were free of violence and corruption, are a credit to Mauritians.

Although pluralism has been the primary factor influencing political development in Mauritius, the small size of the island has also had a profound effect on its politics. As historian Albert Hourani said about Lebanon, before the recent disturbances:

> The very smallness of the country increased the tension. Everyone was involved at few removes or none, in the political process; the mass of unconcerned private citizens living remote from political life, which makes the stability of larger states, scarcely existed. [14]

The respect accorded political institutions in Western countries comes in part from distance, and distance is impossible in Mauritius. People in authority are rarely respected solely because of the office they hold. One way or another, everything about a political figure (usually an unfortunate combination of fact and fiction) is known to everyone on the island; and intensely personal—and usually not flattering—references regarding a political figure's personal behavior usually find their way into the Legislative Council debates. Personality conflicts among leaders are public knowledge. Personal rivalries and petty jealousies determine political behavior as much as do the merits of an issue being debated. [15]

Even where the population is not divided by race and religion as it is in Mauritius, the personal nature of politics in small territories usually promotes factionalism. The description by a nineteenth-century visitor to the island of Saint Pierre, near Nova Scotia and inhabited only by French immigrants, also fits Mauritius:

> The people are gossipy, and in truth one cannot blame them. Shut up on an island, where living is necessarily cramped, they are all over each other as if on board a ship. Lacking more important

ideas, personalities, misfortunes, and disputes are common subjects
of conversation, and when rumour concerns everything, the relations between people suffer, and there are quarrels in which the
ridiculousness of the causes does not rule out animosity.[16]

In a small society where anonymity does not exist, status is ascribed
rather than achieved. Some Mauritians try to change community by
changing names, but no one can escape his or her family tree. Who
one is and who one's relatives are often matter more than individual
merit. Patronage is accepted and efficiency has suffered. Given widespread unemployment and the fact that the government is the second
largest employer, political connections are crucial to finding work.
The fact that one cannot escape one's roots in Mauritius, a result in
part of smallness, has made more difficult the integration of the various social and ethnic groups, an integration some people think is
necessary for political development.

Although it may sound as though everyone knows everyone else on
Mauritius, they do not. Paradoxically, the small and "gossipy" island
maintains, still, divisions that obstruct a real understanding among its
various communities. Because they do not live together, and because
they rarely mix except at official functions, Mauritians generally have
had little understanding of class and social differences within communities other than their own. To be sure, the Chinese shopkeeper is
apt to know the divisions within the Indian village where he works;
and the Franco-Mauritians and Creoles have not been oblivious to
the political advantages of emphasizing caste divisions within the Indian community; but generally each community has a stereotyped
and monolithic impression of the other.

This lack of understanding of another's community, combined with
the tendency to view others in derogatory terms, leads to an atmosphere of suspicion and distrust, a condition fostered both by
pluralism and by the island's size. In this situation, communal loyalties dominate. Individuals join one political party rather than another
because of the group to which they belong, so politics tends to
further separate the communities of Mauritius, confirming
stereotypes and nourishing resentments. Although the fear and distrust have varied considerably in intensity during the nineteenth and
twentieth centuries, they have been major forces in shaping political
behavior on the island. The ways in which each community has been

perceived, and the ways in which each community perceived others, have determined the course of events. Because relations between communities today are influenced by the past, an understanding of how and why each community came to the island and of each community's historical position in the economy and in political life is essential to understanding the current situation.

2. Planters and Slaves
The Franco-Mauritian and Creole Communities

THE FIRST PERMANENT inhabitants of Mauritius were French, settlers who came in 1722 from the nearby island of Réunion (except that it was then called by a more typically eighteenth-century French name, Bourbon). At first life in the new settlement was a struggle, but within about twenty years the first wave of settlers had developed a community that would last, and more settlers began to arrive from France. Following the custom of the day, they imported slaves from East Africa and Madagascar, and by 1789 the island had a population of 3,163 whites, 587 coloreds, and 37,915 slaves.[1] If the people were mixed, the prevailing tenor of the island was French. By 1800 the French community had established its own system of democratic government, dominated by the Colonial Assembly, the French legal system was well established, and a sophisticated and well-educated elite was firmly entrenched.

During the Napoleonic Wars, Mauritian merchant ships and corsairs attacked and looted British trading ships, until in 1810 a British fleet attacked and forced the islanders to surrender. But the British made generous terms: they agreed to take no prisoners of war and to pay for sending French troops back to France. Any Mauritians who wished could leave the colony within two years, taking their private property with them, and the property of those who remained was not to be confiscated. The inhabitants were promised that the new administration would "preserve their Religion, Laws and Customs."[2] The surrender was formally recognized in 1814 by the Treaty of Paris.[3]

So although French administration ended in 1810, French traditions survived, and French influence still pervades the island today.

Franco-Mauritians idealized and tried to preserve a way of life that was nearing its social and cultural peak in the early nineteenth century. Before the British captured the island, Governor Charles Dacaen gave grand balls to celebrate each of Napoleon's victories; the intellectuals formed literary societies and in 1806 founded an elite secondary school, called the Royal College. Mauritian women kept up with Paris fashions and lived in small chateaux complete with mahogany furniture. Their sons often went to school in France and returned with the latest news and styles from Paris. The Franco-Mauritians' sophistication and urbanity led one author to write: "There is less distance between Paris and Mauritius, than there is between Paris and Bordeaux."[4] Another explained, "if there was no public library in Port Louis at the time, it was because each house had its individual library." Stag hunting was already an established sport on the island, and the Mauritius Turf Club sponsored the first horse races in 1812. Opera was an annual feature. Perhaps the roads were in bad condition, the poorly lit streets may have been unsafe at night, and the police were inadequately organized; still, for wealthy Franco-Mauritians, life was as pleasant in Mauritius as it would have been in other parts of the world.[5]

Many aspects of that life have changed little since then. Balls are no longer held, it is true, and the opera no longer comes to Port Louis. But the grand houses remain. Names found today on the list of sponsors for the Mauritius Turf Club and among the members of the Chamber of Commerce and the Chamber of Agriculture appear on a list of members of an 1812 literary society. Many Franco-Mauritian women speak only French and Creole. They remain Catholics, and until the late 1960s were faithful followers of church policy on birth control. But the fact that life has changed only somewhat has some drawbacks. The apparent stability of the Franco-Mauritian community has tended to make its members insular, traditional, unimaginative, and stubborn. Certain strict behavior patterns are expected, and until recently those who deviated usually left the island.

But it was the economic, rather than the cultural or even the political, position of the Franco-Mauritian people that ensured their dominance of Mauritian life. Even when they lost control of the legislature, they continued, through the Chamber of Agriculture, to exercise considerable power on the island.

British Colony, French Community

Franco-Mauritians have differed from many Europeans in British colonies in two ways. First, they have had no home other than Mauritius. Like the Boers in South Africa and the French in Canada, they have lived in Mauritius for so many generations that they no longer have personal ties with their original home. They speak French with a definite accent and an outdated vocabulary. Second, their nationality differed from that of the colonial administrators. If their accent was not from Paris, certainly their language was not from London, and they felt no special loyalty to Britain; the British government in turn felt no special responsibility for them.

After 1810, the first years of British rule were uneasy as the Franco-Mauritians and the British administrators watched one another from a distance. The early governors—military men with the damage inflicted by Mauritian corsairs fresh in their minds—saw themselves holding a post of major strategic importance. By 1900, however, their successors could only consider appointment to the island as banishment to one of the smallest and poorest parts of the empire. Understandably, Franco-Mauritians did not see it that way and considered Mauritius superior to other colonies. Unless a British governor immediately paid lip service to this superiority, he was in for a difficult time. Both the size and the self-confidence of the local elite provided challenges for the island's governor and a mutual animosity that most British colonial governors did not experience elsewhere.

The Franco-Mauritians had no lobby to protect their interests in Britain's Parliament, as the large British sugar importers, such as Booker Brothers, did for sugar producers in British Guiana and Trinidad. Nor did they have relatives voting in British elections as did the settlers of Kenya or Rhodesia. Compared with the Indians in Mauritius, the Franco-Mauritians failed to attract political support in Britain at any time. Letters between the island government and the Colonial Office in London were often filled with charges of bigotry and obstinacy. And yet, for the first century of British rule, the administration could not afford to cross the Franco-Mauritians, who were considered the only politically significant "indigenous inhabitants."

For many years, the Franco-Mauritians had assumed that

Mauritius would be returned to France. Yet when there was a movement to return Mauritius to France in 1919, they failed to support it,
for economic reasons. On the other hand, they refused to meet the
British governor, as a form of protest, as late as 1950.[6] They may have
felt themselves to be French in spirit, but economically they wanted
as much autonomy as possible, and resisted any unnecessary attach-
ments to either of the giants of Europe. As long as British administrators left them more or less alone, and as long as the island remained relatively prosperous, the Franco-Mauritians did not engage
in active protest. Colonial administrators, for their part, regularly
took the easiest path and gave in to their demands. By 1870, such
behavior had become accepted and expected. One of the island's
more outspoken governors, Sir Arthur Gordon,* recognized that "it
require[d] a very great deal of courage, I will say a great deal of self
reliance, to stand up against [the planters'] influence." He was
amazed at "how subservient the government and its officers, whether
executive or judicial, had been to the planting body."[7] But Gordon
knew as well as any other governor that when the Franco-Mauritians
wished, they could bring affairs in the colony to a halt. And they used
that power effectively. They refused to comply with regulations that
did not suit them, and often persuaded local administrators to support them in defying the Colonial Office. Ironically, when their political power was threatened after the 1948 constitutional reform gave
the vote to large numbers of Indo-Mauritians, the Franco-Mauritians
turned to Britain in an attempt to prevent Hindu domination. They
received little help. Although Britain offered compensation to British
settlers in Kenya who fled in 1964 just before independence, no such
offer was made to the Franco-Mauritians. They were British subjects,
rather than British citizens.[8]

The Franco-Mauritians' first direct conflict with their new rulers
after 1810 arose over the issue of slavery and the appointment of an
abolitionist as procureur-general in 1832. The conflict was typical of
such disputes throughout the colonial period. With the sanction of
the governor, Sir Lowry Cole, the slave trade had flourished in
Mauritius in the 1820s. In London, the Anti-Slavery Society argued
that the colony would be a good place to begin abolition, because no
English financial interests would be seriously affected. Mauritian

*For a list of British governors and their dates of service, see Appendix B.

slave owners, taking quite another view, were enraged by the suggestion. Convinced that an armed rebellion would follow emancipation,
they persuaded Governor Charles Colville to let them carry firearms
for self-defense and formed a local militia numbering between 5,000
and 7,000 men.

The Colonial Office, increasingly dismayed by the governor's lack
of concern for the slaves, decided to send to Mauritius a man who
would not bow to the planters' interests. They chose John Jeremie, an
avowed abolitionist, and in 1832 appointed him procureur-general in
place of Prosper D'Epinay, a Franco-Mauritian. Furious that this important legal post had been given not only to an Englishman but to
an abolitionist as well, the planters were determined to prevent
Jeremie from assuming his duties. Interpreting Jeremie's appointment
as a direct threat to their political influence in the island, the planters
demanded his recall. Crowds protested Jeremie's arrival in Port Louis,
shops closed, people refused to work, and the judges who were to
install Jeremie failed to appear. In the face of this pressure, the governor gave in and dismissed Jeremie. But the British secretary of state
sent Jeremie back to Mauritius, along with two frigates and two brigs
that sat off the island ready to intervene if necessary. Undeterred, the
planters, backed by their newspaper, *Le Cerneen*,* and their militia,
forced the secretary of state to dismiss Jeremie. As would often be the
case, the planters won a short-term victory—Jeremie left the island,
this time for good—but in the long run they lost, for slavery was
abolished in 1835.

The Jeremie affair is but one example of the extent of the sharp
differences between the Franco-Mauritian community and the colonial administration in Mauritius and London. For much of the
nineteenth century the greatest differences arose over matters relating to Indian immigration and the treatment of Indian labor in
Mauritius. But the arrival of John Pope-Hennessy as governor in 1882
added a new dimension to the already complex relationship between
the colonial government and the Franco-Mauritians.

John Pope-Hennessy was the only British governor to actively seek
and earn the support of the Franco-Mauritians. Forty-nine years old,
with sixteen years of colonial service behind him when he came to
Mauritius, he had gained a reputation for favoring racial equality and
local participation in colonial administration in Labuan, Lagos, Bar-

*For a list of Mauritian newspapers and their constituencies, see Appendix C.

bados, and Hong Kong. Although familiar with Pope-Hennessy's remarkable ability to misplace dispatches that did not please him, officials in the Colonial Office agreed that he had been a popular governor and considered him especially suited for Mauritius because he was a Roman Catholic.

In the first months of Pope-Hennessy's administration, the rapport between the Mauritian elite and the British governor was greater than it had been since 1810. Pope-Hennessy found the Franco-Mauritians and the educated colored members of the community sophisticated in their tastes and outlook. He disliked the English civil servants as much as the Mauritians did, and was determined to appoint Mauritians wherever possible in order to make "Mauritius for the Mauritians."[9] John Pope-Hennessy became one of Mauritius's most controversial governors, but adversaries and supporters alike credit him with introducing the electoral process into the island's government.

When Pope-Hennessy arrived in Mauritius in 1882, he found the Franco-Mauritian and Creole elites organized and united to combat the British administration, which was trying to enforce an old French regulation about ownership of land on the sides of streams. Believing that the seven nominated members of the Council of Government (provided for in 1831 in the first Mauritian constitution) had failed them, the planters and the Creole professionals demanded a constitution that would enable them to elect representatives to the Council.[10] The secretary of state for the colonies, Lord Derby, opposed their proposals, but he was forced to give in or face a possible rebellion.

A new constitution, finally introduced in 1886, provided for ten elected members, nine appointed members, and eight official members of the Council of Government. A "relative majority" of the unofficial members could determine financial policy and other questions of local interest. The island was divided into nine electoral districts, each returning one member, with the exception of Port Louis, which elected two. The franchise, limited by strict property and income requirements, was nevertheless broader than Pope-Hennessy and the Franco-Mauritians and Creoles close to him had wished.[11] One wonders who the governor and his supporters had in mind as eligible voters, since by 1909 the voting population was made up of less than 2 percent of the adult population, and nearly 25 percent of the registered electorate consisted of civil servants.[12]

The first elections, held in 1886, were contested by two political groups; Pope-Hennessy openly supported one of them. Such direct involvement in local politics eventually brought him into so much disfavor that the Colonial Office ordered a special investigation of his administration. The outcome was that Pope-Hennessy was suspended in late 1886. He returned to England, where he successfully defended himself, and in 1888 he came back to Mauritius and served the final year of his term as governor.

Pope-Hennessy's constitution remained in effect for sixty years, in part because it strengthened the power of the Franco-Mauritian and Creole elites, enabling them to remain in control of politics. They had always controlled economic and cultural affairs, but they had participated in the island's politics only through petitions and newspapers. After 1886 they had significant representation in the colony's legislative body: the ten elected members of the Council of Government participated actively in decision making. Unlike the previous unofficial members, who were chosen by the governor, the elected members could not be considered government stooges. And although an official majority remained in the Council, many major decisions, including some about the island's finances, were left to the elected members.

What had seemed a wide franchise in 1886 was already inadequate twenty years later, but once in power the elite was not willing to withdraw. For its part, the British government, happier with an opposition it knew rather than one it did not know, made no attempt to widen the franchise or to enlarge the Council of Government until forced to do so by discontented Creoles and Indians.

Existing tensions between the colonial administration and the Franco-Mauritians were heightened any time that relations between England and France became particularly hostile. The occupation of Madagascar by France in 1896, the Fashoda crisis of 1898, and the Boer War in South Africa all reinforced opposition to England among the Franco-Mauritians. At that time, if France had tried to recapture Mauritius, most Franco-Mauritians would have supported the invasion. Joseph Chamberlain, then secretary of state for the colonies, wrote in 1900 that "the French inhabitants of Mauritius must be regarded as less loyal than the Indian inhabitants," a strong condemnation for the time.[13]

Aided by their newspapers, most notably *Le Cerneen*, Franco-Mauritians have remained a strong interest group throughout the island's history. They fought to preserve their political and economic interests with extraordinary effectiveness for many decades. When their political power dwindled, their economic power declined considerably. Even so they remained the most powerful economic force on the island until after independence; then they began to develop alliances with the wealthy Indian community. Franco-Mauritians did not hide their own sense of cultural superiority. An insular group, they made no attempt to reach out to other communities until their own self-interest forced them to deal with outsiders. Conspicuous because of their economic and political power and cultural arrogance, the Franco-Mauritians were envied and emulated by a small portion of the island's other groups and hated and distrusted by the rest.

In the early twentieth century, the Creoles became the first group to seriously challenge the Franco-Mauritians' dominant position. Currently composed of nearly 300,000 people of mixed African, Indian, and European descent, the Creole community is, in fact, the most heterogeneous, and as a result has been the most factionalized in Mauritius.[14] Creoles can be found in nearly every job on the economic ladder.[15] But stratification resulting from differences in color, education, and wealth has impeded mobility within the community on this island as in other parts of the world. Fishermen and dockers at the bottom of the social and economic hierarchy generally have darker skins than the urban middle class. On the other hand, many Creole professionals and members of the early political elite were entitled to the same privileges enjoyed by the white minority; outsiders could easily have mistaken them for Franco-Mauritians.

Although non-Creoles tend to view the Creoles as a single group, the social and economic divisions within the community have been so sharp that, except during the ill-fated *Action Liberale* campaign in 1907 and the retrocession movement in 1919, the Creoles failed to act as a political unit until 1963.* At that time the appeal of a charismatic leader, Gaetan Duval, plus the approach of independence and possible Indian domination of the island, finally forced Creoles to overcome their class differences and vote, nearly unanimously, for the *Parti Mauricien*. But up to that time individual Creole politicians had exploited divisions within the community for their own benefit, ac-

---

*For a list of major Mauritian political organizations, see Appendix D.

centuating rather than trying to modify the class differences that separated Creole laborers from the elite.

Divisions on the basis of color have a historical origin. The light-skinned elite are descended from slaves who were freed before emancipation in 1835, whereas most of the darker Creoles are descended from those who were freed that year. The French imported their slaves from the east coast of Africa and from Madagascar and treated them harshly. The British administrators failed to bring about any improvement. Despite the fact that Britain's Parliament abolished the slave trade in 1807 and extended the law to Mauritius in 1813, the slave trade continued, sanctioned by British administrators who were anxious to avoid antagonizing the Franco-Mauritian community. Except for a minor and ill-fated revolt in the 1820s, the slaves did not protest.

In accordance with Parliament's requirements, Governor William Nicolay freed the slaves on January 17, 1835. The slaves, who then comprised nearly three-fourths of the total population, were required to work as apprentices for six years, but this was reduced to four, and in 1839 they left the plantations at last to seek independent lives.[16] Their descendants claim that they would have stayed had they been offered adequate wages, but, for whatever reasons, the slaves scattered so quickly and so completely that by 1872 "they had disappeared from agricultural labor, from the precincts of the plantations, from any contact with the whites."[17] Some began new settlements on the plateau, or went to the coast to become fishermen; others stayed near the plantations and became skilled craftsmen; still others went to Port Louis to work as dockers. By 1900 those who had managed to acquire educations and jobs as teachers or civil servants formed the core of the growing Creole middle class. But in 1835, the newly freed slaves—three out of every four Mauritians—were at the bottom of the socioeconomic hierarchy.

Wedged between the slaves and the Franco-Mauritians in the nineteenth century hierarchy were the light-skinned "free coloureds," the Creole elite. They rarely mixed socially with the Franco-Mauritians, but they did sit in the Mauritian Colonial Assembly, established during the French Revolution, and were equal before the law until 1803, when the French governor issued laws designed to separate free coloreds from whites. The British legally abolished the color bar in 1829, and the Royal College, Mauritius's most prestigious secondary school, admitted its first Creole students shortly thereafter. In 1830, five years before emancipation, there were twice as many "free coloureds" in Mauritius as whites.[18]

This large colored community grew from liaisons between French settlers and their slaves. The French father freed his children, but did not accept them into his family. The children, as they grew up, tried to enter the European community to make it clear that they were not slaves. Creoles, therefore, began to adopt the customs and habits of the Franco-Mauritian community from which they were legally excluded; a white skin, wealth, and a classical education became their goals. Slavery had left them without language or traditions, so like Creoles in other countries, they took on those of the most prestigious and influential community. On Mauritius, that meant adopting the Franco-Mauritian language and religion and participating in Franco-Mauritian politics on the Franco-Mauritians' terms.

Well educated and prominent in society and government, members of the Creole elite were often difficult to distinguish from Franco-Mauritians. Most of the prominent Creoles at the end of the nineteenth century were conservatives. Distinguished lawyers, journalists, and literary figures, they rested their claim to participation in government on their European culture. They were often rewarded with honors, decorations, and knighthoods from the British sovereign—the first Mauritian to be knighted was a Creole. Nor surprisingly, they were rarely sympathetic to the plight of the Creole masses or the Indian indentured laborers. Jealous of their position, they were careful to avoid associating with or even admitting that they knew the lower classes.

When these Creoles asked for constitutional change, they did not suggest that it extend to the Creole lower classes. A large, enfranchised population of poor Creoles was not to their interest, and they joined with the Franco-Mauritians in trying to limit the power of the British administration. Three leaders of the constitutional reform movement of 1892 were Creole: the first, Laurent Louis Raoul, was president of the Chamber of Notaries; the second, Sir Virgile Naz, was an articulate lawyer and a wealthy landowner; the most eloquent of the three, Sir William Newton, had been legal advisor to the Chamber of Agriculture. Two of the three had been nominated by the governor to serve on the Council of Government; two of the three had also given evidence on behalf of the planters before the

1872 commission investigating the condition of the Indian laborers. It was not social change or Creole rights they were seeking, but the power to protect the interests of the Mauritian elite.

Ironically, the elite was first threatened not by the Creole laborers but by the growing Creole middle class, the civil servants and professionals who felt excluded from the special privileges accorded to the few Creoles who were part of the political, if not the economic and social, establishment. Three times in the early twentieth century this group tried to organize politically, but their efforts were haphazard and ineffective. They did, however, try to seek the support of the Creole lower class and therefore to bring some unity to the Creole community.

But in Mauritius, as in the West Indies, the growth of a Creole elite led eventually to the political involvement of the Creole worker. The *Action Liberale*, founded in 1907, became the first political group to solicit the support of Creole workers in Mauritius.

Typical of Mauritian political associations, the *Action Liberale* was not a political party but rather an alliance or *groupement* of men who agreed to work together for a specific objective and for a limited period of time. Its immediate goal was to bring a royal commission to Mauritius to investigate the declining financial situation on the island. More generally, *Action Liberale* leaders—believing that political and economic influence should no longer be in the hands of a few sugar planters who, guided by their private concerns, were unable to make decisions in the best interest of the colony—wanted to protect the interests of the growing middle class.

The *Action Liberale* tried to enlist the support of the Creole community and the Indian middle classes, the petty clerks and the small planters, and in the process created a degree of political awareness among people who had previously been removed from politics. Before 1907 public opinion meant simply what the planters and their allies thought. Now it took on a new meaning. *Action Liberale* leaders went directly to the villages and held weekend meetings in the local open market. Such meetings were not purely political; they were more often than not disrupted by villagers buying vegetables as well as by hecklers from Port Louis, and, viewed with some excitement as one of the few forms of entertainment on the island, were often seen as an excuse for a family outing. But there was some political fallout, and not only for the Creoles.

As the *Action Liberale* sought the support of the Indians, the Indians in turn hoped that the combined efforts of Eugene Laurent and their leader, Manilal Doctor, would succeed in changing their lot. The Indians therefore regularly attended *Action Liberale* meetings. The message was important to them; in addition, the speakers were lively and entertaining. *Action Liberale* leaders, young and energetic men who believed passionately in what they were doing, included elite Creoles and less-than-elite Franco-Mauritians, those who were not from established families. Dr. Eugene Laurent, a member of the colored elite and an ardent, if slightly patronizing and pompous, member of the *Action Liberale*, was the group's central figure: as a municipal councillor since 1892 and mayor of Port Louis in 1905, he was already well known among the artisans, dockers, and colored bourgeoisie of the city.

The differences between the *Action Liberale* and the planters, or Oligarchs as they called themselves, were aired in the press. Obsessed with politics, each of the island's ten daily newspapers was wildly partisan. Libel laws were few, and the editors risked imprisonment only for sedition, so the arguments, though often petty, were usually intense and bitter.

Sir Frank Swettenham, who came to Mauritius in 1909 as chairman of the commission of enquiry, found all Mauritians profoundly lazy except for a

> small class which shows very exceptional energy. I refer to journalists. . . . This colony has more newspapers than any place of its size or importance that I have met with or heard of. . . . To a stranger the number of newspapers must be accounted for in this way: first there is nothing else to read; for in spite of a claim to literary tastes and rather high literary abilities, there is not one bookshop on the island. . . . The higher life of the place is not literature but politics—politics of course on a scale suited to the island and its traditions. . . . Whenever a politician tires of shaking his tongue at the tyrant he lashes himself into a white heat of passion over the doings and sayings and the ancestry of his political opponent. It makes excellent reading, and I have to take this opportunity of expressing my sincere thanks to the press for the entertainment they furnish so punctually every morning and almost every evening.[19]

In 1909 the *Action Liberale* reached its stated goal, and with clear evidence of a declining economic situation (there was a £80,7000

deficit in the treasury in the year 1907–08) persuaded the members of
the Council of Government to seek outside help. Neither the coming
of the Swettenham Commission, however, nor the publication of its
report alleviated political tensions; in fact, antagonisms between the
Oligarchs and the *Action Liberale* intensified. The 1911 election campaign, in the January heat, was the most bitterly contested since 1886.
The *Action Liberale* did win in Port Louis, but the Oligarchs swept
the rural areas and were assured of five more years in power.

The proclamation of the Oligarch victory in Curépipe prompted
only minor skirmishing, but real rioting took place in Port Louis.
Fired by a false rumor that Eugene Laurent had been seriously hurt,
Creoles sacked the office of the Oligarch paper *Le Radical* on the
night of January 18, 1911. Rioting and looting continued throughout
the night and much of the next day as crowds attacked the offices and
houses of well-known Oligarchs in the city.

The governor appointed a local commission to investigate the
cause of the riots. Commenting on the ineffectiveness of the police,
the provocations of the press, and the patience of the Indians, who
had avoided involvement in the skirmish, the commission concluded
that the source of the trouble lay in part with "a feeling of resentment, a belief that the coloured population did not receive impartial
justice." The commissioners then underlined the resentment that
many middle-class and poor Mauritians felt: "There existed amongst
the lower classes a certain feeling of discontent, and of distrust of
their superiors in the social scale, to whom they attributed a practical
monopoly of political patronage."[20] The commission found that the
leaders of the *Action Liberale* were voicing the hitherto unarticulated
views of the lower class.

For the planters, the riots clearly demonstrated the danger they
would face if Creoles were included in the political system. If the
franchise were extended, "the Negro voters might elect to begin with
their half-caste attorneys or such whites (the most disreputable of the
colour) as would court their suffrages, but gradually the black elector
would only vote for black representatives."[21]

With the exception of minor skirmishes between Tamils and Muslims during religious festivals, these were the first riots in Mauritius
since 1832. True, the violence was confined to Curépipe and Port
Louis, and although property was damaged and a few people were
injured, no one was killed. But in a place as small as Mauritius, this

comparatively mild disturbance had major repercussions. The island was swept by fear. The failure of the police to restore calm could have led to a complete breakdown in law and order in Port Louis. This potential for island-wide riots made all Mauritians stop to think. On an island, there is no escape. What would have happened if the Indians had taken sides? Why did the riots happen? Who started them? Would they happen again? The commission report was not enough to answer these questions or still the rumors.

Defeated in the elections of 1911, the leaders of the *Action Liberale* disbanded the alliance. It had brought a royal commission to Mauritius and had instilled a new political awareness in Creole middle-class voters and in some of the disenfranchised lower classes as well. Unable to fight at the polls, they had found and used one means of reprisal: violence. The 1911 riots served as a warning to the Oligarchs that their political domination had been challenged.

Retrocession and Reform

From the founding of the *Action Liberale* in 1907 until the founding of the Mauritius Labour Party in 1936, the Creole community was as united politically as it would ever be again until 1963. During most of this period it tried to build up outside support, sometimes from elements within the Indian community, more often from the progressive members of the Franco-Mauritian community. Once, however, in 1919, Creole professionals organized a political movement without the support of other communities, when the leaders sought a Creole constituency for a Creole cause and tried to win in a national election. Inspired by President Woodrow Wilson's principle of self-determination, a group of young Creoles, mostly from the professional classes, became convinced that Mauritius should again become a French colony.[22] French was still the dominant language on the island, and French customs and the French way of life were very much in evidence. Most of the Creole community was Catholic.

But more than emotional sympathy for France lay behind the movement. The retrocessionists felt that Britain had ignored Mauritius during the war and assumed, illogically, that France would not have. Furthermore, colored Mauritians who had been to South Africa were shocked by the low status accorded the Coloured population in South Africa. Segregation at home contrasted unpleasantly with assimilation in the neighboring island of French Réunion, where universal suffrage ensured that the colored community had political power. Creoles from Réunion even served as deputies in the French Assembly. After a century of British rule, Mauritian Creoles had learned that although equal before the law they were not in fact equal in any other respect to the Franco-Mauritian elite or the British administrators. As the governor, Sir Hesketh Bell, pointed out, in Mauritius Creoles were "British *subjects*. In Réunion they would be French citizens."[23]

There was more to the retrocession movement, however, than a pull toward France. What the retrocessionists believed but did not say openly was that by uniting with Madagascar and Réunion, Mauritius could be saved from the "Indian peril." All around they saw Indians becoming small planters and professionals, and they saw ahead to the day when these Indians could dominate politics and economics in the island. The people most vulnerable to such a change were those in the colored community, who could expect to be pushed out of jobs by upwardly mobile Indians. Federation with Madagascar and Réunion, which would turn the Indo-Mauritian majority into a minority by the simple device of adding more French, offered the only hope for Mauritian Creoles.

Retrocession leaders were mostly young colored professionals with some experience outside Mauritius, such as a young journalist, Raoul Rivet, and two doctors. Edgar Laurent and Maurice Curé. They began their appeal for support at a grand banquet in February 1919. Although it was not considered prudent actually to mention the word "retrocession," the purpose of the evening was fairly evident. French flags were draped around the huge room; the windows were covered with red, white, and blue cloth; and the *Flore Mauricien*, Port Louis's finest restaurant, supplied a gourmet menu. In case the message was still too subtle, the guests drank to the president of the French Republic, to the French colonies, and to the French army and navy; the crowd in the streets outside cheered as they drank. At a later meeting the retrocessionists selected six delegates, Creole professionals who were studying or working in Paris, to promote their cause in Europe.

At first the leaders had reason to believe that the Franco-Mauritian community would be sympathetic, but within a few months it was clear that the retrocessionists would have to rely exclusively on Creole support. Backed by *Le Radical*, *Le Cerneen*, and *The Planter's*

Gazette, Franco-Mauritian planters articulated their sound economic and political reasons for not wanting to give up the tie with England: India and Britain were their best markets for sugar; and Britain was offering prices that were high and going up. Moreover, the Franco-Mauritians feared that the French might grant universal suffrage and thus jeopardize the control over the island's affairs which the elite had held onto for so many years. As Sir Henri LeClezio, a prominent planter and member of the Council of Government, explained to the acting governor, Franco-Mauritians saw that the Creoles on Réunion had many more privileges than did the Creoles in Mauritius, and that was hardly to their liking.[24] The governor, in turn, felt that Franco-Mauritians would have supported retrocession "if a transfer to the French flag did not connote the Republic system of Government, universal suffrage, and the consequent preponderance of coloured influence in the colony."[25] French ties—once again—touched the hearts of Franco-Mauritians only as long as their wallets were not affected.

The Colonial Office understandably took a dim view of the retrocessionists. Governor Bell, whose fluent French made him popular with the Franco-Mauritians, repeated that Mauritius was and would remain British, and he "trust[ed] therefore, that a movement for an impractical object and which could bring nothing but discord and dissention among the people [would] be abandoned." Its leaders, he wrote to the secretary of state, Lord Milner, were "malcontent and mischievous individuals."[26]

For the retrocessionists, the 1921 Council of Government elections represented a test of their influence. The results were conclusive: not one retrocessionist candidate was elected. Even excuses of bribery and intimidation could not account for the solid vote against them. A few years later, with the advantage of hindsight, the staunchest retrocessionists had to consider the whole campaign a farce. Like most political organizations in Mauritius before 1936, the movement was formed by a group of friends who had not thought out the implications of their program. Retrocession had a romantic appeal and provided a means for the growing Creole intellectual class to express its cultural and emotional loyalty to France, as well as an opportunity to suggest to the colonial government that Creoles would in the future demand a greater part in the island's politics. But soon after the 1921 elections, the idea was forgotten.

The failure of the retrocession movement proved that the Creole community did not, at least yet, have a strong enough political base to determine an important national issue, and the 1921 election emphasized the community's dependence on political alliance with some other communal group. Although the days of great Creole leaders were yet to come, none of them, with the possible exception of Gaetan Duval in 1967, would ever believe that the Creole community alone had enough political influence to carry an election. Instead, after 1921 they allied themselves with Franco-Mauritians to halt constitutional change that would give Indo-Mauritians a voice in the political system. Although Creoles resented the exclusive nature of the Franco-Mauritian community, culturally they had far more in common with its members than with the Indians. Both groups were Catholic. Both preferred to speak and read French. And, in any case, until 1948 the Franco-Mauritians had the greatest political and economic power. Any politician could gain more for himself and his constituency by allying with the Franco-Mauritians than by turning to either the Creole lower classes or the Indians for political support. The retrocession movement did have one lasting result, however: it provided political experience for the three Creoles who would dominate the island's politics for the next two decades, Raoul Rivet, Edgar Laurent, and Maurice Curé.

Retrocession died, and constitutional reform, forgotten after the Swettenham Commission Report was published, once again became an issue in 1923. This time, the impetus came from the Creole elite wanting, as in 1886, more control over the government. Similar movements were growing in other British colonies; new constitutions for Jamaica, Trinidad, Nigeria, and Ceylon were under consideration at the Colonial Office, and it seemed obvious to the Mauritian elite that it, too, should benefit from the extension of representative government.

The promoters of constitutional change, called revisionists, wanted a shift in the makeup of the Council of Government, fewer unofficial nominated members, and more elected members.[27] The Council, they suggested, should, "except in matters of paramount importance," have final legislative authority.[28] The revisionists proposed that in addition to those already qualified to vote, Mauritians with 3,000 rupees worth of shares in a recognized stock company be eligible. Since nearly all sugar estates were joint stock companies with Franco-Mauritians and Creoles as major stockholders, obviously this was a strategy to gain ground at the expense of the Indians. Indians who accumulated wealth tended to invest in land rather than business. The revisionists, to make no bones about it, wanted to exclude them from the electorate.

Discussions about constitutional revision provided a background to Mauritian politics between 1924 and 1928. Odd patterns of alliance show up. Because the conservative program of the revision committee was designed to give more power to the elite, for instance, it is strange that the movement received so little backing from the Chamber of Agriculture and the planters. Heavy backers, on the other hand, included people who, as members of the *Action Liberale*, had earned reputations as liberals and friends of the "unruly Creole mob." It must have been this reputation that frightened the establishment; it could hardly have been the program itself, for revisionist demands were extremely modest, unlikely to stimulate a major reorganization of the Council.

Other reactions were predictable: the strongest opposition, naturally, came from the Indians, who had been elected to the Council in 1926. As one of them, Dunpath Lallah, explained:

It would be absolutely rash at this stage of our political development given the heterogeneous composition of our population to grant representative government to this colony. Representative government in such circumstances would be nothing less than government by a minority of the people. In putting forward my reasons against the motion, I must also lay stress on the deliberate attempts made against the Indian population of this island by certain members of the revision committee to keep the Indian population in perpetual subjugation.[29]

Initially, both the governor and the secretary of state seemed willing to consider giving Mauritians greater responsibility for the island's affairs; the secretary of state even went to so far as to suggest a revision comparable to the one introduced in Ceylon in 1923. But when the lack of support for constitutional revision became clear, the governor, Sir Herbert Read, wrote to the Colonial Office explaining that he found "no urgent public demand in Mauritius for a serious revision of the Constitution." Furthermore, he explained that he was opposed to granting greater power to the elected members until he was convinced that the franchise was "sufficiently wide to secure the proper representation of all classes of the people."[30] Once again, an attempt by the elite to strengthen their political position through constitutional change had failed. Within ten years, the same elite would be opposing constitutional change when a new group, the Indian laborers, had become a force in Mauritian politics. Once the franchise was extended to the Indo-Mauritian community, the Creoles could not realistically expect to become politically dominant; on the other hand, an opposition composed of 30 percent of the population could make day-to-day government distinctly difficult. The simple threat of mobilizing this opposition had ensured the position of the Creole community as a political force to be reckoned with in Mauritius.

The Franco-Mauritian and Creole communities, then, were the oldest communities in Mauritius, sharing a common religion but occupying different rungs in the socioeconomic hierarchy of the island. Differences based on color, or at least an awareness of color somewhere in one's ancestry, created a division on the basis of class which still endures today. A small group of light-skinned, well-educated Creoles chose to associate themselves as closely as possible with the power and wealth of the Franco-Mauritian community. But most Creoles were laborers. They worked as dockers and artisans, not as cane cutters, but shared with Indian cane cutters the agonies of low wages and poor working conditions. At first, these Creoles transcended ethnicity and allied with Indians to promote class interests. But they knew that ultimately they would have to compete with the more numerous Indian workers for a larger piece of the pie. During most years before independence, that pie was not growing at a very rapid rate, and as a minority group, the Creoles had to look elsewhere for protection from an Indian majority. Communal interests prevailed and Creole laborers could be relied upon to vote as a block for whatever party and candidates most explicitly offered to look after Creole interests. Their preindependence alliance with the Franco-Mauritians stemmed partly from their common culture and religion, but mostly from a pragmatic conviction that all minority groups needed to band together to prevent majority rule. Franco-Mauritians were always conscious of their ethnicity and community and always fiercely loyal to a common set of values and goals. Ethnic loyalty among Creoles grew markedly as the Indian population began to dominate the political life of the island.

3. Hindu and Muslim
The Indian Community

THE HISTORY of the Indian population in Mauritius stands in sharp contrast to the story of the Franco-Mauritians and Creoles. The most recent to arrive in Mauritius, Indo-Mauritians now constitute the largest group (68 percent). Until recently, they were also the poorest. A few Indians are large planters, with over 1,000 acres of cane; many others work as civil servants or teachers; but even today most are laborers in the cane fields. Once indentured laborers, Indians now dominate the political life of the island, but not without constant compromise, adjusting their interests to accommodate those of the Creoles and Franco-Mauritians. And growing divisions within the Indo-Mauritian community, based on religion and class, only accentuate the problems of Indian politicians.

The Indians Arrive

Before the large-scale immigration of indentured labor began, Mauritius had a tiny Indian community of messengers, seamen, and craftsmen, plus a small number of ex-convicts employed on public works projects. Most of Mauritius's present Indian population, however, is descended from the 450,000 indentured laborers who were brought to the island between 1836 and 1907.[1] After slavery was abolished in 1835, planters needed to find a new source of labor. Some planters imported workers from China and Africa, but most turned to India, where British agents were only too anxious to help with recruitment and transport. With promises of sufficient food, easy work, and good pay, the agents lured Indians, predominantly of lower castes, from areas around Calcutta, particularly Bihar.[2] To meet the growing demand, recruitment stations were also opened in Madras and Bombay. There were numerous difficulties at first in setting up this system, but the planters persisted, spending £200,000 in private funds to cover the costs of recruitment and transport between 1834 and 1838 alone.[3] After 1842, the government of Mauritius assumed the costs. Immigration continued, with only two interruptions, from 1837 until 1907. By 1845 one-third of the population of Mauritius was Indian, and by 1861 Indians made up nearly two-thirds of the island's people.

The Mauritian experiment had effects beyond the island as well. It became a model for other British colonies, and once it proved successful, planters in the West Indies and Fiji also imported indentured laborers on a large scale. The Mauritian government gave its agents an annual quota, the size varying considerably depending on the financial situation in the island that year. To recruit laborers, agents circulated notices such as this one of 1884:

> You will be taken free of expense to Madras. While there you will be fed and properly lodged until the ship which will take you to Mauritius sails, and should you be ill, the greatest care will be taken of you. When a ship is ready, you will be supplied with good clothing. The finest ships are selected and the voyage takes about three or four weeks. The food, medicines and other appliances on aboard are of good quality and your health, comfort and safety will be most carefully attended to. The Indian Government has appointed officers who are most strict and vigilant in securing for you all these advantages. On and after your arrival in Mauritius there is an Honorable Protector of Immigrants in that colony ready to assist you and advise you and there are magistrates from India acquainted with Indian languages to listen to complaints from you. Your religion will in no way be interfered with and both Hindu and Mohammedans are likewise protected. You will find over 246,000 of your countrymen settled there and the greatest care is taken not to separate families and relatives. You will have a house rent free to live in, a plot of garden ground to cultivate and you will, besides, be permitted to breed pigs, poultry and cattle during your leisure hours. When you are ill, medical attendants, medicine and nourishment will be provided free of charge. You will have to work for five years, six days in the week for nine hours between sunrise and sunset, all Sundays and holidays excepted. Besides the rations

of rice, dholl, salt, fish, ghee or oil and slat the men will receive
(Rs. five to seven). Females are not required to work unless they
choose. . . .[4]

Needless to say, such notices bore little relation to reality. The voyage
to Mauritius was a nightmare, and conditions did not improve once
the Indians stepped ashore. On shipboard, the food was inadequate
and the quarters smaller even than those on some slave ships. Appall-
ing sanitary conditions and lack of medical care led to the outbreak of
several epidemics in Mauritius. For those who survived, life was hard.
An immigrant was paid five rupees per month in cash and given rations worth an additional four rupees per month, less than their West
Indian counterparts (one rupee equalled one shilling sixpence, or
about twenty-one cents). Estates also provided a dwelling, usually
without nearby water. In return, the immigrant worked ten hours a
day, seven days a week, since Sundays were seldom holidays (*corvée*
was the term for compulsory Sunday work, originally intended for
those in charge of animals and later extended to all laborers). Malnutrition was widespread because the promised rations did not often
include protein. Immigrant families were separated, and immigrants
were punished severely for minor offenses. Anyone who missed one
day of work lost two days' wages—this practice, called the "double
cut," was unheard of in the West Indies. Besides landing to find a
hellish life, Indians had little chance to leave; by 1871 Mauritius was
"the only coolie importing colony which was not under obligation to
provide return passages after a certain term of residence."[5]

Laws to protect the immigrants were few, poorly defined, and
rarely enforced. The "honorable protector of immigrants," an early
example of false advertising, was not the sympathetic man the recruit-
ing notices described. Between 1859 and 1911 two men held this position: Nicholas Beyts and John Francis Trotter, both, in effect, agents
of the planters. Yet because of their experience, and because they
both spoke Hindustani, the colonial administrators rarely interfered
with their work. John Pope-Hennessy provoked a strong reaction
when he complained of Trotter's "apparent neglect to protect the
immigrants," and to his credit he badgered Trotter to investigate cases
of mistreatment and brutality on the estates.

The number of abuses in the West Indies and Mauritius grew;
epidemics broke out on board three ships in Mauritius in 1837. As a

result, in 1838 the government of India suspended emigration and launched an inquiry into the methods of recruitment in Bombay, Calcutta, and Madras. At the same time, at the other end of the loop, a special commission was established in Mauritius to report on the condition of Indians in Mauritius. The commission report confirmed stories of misrepresentation and deceit, and documented cases of kidnapping, of withholding up to 50 percent of a laborer's wages, and of the hostility of police and magistrates toward the immigrants.[6] Consequently, emigration from India was formally prohibited in 1839.[7] Only when the Mauritian government agreed to reforms in 1842 did emigration begin again; in the next year alone over 34,000 immigrants were processed through Port Louis. The planters followed only the new regulations which suited them, and successfully lobbied for the modification of others, including the regulation requiring planters to provide a free return passage.

In 1867, as the sugar industry began an economic decline, the government consolidated and revised the existing labor laws. The governor was "confident that he was initiating a 'new era of social improvement,'" but the spokesman for the laborers did not agree.[8] Theoretically, the new labor law ensured certain rights and privileges for the laborers, but that was hardly the case in practice. The protective sections of the law were ignored or reinterpreted by the employers; one section, however, was rigidly enforced by the planters: the part renewing the "double cut."

The Labour Law of 1867 also introduced a complex and restrictive system of passes and work permits for laborers who had completed their terms of indenture, and penalties for violating these laws were severe. Immigrants could be arrested without warrant and detained or sentenced to forced labor at the magistrate's whim. In 1869 alone, over 23,900 Indians were arrested for vagrancy, and between 1867 and 1872 Indians paid over £20,000 to the treasury for violating pass laws.[9] For the police and for many Mauritians, arresting Indians became a game. Vagrant hunts were a favorite Saturday morning pastime. Lunch was provided by the government, and teams competed to see how many immigrants they could arrest. In an average hunt, 500 men would be arrested, and of these about 275 would be condemned to a period of hard labor.[10]

The first governor to question these practices or to concern himself at all with the immigrant community was Sir Arthur Hamilton Gordon, who served in Mauritius between 1871 and 1874. The second civilian in that office since 1810, Gordon was one of Mauritius's strongest and most effective governors (in spite of the fact that he disliked the place so much he asked to be returned to his previous post in Trinidad, a request the Colonial Office refused to grant). Gordon arrived from Trinidad and found freshwater streams polluted by waste from the sugar factories, the forests cut down as if to facilitate soil erosion, and the Indian population "subject to disabilities and restrictions which are elsewhere only imposed on criminals under tickets of leave."[11] Whatever his efforts at conservation, the questions he raised on behalf of the Indians were not popular, at least with the Franco-Mauritians. He infuriated the planters when in 1871 he appointed a police commission to investigate charges in a petition signed by 9,140 Indians protesting the pass laws and the double cut. The commission's report concluded that the police had often acted in an "arbitrary and ill-judged" manner, and Gordon himself wrote:

> The timidity of the Protector, the folly and incompetence of the Inspector General of the Police, the extraordinary ignorance of the law shown by the magistrates, as well as its habitual conversion by them were all minutely and mercilessly displayed in the Report which moreover showed it to be proved beyond possibility of doubt or question, that very large sums of money due to the coolie labourers, amounting roughly on the average to some 30,000 dollars annual, have been withheld from them by the planters.[12]

Even the planters could not ignore that, so at their request a royal commission was appointed in 1872 to investigate the complaints of the Indians. The commissioners, William Frere and Victor Williamson, substantiated many of the complaints, even that some laborers had died from severe beatings, and recommended reform of the labor laws. Although many of their recommendations were made law, conditions still did not improve. The double cut was enforced, the planters arguing as late as 1908 that to abolish it would severely hurt them. But in spite of the severe conditions, Indian laborers rarely resisted—presumably because they understood the consequences of provoking widespread violence.[13]

It was not until 1908 that the government again voiced some concern, and in part because the labor picture was once again changing. Immigration was declining; laborers were increasingly reluctant to renew their contracts. Many were not even waiting them out, and there was a rapid rise in desertions. In addition, frustrated with the lack of reform to date, the laborers began to use more dramatic techniques to bring their plight to the attention of government officials. Some went to the extreme of putting their hands on the railway line to be crushed by a train; others set fire to cane fields, preferring to go to prison for arson rather than complete their contracts.[14] Indians even chose suicide as a way of escaping the estates.[15] According to the government, the laborers were most aggravated by the double cut and the *corvée*. In 1908 the protector of immigrants introduced legislation abolishing both.

The elected members of the Council of Government, many of whom were planters, opposed the legislation and argued that immigrants had neither the right nor the cause to expect better treatment. Sir William Newton, who more than twenty years earlier had been a leading advocate of reform, now took the planters' side and summed up the view:

> To change a law which has been for so many years in existence without any complaint on the part of the labourers can only have for its effect to shake the confidence that the labourers have had in their masters to the present moment and to induce them to believe that they are not treated as they should be, of all policies, the worst that can be followed in matters dealing with the relations between master and servant.[16]

In spite of the opposition of the unofficial members (except for one—a Creole), the legislation was approved.

There was more to come on the immigrant question. The Sanderson Commission in London began investigating immigration from India to the British colonies, with an eye to making recommendations that would limit it. When the commission reported in 1910, it found that the treatment of Indians in Mauritius compared favorably with that in other British colonies, but it was the only colony for which it recommended that immigration be discontinued.[17] The island was already overpopulated and there was no land available for the immigrants once their terms of indenture expired. Still, governors of Mauritius, pressed both by planters and by the Public Works Department, whose labor demands had not diminished even though available land had, tried to reintroduce immigration in 1912 and 1915.

Public opinion forced the government of India to abolish the indenture system in 1915. There was a brief flurry of activity in 1923, when
the Indian government reluctantly gave work permits to 1,500 men to
spend two years in Mauritius on a public works project. But the project was a disaster.[18] Most of these workers returned to India, and
further immigration was never again seriously considered by
Mauritius. After several more years, during the Depression, the demand for labor declined and the population so increased that unemployment and overpopulation—not a need for laborers—became the
island's principal worries.

Thus, after nearly ninety years, migration of indentured laborers
from India to Mauritius ended. The history of the indenture system is
long, complex, and generally unhappy. The laborers depended upon
British officials to provide minimum protection, but the officials were
severely limited by the planters' determination to do as they wished.
Some planters treated their laborers better than did others, of course,
but on every estate wages were low, the double cut was a regular
practice, and rations were limited.

By 1923 nearly all Indians on Mauritius belonged to the second
generation; only a few had been born in India. Those who were no
longer immigrants were outside the jurisdiction of the protector of
immigrants, it is true; but they were also without any protection and
had no government authority to whom they could turn for help. By
the 1930s bitter memories of the indenture system and the poor conditions on the estates provided a rallying point for leaders who were
anxious to stir the political consciousness of the Indian community.

Even before the indenture system ended, an Indian peasant class
had begun to form. Sons of the early peasants became the first Indian
professionals, forming the core of the Indo-Mauritian political elite.
These professionals were descended from indentured laborers who
chose not to return to India at the end of their contracts. Attracted by
bonuses and wage increases, some laborers whose terms had expired
signed up for another five years on the estates. Others settled in villages, continuing to work on the estates but now as day laborers. A
number managed to become landowners themselves, and by 1907
Indians owned one-third of the land planted in cane and produced
over one-fifth of the island's cane.

Besides land, the immigrants also began to acquire money.
Nicholas Pike reported that in 1869 Indians had deposited £69,032 in

the savings bank. In 1868, £17,158 was remitted to India on behalf of the immigrants, and additional sums were repatriated through merchants or taken in cash by returnees.[19] Indians used their hard-earned wages to accumulate savings in the bank, and to support their relatives in India. Most Indian landowners had accumulated their wealth by exploiting both employers and laborers. Obviously they were not the ordinary immigrants, for as the 1872 commission observed, "out of £6 per year it would be next to an impossibility for even the greatest miser to save up the large sums reported, namely 1,000, 2,000 and even 5,000 rupees."[20]

The men who saved money were the sirdars. When the first immigrants arrived in Mauritius, the estates selected from among the new arrivals gang leaders, called sirdars, to oversee the work. By the middle of the nineteenth century, the sirdars had increased their sphere of responsibility and worked as job contractors. Indispensable as they were, sirdars were in a strategic position to take advantage of employers and laborers alike. When competition for labor was high, they charged the estates a substantial bonus for each laborer recruited (since it was still cheaper for the estates to pay a bonus to a middleman than to give laborers more money). Responsible for distributing wages to the immigrants, some sirdars pocketed a portion and others charged heavy fines for minor offenses. One job contractor took one rupee per month from the wages of each of the 125 laborers under his charge. Others loaned money at high interest. When the combined pressures of low sugar prices and competition for labor forced planters in 1890 to sell or lease marginal land on deferred terms of payment, many sirdars had managed to accumulate enough money to start their own operations and still keep their jobs on the estates.

In addition to land and money, the Indians also acquired a third commodity: education. In Mauritius it was free but not compulsory. Indians viewed education as the key to a job in town—a step up from working on the estates—so children walked or rode trains for hours to reach schools where they were taught in French and English. By 1924, of the 397 students at the prestigious Royal College, 160 were Indians.[21]

These advances did not go unnoticed. Both the government and the Franco-Mauritians watched the gradually growing class of peasant proprietors in Mauritius with concern. Franco-Mauritians occasionally expressed fear that the Indians would gain too much control. According to Henri LeClezio:

The poor Indian has become the owner of the lands of the colony. The poor Indians are carters and traders. They are those unfortunate people that are sent from India to Mauritius! When they come here, I should not say they are civilized—they are brutes, most of them. They come to this colony in a state of uncivilization. When they have spent a certain number of years in the colony they acquire our civilization, they become landowners, they become traders, they become everything.[22]

British administrators, too, sometimes revealed their dislike and fear of the Indians. George Banbury, receiver general in 1909, reported: "An Indian takes all he can get. . . . There is no need to facilitate Indian loans. The planters can always help them."[23] Graham Bower, the colonial secretary who had earlier warned that the Indian population would compete with the colored community for jobs, wanted the Immigration Department strengthened. Referring to the independence movement in India, he said that the future of the colony depended on the ability of the government "to keep controlling hands over the Indians."[24] And in 1900 when Joseph Chamberlain wrote to Governor Charles Bruce suggesting that he nominate an Indian to the Mauritian Council of Government and consider increasing the number of Indian voters by lowering the qualifications for franchise, Bruce objected:

The Indian community here is totally unfit for the exercise of political privileges. The extension of the franchise would, therefore, have only the same result that has attended the lowering of the franchise in the case of the municipality. It would strengthen the hands of wire pullers and the most disreputable class in controlling the elections by votes obtained by unscrupulous means.[25]

Until World War II, the Indo-Mauritian community was removed from the mainstream of Mauritian social and political life. Unlike the Creoles, Indians did not assimilate or adopt European ways. They continued to live in rural villages. Their East Indian culture was modified and their economic standing improved, but these changes did not make them Mauritians.

If one important distinction existed between Indians and other Mauritians, an equally important division, when considering politics, existed between Muslims and Hindus within the Indian community. Of the total Indian population on Mauritius in 1972, 428,000 were Hindu and 137,000 were Muslim. Muslims constituted 16.6 percent of the total population; Hindus, 51.8 percent.[26] Although most Hindus are descended from indentured laborers, many, particularly the prominent politicians, are descended instead from traders who began arriving in Mauritius in the wake of the indentured laborers. The Muslims, Meimons from Cutch and Surtees from Surat, settled in the towns, opened shops, and soon became prominent dealers in food and textiles. The Meimons acquired a monopoly over the grain trade, while the Surtees became the major dealers in textiles. These Muslims remain distinct social groups to this day, and intermarriage between Meimons, Surtees, and Muslims who are descended from indentured laborers is discouraged.

Deeper than the divisions within the Muslim community, however, is the split between Muslims and Hindus. Having little in common with the Hindu laborers, the Muslim traders formed a separate community for economic as well as cultural reasons. Ancient differences have been accentuated by modern events, such as the creation of Pakistan in 1948. Over the years Muslims have also talked fearfully of Hindu domination, and this fear, as much as anything, has shaped their political behavior in Mauritius. Throughout the constitutional negotiations, Muslims were primarily concerned with safeguarding the interests of their own community.

Poised between the economically powerful Franco-Mauritian population and the populous and often poor Hindu community, the Muslims and the Creoles held the political balance for the two decades prior to independence. For the Labour party, Muslim support was important to an electoral victory; for the *Parti Mauricien*, it was essential. As long as the Muslims could remain united, their political significance was greater than their actual numbers suggested. Since 1948, the Muslim community has been on the verge of splitting into several factions, each representing different interest groups within the community; but only in 1967 did the factions actually fail to unite for the elections.

A number of other linguistic and religious minorities also divide the Indian community. In the 1972 census for Mauritius, 8.5 percent of all Indo-Mauritians reported that Tamil was their mother tongue, and 5.6 percent claimed Telegu; similar percentages of the Hindu community attend Tamil- and Telegu-speaking temples. Approximately 4 percent of the Indo-Mauritians are Christian. Tamil and Telegu holidays have been traditionally celebrated on estates, but only recently have these communities formed a political interest group.

In Mauritius, as in India, the Tamils have adapted more quickly than the Bengalis to "Western ways." Most of the people who straddle the border between the Indian and the Creole communities are Tamils, for some Tamils share Catholicism with the Creoles. They pass from one community to another, frequently changing their names from Verasamy to Jean-Baptiste. The Telegu community, based mainly in the villages, is more directly associated with the Hindi-speaking community.

The question of caste within the Indian community is a delicate one. Most overseas Indians, including those in Mauritius, prefer to deny or minimize its influence. But since the All-Mauritius Hindu Congress was founded, in 1965, with the expressed purpose of improving the position of the lower castes, it has become difficult to ignore the question of caste altogether.

Certainly, though, the caste system as it functions in India has never been successfully established overseas, primarily because the economic and political systems in which immigrants found themselves were not conducive to supporting it. In Mauritius, the colonial administration or else the estate managers took over the functions carried out by the caste associations in India, such as assisting with village organization and administering justice. Furthermore, the indenture system itself weakened the taboos of caste. On board ship or in an estate camp, social restrictions were impossible to maintain; once on land, Indians in Mauritius, as in other places overseas, traditionally left the unclean jobs, such as that of butcher or shoemaker, to other communities. And a number of immigrants may have taken advantage of the anonymity provided by the indenture system to upgrade themselves.

Caste, then, is an extremely sensitive subject in Mauritius, and a non-Indian, non-Mauritian finds it virtually impossible to obtain information that accurately quantifies the place of caste in Mauritius. However, one study suggests that a much higher percentage of Indians could name their caste in Mauritius than in other overseas Indian communities.[27] Certainly caste has been a basis for local factions and a determinant in local elections; since the late 1950s it has had an impact on national politics as well. It is suggested that high-caste Hindus were often selected to be sirdars simply because they could more easily discipline the gangs. Since it was the sirdars who acquired money to buy land, this advantage served the interests of the high-caste Indians.

Once it became clear that Indians would dominate politics in Mauritius, the question became, which Indians? In 1959, lower-caste discontent was responsible for the defeat of older, established, high-caste politicians. By 1963 the Labour party was forced to drop three high-caste candidates in favor of low-caste candidates. The All-Mauritius Hindu Congress appealed directly to low-caste, low-class voters, and their modest success suggests caste was a factor to be reckoned with in political life.

The Indians Enter Politics: 1900–1936

Whereas emancipation helped the Creoles gain entry into politics, experience on the estates impeded the Indians. Indians initially found themselves separated from the rest of society; their education was neglected and their alien characteristics were emphasized. The possibility of returning home may have been remote, but it was still enough to prevent many from taking a real interest in their new country. New arrivals renewed contacts with home for those already in Mauritius, and helped maintain the use of Indian languages on the estates. Regular visits from swamis reinforced religious ties. No wonder things seemed quiet. In 1909 the Swettenham Commission commented on the political docility of the Indian community, reporting that the Indians in Mauritius are "a singularly quiet, law abiding, and easily managed class."[28]

Such docility could not last. An emissary from Gandhi, rather than any local leader, first stirred Indian political consciousness. In 1901 Gandhi, returning to India from South Africa, stopped briefly in Mauritius; six years later, at Gandhi's behest, Manilal Maganlall Doctor came to Mauritius to teach immigrants about the traditions and heritage of their homeland. Believing that non-Indians would not respect Indians until the Indians themselves respected and understood their own background, Manilal was determined to give Indians in Mauritius dignity and self-respect.

From the beginning, Manilal took his mission seriously. He did most of his work in court, where he defended laborers he thought

were being unjustly prosecuted, or in villages, where he met with
small groups of Indians to discuss religion and customs. He founded a
newspaper, the *Hindustani*. But since he did not organize demonstrations or encourage illegal action, the government at first paid him
little attention. Unlike the small Indo-Mauritian elite, which had
been conspicuously silent on the subject, Manilal spoke for the laborers.

In the *Hindustani*, Manilal tried to emphasize the importance of
the Indian community to Mauritius. In the first issue he wrote, "Take
away these Hindustani merchants and the colony will come to a
standstill; take away the Hindustani labourer and the country must
perish." He appealed to the Indo-Mauritians—Hindus and Muslims,
Parsees and Christians—to "sink their little differences, bury their
personal and sectarian jealousies, and unite with one aim, to work for
common ideals and general interest."[29]

He enumerated the abuses on the estates and outlined needed reforms. Manilal called for an end to immigration and for further
financial assistance for the small planter, as well as for greater respect
for Indian religious and social customs. He was opposed by Xavier
Nalletamby, the sole Indian member of the Council of Government,
who believed, with the Swettenham Commission, that the Indians
were content. Of course, as a Christian, a Tamil, and a professional,
Nalletamby had rather little contact with Indian laborers; in fact he
did not speak any Indian language. Nevertheless, when the moment
came to decide whether steps should be taken to include Indians in
the political process, it was Nalletamby's word that mattered. In 1910,
the Swettenham Commission concluded that the Indian population
was not yet ready to participate in government. At the same time, it
was clearly a decision with an expiration date: the commission also
warned it would no longer be possible to continue to view the Indian
as "a stranger . . . who has no real claim to a voice in the ordering of
the affairs of the colony."[30]

Manilal left Mauritius in 1911. He left behind no new legislation or
reforms in the labor system, but he did leave a changed attitude on
the part of a small number of young Indians. Manilal gave these
people confidence in themselves and in their community, and that
confidence opened the door to Indian participation in the social,
economic, and political life of the island.

By the 1920s, a few Indians, encouraged by the formation of the Indian National Congress, began to move into politics, starting newspapers in French and English and standing for election. Following the 1921 election, two Indo-Mauritians were nominated to the Council of Government (provoking cries of horror from *Le Cerneen*); in 1926 two others, Rajcoomar Gujadhur and Dunpath Lallah, were elected to the Council of Government. It would be hard to claim that either Lallah or Gujadhur, both large landowners, were the laborers' champions; both had more in common with their Franco-Mauritian and colored constituents than with the cane cutters. As a matter of fact, both employed and exploited immigrants. They represented a growing Indo-Mauritian elite that was losing touch with the laboring classes, much as the colored elite a century earlier had severed ties with the Creole dockers and lower classes. But for all that, their election was significant: their presence paved the way for other Indo-Mauritians to follow.

In addition to planters like Gujadhur and Lallah, the new Indian elite included some who had studied in France and England during the 1920s, returning to Mauritius as trained professionals: doctors, lawyers, and teachers. In 1935, exactly one hundred years after the first indentured laborers had arrived from India, the Indo-Mauritian elite formed the Indian Cultural Association to organize centennial celebrations in the Indian community. The celebrations did not dwell on the past but provided an excuse to show Franco-Mauritians and Creoles that there were Indians in Mauritius who had acquired European standards of behavior. At the same time, Indian intellectuals and national leaders like Tagore and Gandhi were held up as sources of pride.

Among the leaders of the centennial were Rampersad Neerunjun, a young lawyer, and Seewoosagur Ramgoolam, who was to be Mauritius's first prime minister, both typical of the foreign-trained professionals who would dominate Mauritian politics in the future. A Royal College laureate, Neerunjun had studied law in England, then returned to Mauritius in 1932 to face the same humiliating discrimination Manilal had encountered. The first Indo-Mauritian lawyers had never demanded that closed doors open for them, but Neerunjun was determined to rise to the top. He believed that this could be done by identifying with and joining Creole society. Professionally, he was a success. Socially, that he should even have thought of joining that

most exclusive of Creole groups, the *Cercle de Rose Hill*, shows that
he never fully understood the limitations of the plural society in
Mauritius.

Ramgoolam—unlike Neerunjun, who had been brought up in the
urban atmosphere of Rose Hill—came from a rural background.[31]
His father was a sirdar; although he died when Ramgoolam was
young, he had managed to scrape together enough money to give his
son a primary school education and then send him to the Royal College at Curépipe. From there, with only a few pounds in his pocket,
Ramgoolam set off for England to become a doctor. At the University
of London, he read voraciously—contemporary and socialist litera-
ture, poetry, and plays. T. S. Eliot became his favorite author, and
he memorized long passages from *The Waste Land* and *Four Quar-
tets*. He also became absorbed in politics, following the activities of
the Independent Labour party in India and becoming the organizing
secretary for the Indian Students' Union and a member of its executive committee. In this capacity, he met many nationalist leaders
from India, including Nehru, Patel, Jinnah, and Krishna Menon.

Through letters from home and through Mauritian friends visiting
in London, Ramgoolam kept in touch with events on the island. Returning to Mauritius in 1934, Ramgoolam began writing literary and
social criticism for *Le Radical* and *Le Mauricien*. By the time of the
Mauritian Indian centenary celebrations, he had earned a reputation
as a competent doctor and was an active leader of the Indo-Mauritian
community as well. More than Neerunjun, Ramgoolam remained in
touch with the laborers and peasants, making frequent visits to villages and meeting with Indians of all classes. Underneath, he was a
born politician, sensitive to the feelings of those around him, intuitive
in the art of compromise, persuasive, and honest. He was neither
pretentious nor condescending. When he became a national figure,
he was known as *chacha*, a Hindi term for "uncle" that conveys both
warmth and respect.

Ramgoolam and Neerunjun were prominent figures in the celebrations that took place in December 1935, celebrations that revealed the
deep division between the conservative politicians, such as Lallah and
Gujadhur, of the 1920s and the nationalist politicians of the 1940s.
After the centenary it became obvious that the quiet style of the older
Indian leaders was out of date; younger, more forceful men were
assuming leadership in the Indo-Mauritian community. The new

leaders urged Indians to develop their potential political power. Ramgoolam blamed the colonial government for the existing state of economic affairs. He asked for centralization of the banks and for constitutional revision. But the impetus for change, he saw, had to come from the Indo-Mauritian community:

> This political and economic backwardness is also the result of the Indo-Mauritian being a slave to tradition. He has hitherto lived so much in the past that he has lost all contact with the present. What was good for the contingencies of yesterday seems to be as good for the crises of today. We forget that to move with the world in its progress we must substitute a philosophy of change for a stagnant tradition without intelligence and perspective. . . . Our society must evolve and adapt itself to the new ideas and new inventions, rejecting only that which is meaningless and useless but never disdaining those changes that may give life and vitality. Our barrier of caste and religion must give away to the unification of our race and the brotherhood of man. . . . There must be a great mass movement, but in this mass movement we must not be cheated into giving fictitious importance to what is false, dead and well buried.

> Many great movements have been crippled, many great opportunities lost by the minor spites of the elect. It is only by the subordination of self and by selfless sacrifice and endeavours that this great community of Indo-Mauritians will be saved from being a burden unto itself; and it is through these that will come unity, strength, and the hope of a happy community capable of great achievements like those of our forefathers in India.[32]

Ramgoolam was quoting Aristotle, H. G. Wells, and Fabian Society leaders Beatrice and Sidney Webb. He challenged his community, but for the moment his challenges were for the intellectuals. The concrete result of the Indian centenary was not a mass movement, but the foundation of an Indian Cultural Association, dedicated to promoting the traditions of the Indian community in Mauritius and limited in its appeal to the elite of the Indian community. *Advance*, the newspaper founded in 1940 by Ramgoolam, Aunauth Beejadhur, and other members of the Indian Cultural Association, was a paper for intellectuals. It was filled with philosophical and literary criticism; its editors refrained from attacking the colonial administration, and were reluctant to defend the rights of the laborers.

While the Indians were quarreling about who would direct the centenary celebrations and who would be president of the Indian Cultural Association, and while Ramgoolam talked of the "mass movement" he was later to lead, Dr. Maurice Curé was visiting estate camps, talking to laborers and immigrants about wages and trade unions and human dignity. In 1936 the Indian intellectuals of Mauritius were still not anxious to be reminded of their immigrant past. But on the estates, discontent was growing and the laborers were ready for leadership.

4. Class Politics

The Beginnings
of Mass Participation

THE ETHNIC DIVISIONS between the French, the Creoles, the Hindus, and the Muslims shaped Mauritian society. But just as important were the class distinctions between the elite and the laborers and small planters. Until the 1930s little attempt had been made to bridge the gulf between these two political worlds of Mauritius. During the 1930s the colored elite was making what would turn out to be its final attempt to acquire political power in the Council of Government and the Port Louis Municipal Council. Also during the 1930s, members of the Indo-Mauritian elite established themselves in the professions, generally giving up their Indian customs and maintaining European habits adopted during years of study abroad. Neither group took an interest in the laborers and small planters.

Elite politics in the 1930s centered around the colored intellectuals, particularly Raoul Rivet and Edgar Laurent.[1] Laurent and Rivet were quite different from their nineteenth-century predecessors, who had tried to deny their color and join the Franco-Mauritian community. They had a wider political base, for by 1930 there was a large Creole middle class of civil servants and petty clerks who were eligible to vote and who in Port Louis constituted the majority of the electorate. Unlike the *Action Liberale* leaders, Laurent and Rivet did not seek or need political support from the Indians or the disenfranchised Creoles.

Between 1927 and 1946, these two men dominated the Port Louis Municipal Council, the only entirely elected body in Mauritius, choosing other men to stand with them in their informal alliance, called the *Union Mauricienne*, controlling the municipality's patronage, and together, annually, selecting the city's mayor, who was in theory elected from among the municipal councillors. The governor must have been aware that, if displeased, Laurent and Rivet could rally Creole support and organize a sizable demonstration in the streets of Port Louis.

As the Indo-Mauritian community became active in politics, the ideas of Laurent and Rivet became increasingly outdated. Yet, by challenging the authority of the Franco-Mauritians on the municipal level, they themselves had prepared the way for the most radical demands of the Indian and Creole laborers. Unlike the Creole elite of the 1880s, who had participated in politics on the Franco-Mauritians' terms, Rivet and Laurent had forced the Franco-Mauritians to join the Municipal Council on their terms. At the same time, absorbed by personal rivalries within the council, the problems of the centennial, and the issue of taxation, they were for the most part unaware of what was happening on the sugar estates. From force of habit, they still looked to the governor for an indication of what the future would be like, rather than to the disenfranchised Creoles and Indo-Mauritians.

The principal political issue in the 1930s was the financial condition of the island.[2] The sugar industry had been investigated and pronounced efficient in 1929, but the finances of the colony remained desperate, and in 1932 commissioners came from London to recommend further money-saving programs. Their recommendations included abolishing 303 government posts, reducing civil servants' salaries by 10 percent, and introducing a graduated property tax.[3] Mauritian planters and businessmen, furious, demanded that their representatives go to London; encouraged by the governor, the secretary of state agreed to meet with a Mauritian delegation. He agreed to minor changes which freed six of the nine unofficial members of the Council of Government from their obligation to vote with the government, and persuaded the chancellor of the exchequer to increase the preferential price for sugar from the Crown Colonies and to an increase in Mauritius's quota.[4] But these advantages, unfortunately, were negated by a fall in world prices.

During the 1930s the economic situation in Mauritius became increasingly desperate. And while the elite negotiated with Britain and struggled to maintain their standard of living, the laborers were wondering where their next meal would come from. Hard pressed by the

Depression and encouraged by new leaders, the laborers in Mauritius, like laborers throughout the other colonies, began to demand a better standard of living and some limited participation in government. When their petitions were persistently ignored, they turned to violence. Divisions in Mauritius in 1937 were based primarily on class rather than ethnic community, and so was the violence. Quite suddenly the focus of Mauritian politics shifted away from the elite toward the laborers.

During the boom years of the early 1920s, laborers became accustomed to riding in buses and trains, to eating well, and even to going to one of the island's few cinemas, entertainment possibilities having expanded somewhat from the days of the village meetings. If he worked hard, a day laborer could earn three rupees a day. When sugar prices fell in the Depression, some laborers were deprived of their bus rides and cinemas, but many were forced to turn to the protector of immigrants and to the Poor Law commissioner for survival. In 1929 the Public Health Department reported that:

> Increasing numbers of persons are being seen at the dispensaries whose illness is not any communicable disease but the much more insidious condition of defective nutrition. This is the inevitable consequence of the serious economic depression in the colony. The rising death rate is largely attributable to this and there is no sign of the increase slackening.[5]

By 1932 a day laborer could earn only forty-five cents a day during intercrop and sixty cents a day during the crop. His wife's wages would be half of that.*

Their stories were all much like that of a forty-year-old woman who gave evidence before the 1937 commission of enquiry appointed to study the riots that swept the island in 1936.

> I live at Bon Accueil and I work in the fields at weeding. Sometimes my husband, who is an old man of sixty comes to help me and sometimes I work alone. I have children who help me sometimes. I have too many children and my husband is old. I work and I do not earn enough to live. Sometimes in intercrop for the day I earn twenty-five cents, sometimes thirty. I work from seven a.m. until three or four in the afternoon. In the time of the crop I earn forty

---

*One hundred cents Mauritian=one rupee.

cents and I work until four. Sometimes also they do not give me work. They will tell me that I am too old and I should let my daughters work. We cannot work four or five days a week. I have five children. One of my daughters is married but she has been sent by her husband to live with me. She is fourteen. One of my daughters and my son work in the fields. The daughter earns thirty-five to forty cents a day and the little boy twenty-five cents per day. My husband cannot work.[6]

What happened in Mauritius in the 1930s was not unique. The effects of the Depression, aggravated, according to some, by the failure of the Labour Government of 1929 to implement radical policy changes, were similar throughout the British colonies. But they were particularly severe in colonies that depended on one or two cash crops. Wages in Mauritius, a one-crop island, were among the lowest in the British colonies, and the island's laborers were more heavily taxed than any other economic class. The governor, Sir Wilfred Jackson, was reluctant to establish a minimum wage. If the existing rates were legalized, abnormally low wages might be perpetuated; if wages substantially above the current rate were established, the effect on the sugar industry might be catastrophic.[7]

A few of the more sensitive estate owners recognized that part of the responsibility for the misery in the island was theirs. One concerned planter wrote:

It is unpardonable that after the First World War in 1919 and 1920 when one thought in millions, that one did not seize the occasion to put to one side a large sum for: 1) suitable housing for the labourers, artisans and employees, 2) a retirement pension for the old labourers. One did not dream of the first and one was quiet about the second.[8]

But most planters were obsessed with mounting deficits and took little interest in labor problems. The Poor Law Office tried to help the thousands of people who clamored for help, but its administration was inefficient. Apparently so was its administrator; even the governor considered Lionel Collet unsuited for the job.[9]

In the 1930s the government taxed the laborer, the estates ignored him, and his own people cheated him. As it had been during the days of immigration, actual hiring was done not by the estate owners but by job contractors, usually Indians. The estate owner would pay the job contractor, who was often also the sirdar or overseer of the estate, a fixed sum for each *gaulette* (a measuring pole of ten feet) of cane cut, plus a small percentage of the total wage bill. When measuring the work of one of his laborers, the sirdar usually used a "long" *gaulette* of eleven feet, cheating the laborer out of one-tenth of his wages. Other contractors refused to pay a laborer on the grounds that he had not completed a given task in the given time. As long as the work was done, the estate owners asked no questions. The less the sirdars paid the laborers, the greater their own profits, which they used in turn to buy land for themselves or an education for their children.[10]

The small planters, most of whom were Indian, suffered at the hands of middlemen as much as did the laborers. Most owned four or five acres of land and could grow barely ten or eleven tons of cane an acre.[11] They sold their cane to a cane dealer who in turn sold it to the nearest factory to be milled, taking a sizable cut on the way. It was impossible to bypass the cane dealer, because estates, to avoid buying cane from a hundred or so small planters, would only buy from two or three middlemen. Furthermore, cane dealers served as moneylenders (*bailleurs de fonds*) for small planters, who always needed cash for fertilizer and seed during the planting season. The interest rates were exorbitant, but since the banks refused to lend them money, the small planters had no choice but to borrow from the cane dealers. By the time the estate and the cane dealers had taken their cuts, the small planter received sixty-eight kilos of sugar per ton of cane delivered to the miller. Assuming that there were no droughts or cyclones, the small planter could earn roughly three-hundred rupees, just enough to pay his yearly debts. Cane dealers, on the other hand, often reported annual profits of over four times that amount.

Neither laborers nor small planters had any effective legal means of protecting their interests. What recourse there was proved either illegal or ineffective. Associations or unions of laborers were illegal; laborers were supposed to take their complaints to the protector of immigrants, but they soon learned that a visit to his office was a waste of time. The protector of immigrants usually did nothing, while the trip to his office in Port Louis required a full day, and some estates still practiced the double cut despite the fact that it had been disallowed. Although the Labour Ordinance of 1922 required government inspectors to visit each estate twice a year to ensure that minimum standards of accommodation, health, and safety were met, there was a shortage of staff, and these visits were rarely made.

The first agitation for trade unions came in the boom year of 1921. A typesetter, William Moutou, approached Edgar Laurent, who had just finished a term as mayor of Port Louis, and Arthur Rohan, Laurent's cousin and a prominent attorney. Banding together, the three formed the National Trade Union of Mauritius to obtain fair wages, provide funds for relief, and regulate disputes between employers and employees.[12] In the summer of 1921, a union-coordinated strike of government railroad employees failed. The procureur-general did not recognize the union. In 1925 the new governor, Sir Herbert Read, brought with him a bill providing for the registration of trade unions in accordance with International Labor Organization (ILO) conventions. The bill was referred to the Mauritian government's Committee on Law, and there it died.

After the Labour government was returned in Britain in 1929, the Colonial Office took a new interest in conditions in the colonies. Lord Passfield (formerly Sidney Webb), secretary of state for the colonies, circulated a memorandum asking that all colonial governments introduce trade union legislation, and a newly established Colonial Office Labour Committee regularly sent out model laws. But in Mauritius, as in many colonies, the dispatches and recommendations were virtually ignored.[13] As late as March 1936, the governor, Wilfred Jackson, told the secretary of state for the colonies that labor legislation would have "provoked a great deal of suspicion and factious opposition: it would have created sharp divisions among different sections of the population at a time when this was particularly to have been avoided and would have achieved no real advantage."[14] Furthermore, Jackson argued that Mauritian politicians were not interested in labor union activity. Jackson's conclusion was especially startling in view of both the unrepresentative nature of the Council of Government and the petitions from laborers he had received during the summer of 1935. Since the Colonial Office was unable to effect any change in labor policy, and the local government was unwilling to do so, the impetus could come only from the laborers. In Mauritius, as in the West Indies, strikes and riots finally led to government action.

In 1934, a year of severe drought, small bands of the unemployed began marching on Government House to demand work. The marches continued through 1935, and an organization called *Chomeurs Intellectuels* was formed to monitor the government's efforts to find work for the unemployed. This committee, composed of members of the colored elite, dealt mostly with the problems of skilled urban unemployment caused by the Depression and had little to do with the problems of laborers on estates. (By now, this division, along with all others, was becoming important.) By the end of 1937, the organization had faded away.

The plight of the laborers was taken up briefly by Rajcoomar Gujadhur, then a nominated member of the Council of Government. In July 1935 Gujadhur held a meeting in Port Louis attended by eight thousand laborers to protest the condition of Indian workers on the island, certainly the largest organized meeting of laborers in the island's history. Gujadhur, owner of one of the island's largest estates, saw that the laborers, underfed and suffering from malnutrition, were unable to work effectively. But as he saw it, the blame lay not with the sugar industry and its organization, but with the British government; what was needed, he believed, was increased assistance in the form of preferential sugar prices.[15]

The Labour Party and Dr. Curé

The first Mauritian to attempt to rally the estate workers into a political organization was a Creole, Dr. Maurice Curé. He had gone to England to study medicine just before the outbreak of World War I. In England he had offered his services to the British Army, but had been turned away because of his color. He returned to Mauritius at the end of the war and quickly established himself as a doctor. He was also an active participant in island politics and one of the leaders of the ill-fated retrocession movement of 1919. Through his medical practice, he had contact with laborers on the estates. Appalled by the conditions in which they lived, in 1924 he organized a march on Government House that succeeded in embarrassing the government into supplying workers in one area with good water. Curé ran in the municipal court elections in 1924 and the Council of Government elections of 1926 and 1931, promising to improve the squalid life of the laborers but making no attempt to woo the elite who made up the electorate, an oversight that undoubtedly contributed to his defeat. But in 1934 he won a by-election to the Council of Government, where he quickly earned a reputation as a radical and a troublemaker by advocating trade union legislation and the replacement of the protector of immigrants by a director of labor. The doctor lost his seat two years later. His program, including an extension of the franchise, the appointment to Mauritian courts of judges trained only in England, and the establishment of an agricultural bank to make loans to small planters, could hardly appeal to the Franco-Mauritian or colored bourgeois voters, who believed him to be an agent of the Soviet Union.[16] Curé's bluntness and radical stand ensured his defeat, which in turn led him to form the Mauritius Labour Party.

On January 24, 1936, soon after his defeat, Curé organized a march of unemployed workers to Port Louis. This was somewhat more successful: about four hundred men came on foot and by train. For the next month he wrote earnest petitions to the governor and the secretary of state on behalf of the laborers, and with ten or twelve friends formulated plans to organize a political party. In February, at a public meeting in the Champ de Mars at the Port Louis racetrack, the Labour party was founded to "assure the representation of the workers in Mauritius."[17] Curé estimated that eight thousand people came to his first meeting (though police reports were more modest). He told the laborers that they were entitled to higher wages, better housing, improved hospital care, and the right to form trade unions, but that the government would not recognize these rights unless forced to do so. Before the meeting ended, the enthusiastic crowd approved resolutions demanding that laborers be represented in the Council, that the franchise be extended to the working classes, and that the labor laws in Mauritius conform to the recommendations of the ILO and include provisions for trade unions and old-age pensions.

Maurice Curé was a very unlikely labor leader. Neither a demagogue nor an opportunist, he was actually a poor public speaker; nor did he enjoy spending time gossiping with laborers. But he was ready to risk his reputation and his practice by trying to organize labor, a group which until this time had not even protested to the government. Sir Bede Clifford, who arrived as governor in 1937 prepared to condemn Curé as a fraud, found him modest and sincere, although exceedingly stubborn.[18] Curé was not a strategist, he trusted people too much, and he talked too openly about his plans. But he was determined, and for the first few months he was able to gain popular support without official interference.

Constitutional reform and freedom to form trade unions, Curé's primary concerns, were studiously ignored by the governor. From Jackson's perspective, the absence of trade unions was due to the "lack of organizing capacity among those concerned rather than to any statutory prohibition."[19] He was willing to consider some "moderate" extension of the franchise and a "small" increase in the Council of Government, but opposed any sweeping changes. Officials in London supported Jackson, agreed that Curé had little claim to speak on behalf of the working class, and dismissed him as a "haphazard demagogue" and a "windbag."[20]

Curé's only alternative was to organize effective pressure groups in Mauritius and in London. He had hoped for advice and support from the Indian National Congress and the ILO. The Congress was interested but had no funds to spare; the ILO sent its publications regarding labor conventions and an application for membership. But when Curé protested Britain's failure to apply in Mauritius the conventions which it had ratified, the ILO was forced to reply that it could not accept Curé's representation because it emanated from a political party rather than an industrial association.[21] To meet ILO regulations (as well as Barclay's Bank requirements for opening an account), Curé founded the *Société de Bienfaisance des Travailleurs*, a nonpolitical workers' benevolent society. The officers of the Labour party were those of the *Société*, and the two organizations often met on the same day and used the same minute book. The Labour party became a pressure group without funds, and the *Société de Bienfaisance* was a workers' organization with dues-paying members who would support administrative costs and finance projects to benefit workers.[22]

Legal niceties, it seemed, did not help Mauritius's cause at the ILO, and when the October 1937 meeting of the ILO governing body in Prague came and went without reference to Mauritius, Curé became disillusioned. The pressure, he concluded, must be brought to bear directly on the Colonial Office.

The planters had long kept representatives in London; it seemed logical that the Labour party should do the same.[23] After considerable debate, the *Société de Bienfaisance* selected an Indian, Rajmohunsingh Jomadar, to be the spokesman for Mauritian labor in England. On his arrival in London in 1937, Jomadar contacted both

Arthur Creech-Jones, who by then was taking an active interest in colonial affairs, and after its formation in 1940, the Fabian Colonial Bureau, which, through its connections with Labour party members of Parliament, and its regular publications, served as an effective lobby in London on behalf of laborers in all British colonies. Both Creech-Jones and the Fabians encouraged Jomadar to keep in touch, which he did until the Labour party lost most of its support in 1941. He then lost contact with Curé, and was of little further use to the party in London.

By the summer of 1936, both the party and the *Société* were firmly established, claiming four thousand members and holding meetings at least weekly. Curé appointed a number of village agents to explain the aims of the party and the *Société* to all laborers and to sell *Société* membership cards for twenty-five cents a month. Part of the fee was kept by the agent (another middleman in the life of Mauritius) and the rest Curé planned to use for operating expenses, unemployment relief, and, eventually, a headquarters.

Unlike previous political groupings, the Labour party was not controlled by a small clique. Its leaders were a heterogeneous group who believed that the laborers themselves had to organize to force a change. Curé's principal assistant was Pandit Sahadeo Rama, a diminutive and unpretentious follower of Gandhi who had campaigned for Curé in the 1936 election. Sahadeo explained the purpose of the party to audiences in Hindi, still the first language of the large majority of laborers. He also provided the main link between the party and the Indian National Congress. He had met Gandhi in 1925, and returned to India to put the case of the Labour party before the Congress in 1938 and again in 1940. At no time, however, did the Congress help the party in any significant way.[24]

The Labour party gained momentum when Emmanuel Anquetil joined at the end of 1936. The son of a nurse, Anquetil left home when he was very young to work as a ship's carpenter. One of his early trips took him to England, where he married and settled for twenty-five years. An admirer of G. D. H. Cole and J. M. Keynes, Anquetil was organizer and secretary of a local branch of the National Union of Shipwrights. When World War I began he tried to enlist in the Royal Navy, but he, too, was turned away because of his color. A ship took him to the United States, from which he was deported in 1931 because he carried no passport. In England during the

Depression, Anquetil could find no work, and the Home Office, after considerable debate, repatriated him and his son to Mauritius in 1936.

Already embittered by his experiences abroad, Anquetil was horrified by conditions on the estates, which he saw as worse than when he left. Within days after his return he had joined the *Chomeurs Intellectuels*, from which he resigned in 1937 to join Curé. More militant than the physician, Anquetil worked with religious devotion. But he lacked the flamboyance of his successor, Guy Rozemont, although the intensity of his concern made him popular among the laborers. And his familiarity with trade union organization in Britain and his grasp of facts and figures was an immense help to Curé's comparatively amateur efforts.

Since the founding of the Labour party, the police had attended every meeting, listening conscientiously for seditious phrases. But its leaders were careful. In pressing for trade union legislation, Curé cited the examples of Cuba, where laborers were permitted to strike, and closer to home, the nearby island of Réunion, whose laborers had just organized a legal strike for higher wages, to remind his audiences that unless laborers in Mauritius took some action themselves, their lot would never change. But not once did he publicly advocate a strike or violence.[25]

Despite the governor's conviction that the Labour party was not "in any sense a political organization of a representative character," it was in fact Mauritius's first political party.[26] Furthermore, it was the first political organization to call itself a party. It had an elected executive which met regularly, kept books and records, and charged membership fees. It had an ideology and a program, albeit one copied to a large extent from that of the British Labour party. Shared beliefs rather than personal friendship held the party together in its first years. Antagonisms within the leadership would weaken the party, but they would never destroy it in the way that such quarrels had destroyed the *groupements* based on friendship that characterized politics in Mauritius before 1936.

The Mauritian government clearly had little patience with the Labour party, and would have welcomed a chance to silence its leaders. Some colonial administrators felt that force was the best way to keep Mauritius calm, but officials in London were beginning to look for other solutions. One colonial official wrote in 1937:

My own instinct is that if we are to avoid storms we ought to set our political course a few points to the left. The situation of the working classes is deplorable. The white planters are excessively *ancien regime*. The *bastille* seems not yet to have fallen. They have, under the present constitution, an overweighted political power. They have their representative in London and understand the technique of making things uncomfortable for the Governor unless he moulds his policy generally to conform with their views and commercial interests.[27]

But it was too late. The cane fields were already burning.

Confrontation: The 1937 Riots

In June 1937 the police, fearing that Mauritians might be influenced by recent strikes and riots in Trinidad, intensified their watch on the Labour party. Their reports note that the emphasis of the speeches had changed (probably as a result of Anquetil's influence) from explicit political demands, such as constitutional reform and a wider franchise, to economic demands, specifically higher wages.[28] But employers gave no indication of raising wages to correspond with the higher prices they were receiving for their sugar.[29]

On August 1, 1937, the Labour party held its last meeting of the year. The leaders themselves seemed caught up by the excitement, and the police, particularly sensitive after the West Indian riots, were disturbed by the tone of the last meeting. They called Anquetil's speech "inflammatory" and accused him of arousing racial antagonisms. Before the police had decided what action to take, strikes and riots broke out and the party was banned.

Laborers were not the only discontented Mauritians; by 1937 the nearly twenty thousand small planters were also starting to voice their grievances.[30] Producers of one-quarter of the island's crop, they objected to the "limitation of area system" which forced planters to send their cane to a specified crushing factory, which in turn meant a specified cane dealer. Although the thirty-eight miller-planters believed this system prevented wasteful competition, the small planters claimed they could get more for their cane if they were not required to sell to one factory. They further objected that they had no opportunity to verify the accuracy of the scales or the honesty of the weighers. But it was the Uba cane question that sparked the small planters into action in 1937.

Uba cane was an especially hardy variety first imported from South Africa in 1917. By 1924 the big estate planters had learned that Uba produced less sugar per ton of cane than did other varieties and had stopped planting it. But it remained a favorite of the small planters because it required less care and withstood the heavy winds of the cyclone season. In August 1935 several estates with factories warned that in the following years they would reduce the price for Uba; a few even warned middlemen and planters that they would refuse to accept the cane at all. The small planters paid no heed. The warnings were repeated during the 1936 crop season. In 1937 the Rich Fund Estate reduced the price for Uba cane by 15 percent. The small planters sent a petition to Curé, who forwarded their protest to the government with the comment that it needed urgent attention. Neither quick nor decisive action was likely, however, for the governor was absent and his colonial secretary was in charge.

At this point the laborers and small planters, already aroused by Curé and Anquetil, decided to take matters into their own hands.[31] In the middle of the morning of July 30, laborers on the Rich Fund Estate walked out. To be sure, they were back at work two days later, but the unrest quickly spread to other estates. On August 8, eight hundred determined men began a march to Port Louis to see the protector of immigrants. Armed police prevented the crowd from reaching the city; instead, its leaders met with two representatives from the Office of the Protector of Immigrants and the managers of the three troubled estates. Complaints of low wages, exploitation by the sirdars, and reduction of the Uba cane price were hardly new to the estate managers, whose only reply was that they had posted warnings for two years that the price of Uba was going to be cut. The police apparently felt that permitting the laborers to express their grievances would solve the problem. But the laborers wanted more than a platform: they wanted assurances that their requests would be granted, not vague promises that someone would try to look into the matter.

On the estates, things were heating up. Laborers began to set fire to cane fields, picketers prevented people from going to work, crowds overturned trucks and cut telephone wires. As soon as the police dispersed one group and moved away, another group formed. Not having had to deal with riots since 1911, the police were neither well trained nor experienced. The acting governor's response, a cable to the Colonial Office in London asking that a cruiser be sent immediately, did little to ease the situation. On August 12 the manager of Union Flacq, Ackbar Gujadhur, the brother of Rajcoomar Gujadhur and co-owner of one of Mauritius's largest estates, asked the commissioner of police and the procureur-general for additional protection. His request was refused; the commissioner had no extra men available. When Gujadhur asked what he was to do if the laborers marched on his estate, the commissioner replied, "My only advice to you is to stop your mill, to mobilize yourself, and to inform the police immediately. We will come to protect you."[32] Did the commissioner mean that the managers of Union Flacq Estates should arm themselves? Gujadhur thought so and ordered rifles and ammunition.

The next morning armed Union Flacq managers met nearly two hundred Indian laborers brandishing sticks and sugarcane. After some futile attempt at negotiation on the part of the police, the angry crowd moved to attack the factory with stones. One of the Gujadhur brothers fired over their heads. Still the mob did not retreat. Terrified, several members of the estate staff fired directly into the mob. The mob scattered and fled, leaving four dead and ten wounded—the first Mauritians ever killed in riots in the island's history.

What had been trouble on three estates was now an island-wide conflagration. During the next week, unrest spread. Strikers armed with sticks and stones intimidated and threatened any strikebreakers they met and blocked lorries attempting to carry people to work. Factories were sabotaged. Cane fields smoldered everywhere. Detachments of police and soldiers, trying to move from one village to another, could not keep up with the growing crowds.

Immediately after the shooting at Union Flacq, Curé cabled D. N. Pritt, a lawyer well known for defending laborers in the colonies, and sent telegrams and letters of protest to the secretary of state. There was no immediate reaction in London; nor did either of the Indian representatives on the Council of Government speak up on the laborers' behalf. Both were part of the establishment; neither wanted to side with the lower classes. (Later, they would pay dearly for their silence, for after the 1948 constitutional reforms, the new leadership, which celebrated the 1937 strikes as a turning point in Mauritian history, would turn its backs on them.)

The acting governor refused to intervene directly, sending a letter to the Chamber of Agriculture asking them to submit proposals for settling the dispute between laborers and employers. The Chamber of Agriculture promptly recommended that the mill owners pay hard-working laborers Rs 1.50 a day and reduce the price cut for Uba cane from 15 percent to 5 percent. Individual estates, especially those most threatened, began at once to raise wages to meet the suggested standard; three days later the police commissioner requested both the police and the army to resume normal duties. The commissioner, however, was too optimistic, and his command premature. Crowds continued to gather, especially in the south, and on August 27, six hundred men began throwing stones at the police station in L'Escalier. The police fired, killing one man and wounding another. But although excited crowds gathered in protest throughout September, those shots marked the end of the violence for the crop season. As the number of disturbances diminished, all parties settled down to the task of preparing evidence for the commission of enquiry which the acting governor had appointed.

The makeup of the commission said almost as much about Mauritius in the fall of 1937 as its findings could. In spite of Curé's protests, the commission was composed only of planter and government representatives. It heard evidence from 116 witnesses—estate managers, politicians, civil servants, and day laborers—and during the hearings the naïveté and isolation of the planters became apparent. They seem to have been living in a dream; without exception, the planters told the commission that they had been shocked and surprised by the riots, that they deeply resented any suggestion that they had mistreated the laborers. They did their best to persuade the governor that the violence was the work of agitators who had stirred up the otherwise docile and contented laborers. One man in particular, they felt, was to blame—Curé, whose "subversive agitation, carried on with systematic persistence, has undoubtedly created an atmosphere propitious to the hatching of grievances."[33]

The planters' and estate managers' testimony revealed that few were even familiar with the employment policies practiced on their own estates. The commission found that the methods for paying laborers were often haphazard, inviting corruption on the part of the sirdars. But the planters defended the system, one of them, writing after the report was published, even going so far as to claim that the laborers' demand for higher wages was "grotesque" and the small planters' demand for more sugar per ton of cane "preposterous." Since Mauritius was so remote, he felt it was "the law of things" that the laborers' level of living should be lower than in other countries.[34] Another planter was convinced that if wages were increased, the laborers would only spend the additional money on drink.[35]

Curé, for his part, denied responsibility for the riots. Repeating the grievances of the laborers and the small planters, he opened the account books and the minutes of the Labour party for inspection, while the laborers and small planters themselves told poignant stories of economic distress and corrupt cane dealers and sirdars.

The findings of the commission, known as the Hooper Report, were finally published in 1938, and somewhat surprisingly, the commissioners found most of the small planters' and laborers' complaints justified. They came up with recommendations designed to remove some of the inequities in the existing system: that the cane dealers be replaced by cooperative banks; that a government inspector be present at every weigh-bridge and be able to inspect without warning; and that small planters be permitted to watch the weighing of their own cane. On the estates themselves, they recommended that job contractors be licensed and required to keep books showing the name of each laborer employed, the number of hours worked, and the amount paid to him. They suggested, in addition, that the protector of immigrants be replaced by a director of labor. The new labor department should set standards for food, housing, and hospital care, and should guide the establishment of trade unions. After weighing the evidence, the commission determined that the Labour party was not responsible for the violence. Party activity had created an awareness among the workers of their right to higher wages and better conditions, but none of the strikes and riots were directed by a central organization. And Curé himself, they concluded, had not been involved in the actual disturbances.

The commissioners' conclusion was best summarized by a prominent conservative Indian:

The present struggle with its accompanying tales of sharp rifle shooting, misery and grief might have been avoided, had the government enforced the Minimum Wages Bill, or had the masters seriously attempted to bring representatives of both contending

parties together to settle the disputes. . . . Neither government or
masters, we believe, paid any heed to the prayers and petitions presented on bended knees so to speak for better treatment; or they
both sadly lacked psychological acumen in weighing too lightly the
growing force of the proletarian propoganda. It should be kept in
view that the worker has begun to think, feel and be himself more
and more and is developing a sense of manhood and independence.[36]

The strikes and riots in Mauritius were but one example of a series
of labor disturbances throughout the British colonies in the late 1930s
protesting an inadequate colonial policy and economic depression.
The Hooper Commission that reported in Mauritius was a local
commission. A royal commission, under the chairmanship of Lord
Moyne, was dispatched to the West Indies to report on riots there.[37]
The findings of the Moyne Commission were to have a profound effect on future colonial policy, a fact that was important for Mauritius,
for nearly every recommendation of the Hooper Report was echoed
by the Moyne Commission—which carried greater weight in the
Colonial Office. The following summary paragraph in the Moyne
Report could easily have been taken from the Hooper Report:

> The discontent that underlies the disturbances represent[s] no
> longer a mere blind protest against a worsening of conditions, but a
> positive demand for the creation of new conditions that will render
> possible a better and less restricted life. It is the co-existence of this
> new demand for better conditions with the unfavourable economic
> trend that is the crux of the West Indian problem at the present
> day.[38]

Like the Moyne Commission, the Hooper Commission, too, was
distressed that local government was so unwilling to act on Colonial
Office recommendations for establishing trade unions. In the absence
of unions, responsibility for labor relations inevitably lay with the
local governments, yet their failure to really take on this responsibility
was painfully evident during the years that led up to the disturbances
However, in neither Mauritius nor the West Indies would the riots
have been possible if the estate laborers had not become aware that
there were alternatives to their traditional lot as underpaid, underfed
cane cutters.

In neither Mauritius nor the West Indies, moreover, was the basis
of labor organization community: it was class. The laborers and small

planters acted as an economic pressure group. Yet since most of the laborers and planters in Mauritius were Indian and most of the factory owners Franco-Mauritian, class and community coincided. In the 1930s, however, class was the principal basis for political division in Mauritius. The issues were class issues; Creoles and Indians worked together to bring them to the attention of the government.

After the riots it was obvious that laborers could no longer be ignored or excluded from the political process—but just how they would be incorporated into the system still remained a crucial question. Each of Curé's major demands, except the demand for increased representation in the Council of Government, was included as a recommendation in the Hooper Report. Implementing these recommendations, on the other hand, would depend upon the new governor, Sir Bede Clifford, his staff, and the 1938 session of the Council of Government.

A Catholic and an aristocrat, Sir Bede Clifford had served as secretary to the high commissioner and as special representative from Britain in South Africa for seven years. He came to Mauritius after five years in the Bahamas. Far more interested in economic development than in politics, Clifford made a detailed study of the hydroelectric resources of the island, a study that later governments used to make recommendations for dam sites and irrigation schemes. Sir Bede and his lively American wife thoroughly enjoyed the luxuries of Mauritius, the deer hunts with Phillippe Raffray and the balls at Le Reduit. (In 1937, governors still never mixed socially with any of the local people other than the Franco-Mauritians and the colored elite.)[39]

Soon after his arrival, Clifford sent a long memorandum to the Colonial Office outlining his priorities. Believing that industrial reorganization had to precede political change, his immediate plan was to transform the Poor Law Office and the Immigration Department into a Labor Department, and set up machinery for settling labor disputes. Direct contact between laborers and employers would be the best way to protect the interests fof both. Clifford readily agreed that labor conditions were well below standard, but also recognized "the vulnerability of the mills and cane fields to sabotage and incendiarism," and the need to defend the industry from "organized or sporadic attack."[40]

Constitutional change was inevitable, but inevitable did not have to

mean imminent. Clifford believed it should be delayed. In the meantime, labor interests needed to be defended in the Council of Government. The governor feared that members of the "intelligentsia,"
such as Laurent or G. M. D. Atchia, an ambitious and influential
Muslim trader, or "self-appointed" leaders such as Curé and Anquetil, would exploit the situation. On the other hand, the laborers
themselves might be too inexperienced to plead their own case. He
concluded that they would best be represented by officials. At the
same time, efforts to extend primary education and to form a responsible electorate were essential. Universal adult suffrage was unthinkable in 1938, and widening the franchise, using either education or
property as criteria, would not help the laborers. Clifford's cautious
approach was supported in London. In the Colonial Office, P. Rogers
minuted:

> The population are particularly excitable and as the planter ele-
> ment is Latin in temperament and equally volatile, it may be fairly
> said that the place is a tinderbox, and that any suggestion of re-
> form, however necessary, will have to be extremely carefully han-
> dled and firmly handled too.[41]

During his first months in office, Clifford did nothing to restrain
Curé, and the Labour party, strengthened by the report of the 1937
commission, gained new membership. On May 1, 1938, Curé organized the largest of the party's prewar meetings. Special trains brought
workers from all over the island, and by 11:00 A.M. some twenty
thousand people carrying signs and placards were assembled in the
Champ de Mars racetrack.

The meeting lasted well into the afternoon, and at the end a special
train carried the crowd back to the villages while the band played
"God Save the King" and the "Marseillaise." Curé and Anquetil were
happy and hopeful. The new governor seemed sympathetic. In two
years they had organized and built a party, the first real political party
in Mauritius. Now, instead of a few dozen people, thousands came
from all over the island to hear them speak. The Labour party
seemed firmly entrenched and the success of its leaders could not be
doubted.

5. Labor Organizes

Parties, Unions, and Cultural Organizations, 1938–1948

DURING WORLD WAR II, changes in Britain's colonial office policy influenced political and economic developments in Mauritius. Even though Britain was preoccupied with the war, the Colonial Office did attempt to revise the relationship between Britain and its colonies, to put aside an approach that alternated between neglect and paternalism and to provide greater opportunities for local participation. The Moyne Commission Report, more than anything else, had forced the Colonial Office to reassess its policy, but even that report was just one of many documents of the 1940s that, as a Fabian Society official wrote, "rarely led to immediate action, but contributed towards the shaping of a state of mind which would, eventually and inevitably, demand that some action, any action be taken."[1]

In 1940, Parliament approved the Colonial Development and Welfare Act, and for the first time large quantities of funds were available for the colonies. In the colonies, too, there was new legislation. Labor departments recommended in the 1930s were established in the 1940s, trade unions were promoted, and constitutional reform was considered, although actual reforms were usually delayed because of the war.

Except during 1942, when a Japanese attack appeared imminent, Mauritians did not worry that they would be directly involved in World War II. Nonetheless, they felt its impact. Mauritians fought in the Middle East and in North Africa and became caught up in a mutiny in Madagascar provoked by tensions among British, Franco-Mauritians, and Creoles in the military. For those at home, food shortages were acute, and corruption and bribery, hardly new to the island, became institutionalized. Britain controlled sugar prices, so Mauritius could not benefit from the fact that the years 1940 to 1944 were good crop years. Lack of shipping forced a reduction of imports, and a population that depended on imports for everything from manufactured goods to food had to go without. To feed the island, the government first tried applying economic and moral pressures, then finally resorted to legal measures that forced planters to take thousands of hectares out of sugar and replant them with potatoes and vegetables.

Even so, Mauritius still had to depend on imported food. A Food Control Board was appointed as early as 1939; rationing began in November 1942. The fall of Burma cut off the island's rice supply, and by the end of April 1943 stocks were exhausted. Before the end of the war, wheat, maize, edible oils, and lentils were added to the list of rationed goods. There was almost no meat. In spite of committees on profiteering and even a profiteering court which levied heavy fines, the black market flourished. Importers reaped huge profits at the expense of the laborers, so much so that Anquetil and Rozemont cabled both the Fabian Colonial Bureau and Creech-Jones to ask them to intervene. Their protests to the Colonial Office had no effect; food shortages forced *Le Cerneen*, *Le Mauricien*, and *Advance*, the newly-founded paper of the Indo-Mauritian intellectuals, to merge, although each retained its own editorial column. It must have been an uncomfortable alliance.

Although the war increased the anxieties of colonial officials, planters, and laborers alike, it did not halt the pressures for labor reform—and the consequent disputes about the nature of such reform. Both government and labor agreed that the 1937 riots showed the necessity for strong and representative labor organizations. But they could not agree on how these organizations should be established or who should lead them. The governor hoped to substitute a government labor department for the Labour party. His success was limited. He destroyed the Labour party, but between 1938 and 1948 two other labor movements emerged to fill the vacuum: one was an agricultural laborers association, the other a semipolitical movement stressing the revival of Hindu culture. These two movements (the Mauritius Agricultural Labourers Association and the Bissoondoyal movement) in turn survived the renewal of the Labour party in the 1950s and retained a significant place in Mauritian political life until independence.

The Government and the Labour Party

Immediately after the publication of the Hooper Report in 1938, Sir Bede Clifford began to turn the wheels to put its recommendations for political, economic, and social reform into practice. While he made it clear that the laborers' interests would be looked after by the official members, he did appoint two representatives of the small planters to the Council of Government. Other legislation established committees of representatives from the estates and the small planters to regulate payment for cane, boundaries of factory areas, and transport of cane to mills. To improve communication between the laborers and the estates, Clifford merged the Poor Law Office and the Office of the Protector of Immigrants into the Labour Department and appointed six labor inspectors, four of whom were Indian, to serve as a link between the two groups. Finally, the Council of Government passed the 1938 Labour Ordinance, which outlined minimum standards of health and diet for workers and required payment of wages in cash. On paper, it promised improvements, but although the Labour Ordinance provided the machinery for ameliorating conditions, there was, in fact, little change. The wheels turned very slowly. The government, anxious not to alienate the planters, only halfheartedly enforced the legislation.

The Industrial Association Ordinance, legalizing a limited form of trade unionism, was passed in May 1938, and in the next twenty months one employers' federation and forty-eight employees' associations were registered. By 1943, however, nearly all these associations were dissolved or inactive. The strong trade union movement envisaged by the Hooper Commission did not emerge. Government, employers, employees, and the legislation itself were all to blame for this failure. The government lacked administrators with trade union experience or sympathies. Labour officers, preferring to follow a policy of peace at any price, were reluctant to enforce the legislation and, having little interest in the success of the associations, were no help at all to local leaders. The employers, hostile to the associations, claimed that relations between themselves and their workers were a private matter in which the government had no right to interfere. The laborers had, unrealistically, expected immediate and magnificent results from the legislation and were doomed to be disappointed. With no experience at collective bargaining, and at a further disadvantage because they were not educated, they looked to an un-enthusiastic government for advice and help. It was not forthcoming. Illegal action still seemed the laborers' only recourse, and new riots broke out in 1943. It was this second outbreak of violence which at last made clear to the government that the laborers needed more than institutions and laws to protect their interests; they needed proof that the government understood and sympathized with their prob-lems and that the attitudes of the estate owners were changing—or being forced to change.

By June 1938, Labour party leaders had begun to question Clif-ford's sincerity and motives. Part of the problem stemmed from differ-ing views of time and differing expectations that always typify rela-tions between interest groups and governments. Curé and Anquetil complained that Clifford was moving too slowly; Clifford justified his delays by saying that he had to cope with pressure from estate owners who had grown used to influencing colonial administrators.[2] From the governor's dispatches, however, it is clear that he did not respect the Labour leaders and was not eager to see their influence increase, for he was convinced that "they were more interested in personal prestige than the material needs of the workers."[3] In describing Labour party meetings, Clifford wrote in 1938:

> It would appear that the utterances of Dr. Curé are mainly con-cerned with local politics, those of Anquetil with international Bol-shevism, while Sahadeo (who is frankly seditious) appeals to the religious fanaticism and racial animosities of the Indians with the obvious intention of arousing anglophobia, and of provoking a dis-turbance of the peace.[4]

By the middle of 1938, Anquetil, the only labor representative with union experience, withdrew his support of the Labour Department, objecting to the inadequacies of the legislation and the incompetence of the department's staff. In his view, the legislation did not permit real trade unions, since it prohibited island-wide organizations and required that associations be limited to certain industries. No unem-ployed person could be a member of an association, yet because of the seasonal nature of employment in the sugar industry, most work-ers were automatically unemployed from December to July. Moreover, no person could be a member of more than one associa-tion, and since one laborer often worked on many parts of the island during the crop season, Anquetil believed he should be eligible to join more than one association. Above all, Curé and Anquetil objected to the ineffectiveness of the Labour Department and to the fact that four of the labor inspectors, although they were Indian, came from the elite and had stood aloof during the 1937 strikes. Clifford, whom Anquetil and Curé had welcomed enthusiastically to Mauritius, soon became their greatest opponent. Clifford and the Labour leaders may have distrusted each other mutually, but Clifford's power was greater than the Labour party's, and the Labour party proved unable to withstand the concentrated effort by the government to diminish its influence and eventually destroy the party. By 1938 the popularity of the Labour party began to decline. By 1942 the party was virtually nonexistent.

In July 1938 Clifford took the initiative. Using legislation passed that May, which empowered the governor to investigate the island's friendly societies at his discretion, the procureur-general launched a full-scale investigation into the financial affairs of the *Société de Bien-faisance*.[5] While the *Société's* books were in order, and charges that Curé had embezzled funds could not be substantiated, the government identified three expenditures that did not fall within the expressed aims of the *Société*: two were fees for newspaper articles, and the third was money given to the Labour representative, Jomadar, for transportation to London. Curé agreed to make the payments for the newspaper articles, but he argued that he could not and would not repay the cost of Jomadar's transportation. Other organizations provided scholarship money for members to study abroad, and he did not feel his action was irregular. The governor disagreed, and in January 1939 the *Société de Bienfaisance des Travailleurs* was erased from the register of friendly societies. The planters' paper, *Le Cerneen*, ran a headline saying "Bravo." The assets of the *Société* were distributed by the governor to charitable organizations in Mauritius, and Curé was left disillusioned but determined to reconstruct the organization. In an effort to balance the ledger he asked the governor to invest comparable time and energy in an investigation of the Sugar Syndicate, but his plea went unheeded.

The failure of a dock strike in September 1938 only added to Curé's woes. Port Louis dockers, mostly Creole, decided to strike for higher wages. They refused to submit their grievances to the Conciliation Board as required by the new law; instead, they chose to challenge the legislation and the power of the government to enforce it. They began the illegal strike when the harbor was filled with ships waiting for cane.[6] Since sugar spoils quickly if not stored properly, each day's delay had grave economic consequences. And because countries were stockpiling in fear of war, the ships, too, were in great demand and ship owners were in no mood to wait out a long strike in Port Louis.

The governor declared a state of emergency. He rejected the planters' demands for police and army interference, but was nevertheless determined to break the strike, if only to prove the effectiveness of the new Labour Ordinance.[7] He therefore brought laborers from the estates to serve as strikebreakers. Seven days after the strike began, the dockers agreed to return to work and present their grievances to the Conciliation Board as required by law. The government had succeeded in forcing them to deal within the bounds of the Labour Ordinance.

Clifford, blaming Anquetil and Curé for the dock strike, was determined to prevent them from causing further trouble. Anquetil was deported to the island of Rodrigues for three months, and Curé, although claiming—probably correctly—that he had nothing to do with the dock strike, was placed under house arrest for a month.

Only three months after the end of the *Société* case, however, Curé was back in court again, this time suing a popular local singer who had accused him of using Labour party funds for his own personal use. Curé won the case, but the damages awarded were far short of what he had sought, and there were few witnesses on his behalf. By 1940, the Labour party had lost much of its following. Curé and Anquetil were full of promises, but could claim no achievements, and had no money, no legal organization, and nothing to show their followers.

As a final effort to revive interest in the party, its executive committee began a newspaper, *Le Peuple Mauricien*, edited by Anquetil and aided by the young enthusiast Guy Rozemont, who rented a tiny room in Port Louis and worked day and night to publish each day's edition. But a little over a year later Curé was forced to sell the press to pay off his debts. Too exhausted to carry on, Curé resigned as leader of the party and designated Anquetil as his successor in May 1941. Bankrupt, leaderless, and with a depleted following, the Labour party in 1941 seemed doomed. It had collapsed as fast as it had risen.

Since its formation, Labour had been a class party. Anquetil called his meetings to protest against "the means of treating in one particular way the class of the most poor of the community."[8] Both Anquetil and Curé regarded the Indo-Mauritian intellectuals as much their opponents as the Franco-Mauritian estate owners. Curé in particular feared that in the future the Labour party would become a party for Indians rather than a party for laborers. At the conclusion of the 1940 annual meeting, he issued a warning that some have called prophetic:

> The workers, Creole or Indians, are all basically the same colour, with the same interests united under the same banner. Today the leader of the Labour Party is a Creole; tomorrow it will be an Indian. That is right, but the workers are to beware of the Indian intellectuals who one day would try to found a party ostensibly for the labourers but in reality for themselves.[9]

Curé knew that he had lost his popular following and that the laborers would find a new leader. But he did not want his influence to pass to an Indian who had not participated in the struggle since the beginning, to members of the elite who had "severed all connections with the labouring classes," most of whom were employers of labor.[10]

The vacuum created by the Labour party's decline was partly filled by the Labour Department, headed by Edward Francis Twining. But the Labour Department was never really able to gain the confidence of those it was to serve. It failed, first of all, to follow the recommendations of two official reports outlining the changes necessary to improve conditions on the estates.[11] The inspectors, too, were suspect because they were part of the educated elite; certainly they never gained the laborers' confidence. As it worked out, the role of the Labour party was more effectively assumed by two new organizations—an association of agricultural workers, the North and Central Rivière de Rempart Association, concerned mainly with the wages and privileges of the cane cutters; and a presumably nonpolitical movement to revive Hindu culture.

The Agricultural Workers Unite

Encouraged by Anquetil, the only labor leader with trade union experience, Harryparsad Ramnarain organized the North Rivière de

Rempart Employees Industrial Association and the Central Rivière de Rempart Labourers' Industrial Association. The son of a sirdar and a laborer on St. Antoine Estate, Ramnarain had been working in the fields since he left primary school. He was also an active Labour party member who visited estates with Curé in 1936, and he became an agent in 1937. In 1941 his two associations merged and he rapidly gained a kind of influence that was outside the limits prescribed by the law and yet sanctioned by Twining.

Ramnarain and Twining had an unusually close relationship; Twining, realizing that Ramnarain could communicate with the laborers better than the inspectors could, frequently asked for his advice in settling disputes. Both government and workers, whether members of the association or not, relied on him as a liaison. Twining formalized his relationship with Ramnarain in 1942 by arranging to have the Information Office employ him as a "propaganda agent" to explain as persuasively as possible to the workers the demands which the war imposed upon the economy, and therefore upon them.[12] Ramnarain in turn was allowed to extend his influence. With Twining's consent he even secretly enrolled members in his association (for estates were known to dismiss employees who joined industrial associations).

Despite these arrangements, discontent on the estates increased, fostered by rising prices and shortages due to the war. The government seemed slow to respond to obvious needs and virtually ignored two reports that strongly urged reform. The first, written in 1940 by S. Ridley, who had been sent by the Indian Civil Service from South Africa to study the condition of the Indian community and that of the laborers in particular, included a list of twenty-three recommendations ranging from direct payment of day laborers by estate managers rather than by job contractors to the strengthening of the Industrial Association Ordinance and the extension of the franchise.[13]

The second report was by Major Granville Orde-Browne, the labor adviser to the secretary of state for the colonies, who had already reported on conditions in Tanganyika, West Africa, and the West Indies. Orde-Browne spent one month studying the situation in Mauritius in 1941 and had little to say in its favor. Dismissing accusations that industrial associations were incapable of conducting their own affairs, Orde-Browne was "impressed with the business-like way in which proceedings were conducted."[14] At the same time he noted that although wages had remained the same since 1914, the cost of living had more than doubled. In fact, wages in Mauritius were lower than those in the West Indies. Output per laborer was also less, possibly because of malnutrition:

> The picture is, therefore, that of a poorly paid, undernourished, sickly population, capable only of such a limited output of work that an increase of wage offers little promise of improved performance. Such a position must obviously be equally disastrous for the employer and the worker.[15]

Although the Orde-Browne Report was not published until 1943, the Mauritian government was aware of its recommendations in 1941. But no one in the Labour Department took any initiative. Once again, the failure to respond to labor's demands, even after they had been underscored and supported by official reports, led to violence. The pattern was becoming familiar.

In early 1943, laborers from the north began a series of marches to Port Louis to protest low wages and shortages of food and clothing. The Labour Department promised to look into the situation after each march, and the laborers returned to their homes. But Twining was not sympathetic. He wrote to Ramnarain on March 16:

> Work at present is plentiful and if a man works five or six days a week he can earn good wages. It is no use making general complaints. If you can bring particular cases to my notice, I will investigate them. If wages are so low as is alleged, it is surprising that the labourers who take part in the demonstrations can afford to lose a day's pay and pay the train fare to Port Louis and back.[16]

Wages varied in the north in 1943, but everywhere they were below the legal minimum prescribed in 1941. After the 1943 crop began, however, the manager of one estate, influenced by the rising cost of living, increased wages 20 percent, gave all workers an additional month's pay, and offered a war bonus to those who worked five days a week. Soon after, an agreement satisfactory to the workers was negotiated with a second estate. Strikes led to a settlement on a third estate, although not before the police used batons and tear gas to disperse the threatening crowds.

Meanwhile the laborers at a fourth estate, Belle Vue Harel, were also complaining. The Conciliation Board compelled Ramnarain, who was secretly employed by the government, and his younger cousin, Mohunpersad Jugdambi, the laborers' representative, to accept an agreement which, although consistent with those on other estates, fell short of the workers' extravagant demands. Refusing to ratify the agreement, the laborers went on strike on September 23, 1943. On the fourth day of the strike, a group of laborers attacked a plainclothes policeman visiting the estate.[17] When the police came, a crowd of two or three hundred had gathered, and some of the men were armed with sticks. The police ordered them to put down their sticks; the men refused. Tensions built and the crowd threw sticks and stones at the police; even a baton charge did not deter them. Finally the deputy commissioner of police ordered three men to fire; the police injured sixteen people and killed three—a man, a woman, and a child. For the rest of the day there was a stunned quiet.

The immediate results of the shooting were reprisals against the workers. Labor leaders found themselves without work; women were no longer permitted to come to the estates to cut grass; and manure, which had traditionally been left for the workers to use as fuel, was collected by the estates. Ramnarain resigned as an information officer and retired to the Hindu temple at Goodlands where he fasted for eight days, until the government agreed to appoint a commission of enquiry into the disturbances. Ramnarain's decisive action following the strike enabled him to maintain credibility in the eyes of the laborers, who still did not know that he had been employed by the government as an information officer.

Three people dead is not a great toll for a riot in some countries, but as in 1911 and 1937, the 1943 disturbances shocked the island. Since it was wartime, anxiety was especially great. Were these riots a sign of more to come? Neither the British administrators nor the Franco-Mauritians felt particularly at ease in their symbiotic relationship with the vast crowd of illiterate Indian laborers. They did not comprehend the workers' grievances; they did not understand their way of thinking. Lack of communication led to fear. Class and culture were for the moment barriers too great to overcome.

The commission of enquiry was headed by Sydney Moody, the procureur-general, and included one Franco-Mauritian justice, one Hindu, and one Creole, Edgar Laurent. Civil servants, planters, and laborers all gave their versions of the riots and their opinions as to the cause. The testimony underscored the gap between estate managers and laborers. One Franco-Mauritian was particularly outspoken:

James LeMaire: I am against industrial associations. I do not be-
lieve that the associations can ever be directed properly. The
Indian labourers are like children.
Laurent: What do you think of the labourers?
LeMaire: They are very good children and you must tutor them.
Laurent: What do you think of the Minimum Wage Board?
LeMaire: I see no reason why there are minimum wages.[18]

Lemaire then said he had never been in direct contact with any
laborers, but he was convinced that the government should take immediate measures to prevent them from becoming alcoholics, as he
felt many were in 1943.

When the Moody Report was published in 1944, it was a victory for
Ramnarain. The commissioners found the grievances of the laborers
justified and recognized Ramnarain as the leader of the cane cutters
in the north. Like the commissions of 1911 and 1937, the 1943 commission found police action inappropriate. But the main cause of the
discontent, the report cited, was conditions on the estates. Although
six years had gone by, little had improved since the Hooper Commission reported in 1937; legislation had not changed habits, partly because the Labour Department had not enforced the law. Showing a
remarkable understanding of the mutual resentment between employers and employees, the 1943 commission saw that its causes were
as much social and psychological as economic and legislative. Relations between the estates and the laborers could not improve until
both parties, through education and interest, better understood the
problems of the other. A beginning step would be to implement the
suggestions of the Hooper Report, the Ridley Report, and the Orde-
Brown Report, all of which had so far been largely ignored.[19]

The riots of 1943 also had a profound impact in London. The Fabian Colonial Bureau, which had until now taken only a passing interest in Mauritius, began producing lengthy documents for internal
use. Using the 1943 commission report and later letters from Anquetil
and Ken Baker, who came to Mauritius as trade union adviser, the
Fabians condemned officials of the Labour Department for "bul-
ly[ing] workers to sign agreements," and the police for being "in
league with the employers" and for involvement "in conspiracies to
hush up illegal actions." The Fabian Report continued:

Mauritius is an exceptionally bad case by no means typical of all
colonies; and we all know that there are dozens of colonial officials

of the highest calibre. But the fact that in any British colony there
could have been such disastrous mishandling at a time the pro-
nouncements from London have been at their noblest must give us
furiously to think.[20]

Nagging from the Fabian Bureau and its "representatives" in Par-
liament forced the Colonial Office to pay some attention to
Mauritius, but it was wartime, and the island had very low priority.
The 1943 riots were a shock and an awakening, but they failed to
provoke immediate reform. "Furious thinking" about conditions on
Mauritius would have to wait for another day.

Trade Unions, 1944–1948

By 1944 most of the industrial associations had collapsed. With the
exception of Ramnarain's North and Central Rivière de Rempart Industrial Association, which had been renamed the Mauritius Agricultural Labourers' Association (MALA), the few that remained on the
registers were inactive. In 1945, however, the situation changed. Between 1945 and 1948, trade unions were formed on a countrywide
basis, and during these years acquired as much political influence as
at any time in the island's history. The impetus for stronger unions
came from Ken Baker, the union adviser sent from England in early
1945.

An ardent socialist, Baker had been president of the Fire Brigade
Union in England, but had had no experience in the colonies. He
adapted quickly and was one of the few colonial officers to gain the
confidence of Mauritian labor leaders. When Baker arrived in
Mauritius, he found the industrial associations in an embryonic state,
and quickly urged that their status be raised to that of trade unions.[21]
He urged the consolidation and clarification of existing legislation and
the strengthening of the Labour Department. One of his concerns
was the possibility of retaliation against the workers: laborers hesitated
to pay a visit to his office for fear of being dismissed. Employers
threatened reprisals more often than they carried them out, to be
sure, but the threat alone was a major check to the development of
strong organizations. Until laborers could talk freely with union leaders and Labour Department officials, there was no way that unions
could be established.

Baker's primary concern, however, was education. Education was the key to establishing unions, and the lack of it, he claimed, was the reason for the failure of the associations founded in 1938. Rather than set up a separate organization to provide education, Baker hoped to use the *baitkas*, the meeting places or clubhouses that often served as the center of religious and community activity for Hindus in village neighborhoods. Villages with a large Hindu population often had more than one *baitka*, one for each sect or caste grouping, and *baitka* presidents were usually among the more prestigious men of the village.[22] Baker had quickly recognized the importance of these institutions and the potential network they offered, and was the first colonial officer in Mauritius to try to work through rather than around them.[23]

Baker hid neither his sympathy for the laborers nor his antagonism toward most government officials. After a brief settling-in period, he and the governor, Donald Mackenzie-Kennedy, who had replaced Clifford in 1942, were at loggerheads. The governor called Baker "subversive"; Baker, for his part, began by recognizing that the governor had a "difficult job," but a year and a half later, after a meeting with Mackenzie-Kennedy, the union adviser was writing: "Many obstacles are being put in my way, mainly by the Governor. . . . He made a complete fool of himself, raved at Anquetil, threatening to send him to prison. . . . He [the governor] goes next March. For God's sake send someone with some democratic intelligence."[24]

Both Baker and Mackenzie-Kennedy, each in his own way, were cynical about Mauritius. Mackenzie-Kennedy found the "local population very difficult to move, self-satisfied, conceited, arrogant, and intellectually terribly dishonest."[25] Baker was equally discouraged and told the Fabians, "The average person here is anti-native, anti-Indian, anti-semitic, and anti-social. You may think I am exaggerating, but this is not so."[26] Despite his reservations, Baker threw himself wholeheartedly into the job of helping the laborers, and ensured the development of a strong and lasting trade union movement.

In 1945, the two largest and most active unions were the Engineering and Technical Workers Union and the Mauritius Agricultural Labourers' Association. The first was an association of artisans under the direction of Anquetil, the second, the successor to the North and Central Rivière de Rempart Industrial Association. Antagonism between the leaders of these two unions, Anquetil and Ramnarain, proved to be a major block to union growth between 1945 and 1947.

When Baker arrived in Mauritius, Anquetil's Engineering and
Technical Workers Union (ETWU) was only a few months old, but
already well known because of its services during the cyclones of
1945. The most devastating of these swept the island in January and
left thousands without homes or shelter. While some builders took
advantage of the desperate state of the population and demanded exorbitant fees, the members of Anquetil's union agreed to work at reduced rates and temporarily gave up demands for an increase in
wages. Anquetil was proving that responsible leadership could create
responsible trade unions, and was praised even by the government.

Baker and Anquetil became friends. Both socialists, they had much
in common, although Baker did find Anquetil somewhat inexperienced. With Baker's help, Anquetil and Rozemont succeeded in making the ETWU into an island-wide union with a membership of four
thousand. Anquetil provided the technique and the discipline;
Rozemont attracted the membership. The new union's first strike, in
1946 in the south, proved that Mauritian artisans, organized into a
single union, could conduct an orderly and disciplined strike within
legal bounds. The union forced employers, government, and non-
union laborers to recognize a new influence in Mauritius.

While Rozemont and Anquetil were building up their artisans'
union, Ramnarain was extending his influence among the agricultural laborers and trying to persuade the estates to raise wages. He
began by taking an interesting step, strategically: he tried to get the
laborers to give up rum. The government and the estate owners
charged, as they had in the past, that Indian laborers used their wages
to buy rum, and that if wages were increased the laborers would just
drink them up. To disprove this allegation, Ramnarain traveled
throughout the island expounding the evils of the "drink habit." He
told his followers: "All alcohol is on the side of the enemy and . . .
every regular drinker is lessening his efficiency and abilities to help
him in winning a victory. . . . For our workers it is essential that there
should be places to spend leisure where strong drink is not served."[27]
The campaign met with considerable success: the government began
losing revenue from the liquor tax; and Ramnarain became a familiar
figure throughout the island, not just in the north. The governor,
who had from the beginning distrusted Ramnarain and feared his
growing popularity in the villages, was sufficiently worried to detain
him for ten months without bringing specific charges.

Rivalry between Anquetil and Ramnarain was intense. At Anquetil's urging, the government refused Ramnarain permission to expand his association and attempted unsuccessfully to dissolve it for not complying with the Industrial Association Ordinance. The government urged that the two work together, but Anquetil was clearly the favorite. Anquetil's friends were permitted to register in a rival agricultural association, the Mauritius Agricultural Labourers' Union (MALU). But Anquetil's agricultural union did not detract from Ramnarain's, and the government finally was able to persuade the two to merge in 1946. The MALA remained dominant, and between 1947 and 1950 it was the only agricultural workers' union in Mauritius, claiming over twelve thousand members.

By the end of the war, the two unions that were to dominate Mauritius during the next decade had been established with Baker's help. Anquetil and Rozemont had extended their Engineering and Technical Workers Union to include nearly all artisans on the island, and Ramnarain had emerged as the principal leader of the agricultural workers. Much of the credit must be given to Ken Baker: he had improved internal organization, established negotiation procedure acceptable to trade union representatives, and created a trade union council with which most unions were affiliated. Perhaps even more important, his efforts had at last given the laborers confidence in the power of trade unions to protect their interests.

In 1946, Baker was transferred from Mauritius, possibly at the request of the governor. His departure was followed by Anquetil's death from tuberculosis in January 1947. According to a Labour Department official, Anquetil's death was "a blow for all trade unionists and for all outside trade unionism who hoped for a speedy development of strong and responsible trade unions. No one of his personality and experience had risen to take his place."[28] Their absence—when their presence had made such a difference—was marked, and mourned (at least by some). But Baker's departure and Anquetil's death did not result in the disintegration of the unions.

Rozemont now became the leader of both the Engineers and Technical Workers Union and the weakened Labour party. Immensely popular among the Creole dockers and artisans, Rozemont had a rapport with workers that no previous Labour party or union leader had been able to develop. Unlike Curé and Anquetil, Rozemont happily spent afternoon after afternoon drinking rum with the laborers, listening to their grievances and telling them stories. Creole was his favorite language, and his vivid images and lively delivery are a legend in the island today. The governor was less enthusiastic. He called Rozemont "a self-inflated windbag, of little experience in any form of administration. A stump orator with a stentorian voice and the usual terrible inferiority complex of a black Creole intellectual."[29]

When Rozemont spoke, he made no distinction between his roles as president of the Labour party and president of the Engineers and Technical Workers Union. He assumed that all union members were party members, and, as a result, the party acquired new influence. But the revitalized Labour party in 1946 was very different from the one Curé had founded ten years earlier. Then, Curé's principal support had come from Indian estate laborers. Now, a few Indians remained loyal to the Labour party and to Rozemont, but the party membership was dominated by the Creole dockers and artisans, and they were committed to a man, Rosemont, rather than to an ideology.

Bissoondoyal and the Hindu Cultural Revival

Unions and formal associations of laborers were not the only organizations to appeal to the poor in Mauritius. Soon after the 1943 riots, a traditional movement focusing on the revival of Hindu culture began to gather support, led by Basdeo Bissoondoyal. The movement was very much like that of the independent schools and churches which began in many colonial countries in the early days of nationalism.[30] Basdeo, a Hindu missionary with an M.S. from the University of Calcutta in religion and philosophy, was its main inspiration until 1948. His brother, Sookdeo, was his right-hand man, but as a government school teacher, Sookdeo's political activity was limited until he resigned from his teaching post in 1946.

Since the departure of Manilal in 1911, the Indo-Mauritian community had lacked traditional leadership. Community spokesmen, such as R. Boodhun and Gujadhur, elected representatives to the Council of Government, had European attitudes. In 1939 a reporter for the Calcutta *Statesman* visited Mauritius and found that "There was, in fact, nobody who had any real authority or power enough to sound the trumpet call that would rally the Hindus together, retain them within the Vedic fold, and bring about the unification of the various sects and creeds that composed the great Hindu tradition."[31]

Basdeo Bissoondoyal learned about the Labour party activities when he was studying in Calcutta, but when he returned to Mauritius he decided to start a separate movement.[32] Like Manilal three decades before him, he believed that if he taught Indians in Mauritius to read and write their own language and to understand their own religion and culture he would be giving them pride in their heritage. Known as "the Professor," Bissoondoyal founded schools for Indian culture and language, holding evening sessions for the workers, and afternoon sessions for children, most of whom attended government schools in the mornings. In addition, Bissoondoyal held special meetings for the women, who had been ignored by the Labour party in spite of their considerable influence in the family. Although Bissoondoyal and his brother lived in Port Louis, their first schools were in the south, where they could avoid conflict with the powerful Ramnarain. To staff them, Bissoondoyal trained over eight hundred teachers and supplied them with a Hindi grammar and children's readers that he had written.

Public meetings were forbidden because of the war, but Bissoondoyal was not deterred; he went to jail three times between 1943 and 1944 for holding illegal gatherings. Like Baker, his meetings were usually held in *baitkas*, meeting places or clubhouses that often served as the center of religious and community activity for Hindus in village neighborhoods. He understood—even better than Baker—the value of *baitkas* and local village organizations, and assiduously cultivated the traditional Hindu leadership. Consequently, *baitka* presidents approved of Bissoondoyal's efforts and were honored when he held meetings on their premises. The Professor was also an avid pamphleteer and wrote at length about his personal experiences and philosophy. He had access to one press in Calcutta and another in Mauritius, and his pamphlets in English, French, and Hindi, glorifying his teachings and the Hindu religion, soon could be found everywhere. Just as the Creole laborers were committed to Rozemont, the Indian laborers gravitated to Bissoondoyal the man. A personality cult grew around him. There were accusations that he was exploiting his followers for his own financial benefit (even though the money he collected paid for teachers and books, it also enabled him to live comfortably in Port Louis), but these accusations did not detract from his support.

By 1946, Bissoondoyal's influence, which had begun in the south, extended throughout the island. The police watched closely, concerned that his hold over his followers might approach that of Gandhi's in India. They realized that Bissoondoyal lacked Gandhi's intellectual ability, but they feared that in a community devoid of leaders, charlatans and demagogues could as easily gain a following. In January 1947, the deputy commissioner of police persuaded the governor that "the Bissoondoyals were about to pack up, having made a lot of money in the last few years."[33]

Indian intellectuals as well, particularly those on the fringes of politics, shared the British distrust of Bissoondoyal. They were anxious to keep the Indian community united under their control, and saw him, jealously, as a divisive force. At the same time, it would have been heretical to criticize directly someone who was promoting Indian customs and language. The intellectuals therefore chose silence; their newspaper, *Advance*, did not usually report Bissoondoyal's activities or public meetings. Curiously, the only recognition Bissoondoyal ever had from the established press was from *Le Mauricien*: under the editorship of Raoul Rivet, the paper gave Bissoondoyal's meetings full coverage, hoping to weaken the Indian community by emphasizing the differences between Bissoondoyal and the intellectuals.

The professionals' disapproval did not affect Bissoondoyal's popularity. To the Indians in the villages, his lessons from the ancient Vedas seemed more relevant than the Western and still foreign ideas of those who had just returned from England and France. Today, many Mauritians who grew up in villages in the 1940s and find themselves now in positions of responsibility do not hide their debt to Bissoondoyal, who gave them a feeling of self-respect and pride in their heritage, and a self-confidence that was essential to success. Certainly during the war the popularity of Bissoondoyal and Ramnarain was greater than that of either the Labour party or the Indo-Mauritian professional elite. And when the time came to discuss constitutional reform and an extension of the franchise, Bissoondoyal could not be excluded. Some of his achievements were highly practical, as well: Bissoondoyal deserves credit for the large number of Indians who were able to pass the literacy tests required of voters in 1948. When the 1948 elections were over, it was clear that among the beneficiaries of his education program for the masses were the Indian elite who so mistrusted him—they owed their new seats to the constituency which he helped create.

In 1946, ten years after Dr. Curé founded the Mauritius Labour Party, laborers in Mauritius still had no representation in the Council of Government, but they had found an effective way to express their discontent through associations, unions, and cultural organizations. Each organization—the Mauritius Agricultural Labourers' Association, the Engineering and Technical Workers Union, and Bissoondoyal's Hindu cultural revival movement—represented the poorly paid workers who lived and worked at the bottom of the social and economic ladder. At the same time, because of the coincidence between occupational and communal divisions, these organizations gave an indication of the communal politics that would emerge in the future.

Ramnarain's MALA was composed of cane cutters on the sugar estates, nearly all of whom were Hindu. In part because its leaders were not Hindu, the government-supported Mauritius Agricultural Labourers' Union had failed. The Engineering and Technical Workers Union, organized by Anquetil and Rozemont, included the artisans of the island, who were Creole. Finally, Bissoondoyal, desperately determined to raise the level of education and the aspirations of Hindu villagers, organized Hindus throughout the island. In 1946, despite their ethnic differences, these organizations had more in common with each other than with the elites who were members of the Council of Government. All focused on the quality of life and the standard of living of the poor. Antagonisms based on communal differences were rarely articulated, although the two unions, at least, were composed of members from different communities.

After 1948, however, the basis of Mauritian political divisions began to shift subtly from class to community, and it became apparent that divisions between the unions were such that they, too, could easily shift from class to communal politics. At the same time, once union leaders were integrated into the political process through membership in the Legislative Assembly following 1948, the political role of the trade unions declined. As a force separate from the established political leadership, union leaders had been in a better position to oppose the government. Once these leaders became part of that government, they were less effective as union representatives.

As always in Mauritius, the quality of leadership and the characters of the individual men had an impact on the effectiveness of any organization. Rozemont, appealing though he was, was not able to establish the island-wide support that he needed to keep his union strong. There was little substance to back up Rozemont's charisma, and the dynamic storyteller quickly yielded his position of leadership to those who took pleasure from mastering parliamentary procedure. Ramnarain, the skillful go-between, stayed aloof from elective politics, failing to understand that the power to make decisions about wages and conditions on the estates was shifting from the union to the legislators. Only Bissoondoyal, through his brother, Sookdeo, managed to maintain an effective, village-based organization and develop a base, however small, in the Legislative Council. An understanding of how major constitutional reform would change the nature of politics in Mauritius eluded all but a very few on the island.

6. Constitutional Reform

1938–1948

EVEN BEFORE World War II, the Colonial Office recognized that constitutional reform was necessary in a number of colonies; but most of them, to London's eyes, were larger and more important than Mauritius. On Mauritius, the governor, Sir Bede Clifford, knew that constitutional reform was inevitable; but with his attention riveted on questions of economic viability, he did not think the outdated constitution was the most significant of the island's problems. The combination of a reluctant governor and a distracted Colonial Office ensured that little progress was made during the war. However, Clifford's successor, Donald Mackenzie-Kennedy, saw the constitution—and specifically the franchise and the resulting system of representation—as primary reasons for the tensions in Mauritius, understanding that until the political tensions were reduced, there could be few advances in other areas. Thus, during his term as governor he turned his attention to the constitution, concentrating on two main questions: What should be the nature of Mauritius's next constitution, and to what extent should Mauritians be involved in shaping it? From the Mauritian point of view, the delay in effecting reform continued to seem endless. But without Mackenzie-Kennedy's commitment and persistence, it is unlikely that the Mauritians would have had a new and radically different constitution as early as 1947.

In 1942 most Mauritians had little sense of what they wanted. But any outside observer could tell that the new constitution would have to incorporate into the political system many who had previously been excluded. The franchise would have to be widened and the number of elected representatives increased. The activities of the Labour party, Ramnarain, and Bissoondoyal left no other choice.

Just as important as the nature of the new constitution was the process of shaping it. Mackenzie-Kennedy's style was open and consultative, and as a result, many Mauritian politicians, elected or self-appointed, joined the newspapers in wide-ranging and endless debates about Mauritius's needs, arguing intensely over qualifications for franchise and methods for ensuring that the interests of all communities would be protected in a new council. The discussions began to seem interminable, but the very process of discussion enabled many people with no prior political experience to perfect their skills at filibustering and to learn something about the need for compromise. Moreover, the discussions served as a warning to the more thoughtful Franco-Mauritians that they were going to have to share political power on the island with other population groups.

Prelude to Change

During the war, the Council of Government elections were repeatedly postponed, but regular municipal council elections in Port Louis acted as a barometer, reflecting changes in the views of the island's voters. The Municipal Council elected in 1940 was decidedly conservative, and the Creole elite, led by Laurent and Rivet, remained in control. Ramgoolam protested the dictatorial manner in which the mayor was selected, but his objections went unanswered. So did his charges that Rivet had insulted the Indo-Mauritian community during the election campaign.[1] But a few years later, in both 1943 and 1946, younger and more radical candidates were elected to govern Port Louis. Laurent and Rivet had lost their hold on municipal politics, and neither stood in the 1946 elections. The 1946 Council included Edgar Millien, an outspoken opponent of the Franco-Mauritians and editor of his own newspaper, L'Oeuvre, which reliably supported the interests of the poor and the Creole community; Jules Koenig, a young Franco-Mauritian lawyer who would later become president of the Parti Mauricien; Razack Mohammed, an outspoken Muslim trader beginning a career as a quixotic but powerful leader of Mauritian Muslims; and Rengaden Seeneevassen, a Tamil attorney who had spoken on Curé's platform in 1938 and a close friend of Ramgoolam (who would have succeeded Guy Rozemont as president of the Labour party in 1956 had he not died).

While shifts were taking place in the Municipal Council, it was business as usual in the Council of Government. Most unofficial members supported officially proposed legislation. Only Ramgoolam, who had been nominated to the Council in 1940, tested the established interests at all, and when he spoke out on behalf of the Indians, the laborers, and the small planters, his was the only voice. His accusations that the 1943 budget was "a budget of the upper class, a budget from which anything concerned with the welfare of the working classes had been entirely left out" were ignored, as were his demands that the Industrial Association Ordinance and old-age pensions be revised.[2]

In Ramgoolam's view, needed social and economic reforms could happen only after—and if—there was constitutional reform. It was as clear to the Colonial Office and the local government as it was to Ramgoolam and the Indian professionals that the constitution, last rewritten in 1886, was an embarrassing anachronism. Visiting Mauritius in 1939, Lord Dufferin, parliamentary undersecretary of state for the colonies, became the first official spokesman to suggest that constitutional reform in Mauritius was a concern of the Colonial Office.[3] In 1941 George Hall, then parliamentary undersecretary of state, told Creech-Jones that political reform in Mauritius had not been lost sight of, but "it was not practicable to carry matters forward under present conditions."[4] A year later the secretary of state, Colonel Stanley, was "looking into the matter,"[5] and in 1943 Sir Cosmo Parkinson, permanent undersecretary of state for the colonies, visited Mauritius to discuss the question with the new governor.[6] The war prevented decisive action, and led the governor to postpone elections each year.[7] Even with all the "discussions" and "looking into the matter," however, no one in 1940 foresaw that constitutional reform would be delayed as late as 1947, and elections until 1948.

Donald Mackenzie-Kennedy replaced Sir Bede Clifford as governor in 1942. After twenty-two years of colonial service, Mackenzie-Kennedy was disappointed in the Mauritius assignment because he had a special fondness for Central and East Africa. But London had persuaded him that Mauritius in 1942 was strategically located and that a man of his caliber and background was needed. Although never very happy there, Mackenzie-Kennedy, like Sir Arthur Hamilton Gordon sixty years before him, took pride in doing his duty as best he could no matter what the circumstances. And he had a keen sense of justice. He disliked the trade union leaders, for instance, but he wanted to see conditions on the estates improved and Indians given some say in government. However, he never won support of the Indians (who, among other things, strongly objected to his son's marriage to the daughter of a leading Franco-Mauritian, "a Mauritian lady of the reactionary class"[8]).

Once the island seemed safe from Japanese attack, Mackenzie-Kennedy devoted himself to constitutional reform, spending hours laboring over drafts he knew would have taken the Colonial Office months to produce. He knew he could not expect unanimity of views from the various communities. But he at least wished to hear all opinions before he presented his recommendations. To provide a basis for discussion, the governor proposed that a legislative council with thirty-two members replace the existing Council of Government. Of the thirty-two members, eight would be official and twenty-four unofficial, sixteen elected and sixteen nominated. He proposed that in four of the constituencies, at least one elected member be from the Indian population. The franchise would be restricted to those who could pass a minimum property or income requirement or those who had a standard school certificate.[9]

Mackenzie-Kennedy's proposals and subsequent modifications were discussed by two constitutional consultative committees. The first had twenty-five members, including the eleven elected members of the Council of Government. Although it included representatives of the Indo-Mauritian community, it did not include representatives of the workers. This first committee, meeting between March 6 and May 20, 1945, spent most of its time deliberating the relative merits of communal representation.

The idea was not new. In 1927 a group of Creoles sent the Colonial Office detailed proposals for a system of communal representation, saying it would be "the ideal form of representation for Colonies with a heterogeneous population."[10] When major constitutional reform again became an issue in 1939, Bede Clifford revived the idea. He had proposed a council consisting of forty-two members, including twenty-one nominated members and twenty-one elected representatives—seven Franco-Mauritians, seven Indians, and seven Creoles. Ensuring that the number of nominated and official members was equal to the number of elected members, Clifford believed,

> would prevent the French and Creole sections from passing legislation manifestly unfair to the Indian section or the Creole and In-

dian section passing penal legislation against the French. In short, the Government would hold the balance between the sections as the Governor as President would have a casting vote to avoid deadlock.[11]

The problem in Mauritius, as in other colonies with plural societies, was to reconcile majority rule with minority rights. Communal representation had been seen as the solution in Ceylon and in Central Africa as well as in Fiji. In Africa it was devised solely to protect immigrant communities who had no claim to political power on the basis of numbers or nationality. In Ceylon and Fiji it was viewed as a way to prevent majority rule at the expense of the minority, but the Colonial Office soon learned that at least in Ceylon communal representation could also perpetuate communal rivalries. By 1928, only five years after the constitution providing for communal representation had been introduced in Ceylon, the Donoughmore Commission concluded that

> Communal representation is, as it were, a canker on the body politic, eating deeper and deeper into the vital energies of the people, breeding self-interest, suspicion and animosity, poisoning the new growth of political consciousness and effectively preventing the development of a national or corporate spirit. . . . There can be no hope of binding together the diverse elements of the population in a realization of their common kinship and an acknowledgement of common obligations to the country of which they are all citizens so long as the system of communal representation, with all its disintegrating influences, remains a distinctive feature of the constitution.[12]

By the time constitutional revision was discussed seriously in Mauritius, Britain had learned the lessons of Ceylon. Wilfred Jackson, who had been appointed governor of British Guiana following his tour on Mauritius, advised Mackenzie-Kennedy, "If you have never had a communal system it would be madness to introduce it."[13]

Some leading Mauritians, however, strongly advocated this system. Jules LeClezio, backed by the Chamber of Agriculture, supported Clifford's plan for reserved seats with separate electoral rolls for each community.[14] He was joined by some Creole intellectuals, including Laurent, who warned that "No constitution should be framed which is likely or susceptible to give them [the Indians] a predominant part in the Council." Laurent concluded:

> . . . to believe especially after what we have heard during our sittings, that the grant of a constitution would change the mind of the electors over night, that henceforth the electors in the Colony would no more think and act communally, and to say that a revision of our constitution and the grant to us of a more liberal constitution would see us all united in the defence of our common interests irrespective of class, creed or religion, is to my mind, a fallacy. I am, Sir, under no delusion.[15]

Rivet led the opposition. In a memorandum to the first consultative committee, he pointed out the difficulty of determining who belonged to what community. Creole intellectuals, in particular, resented being permanently set apart from the Franco-Mauritian community they wanted to join.[16] But the real problem was that communal representation would exacerbate existing conflicts. In Rivet's view,

> No ethnic group in the colony has interests which are not shared, more or less, by the other groups, and it is therefore on the safeguard of these interests that the peace, development and prosperity of the colony depends. Reserved seats would, in my opinion, create an impression of distrust and be a consecration of the principle of communalism.[17]

The Indians also opposed communal representation. They argued that it would prevent a Mauritian nation from ever being created.

The Mackenzie-Kennedy Proposals

With a briefcase full of suggestions, the governor left for England in mid-1945 to discuss drafting a new constitution, and did not return until 1946. In London, Mackenzie-Kennedy was not impressed by the efficiency of the Colonial Office. His patience tried, he noted in his diary, "Conferences at the Colonial Office and delay after delay while people go on leave or mess about. What a show."[18] Of course, the Colonial Office was overwhelmed with countries "clamouring for new constitutions," and Mauritius had lower priority than Ceylon, Nigeria, and the Gold Coast. Then, when the Labour government came to power in Great Britain in 1945, Mackenzie-Kennedy had to start negotiations again.

For Creech-Jones, the central purpose of British colonial policy was "to guide the colonial territories to responsible government within the Commonwealth in conditions that ensure to the people concerned both a fair standard of living and freedom from oppression."[19] Colonial officials and Mackenzie-Kennedy were free to cull from those constitutions already drafted or being drafted any elements that related to Mauritius. In this respect, constitutional change in Mauritius was very much a part of the pattern of postwar constitutional reform throughout the colonies: the final package could well be made up of parts and pieces of the constitutions of other colonies.

In an effort to speed up the process, the governor did considerable research in the Colonial Office library and with some temerity drafted the proposals for the electoral law himself. On October 29, 1946, nearly a year and a half since the first consultative committee had met, a draft of a proposed constitution was presented to the Council of Government. It provided for a legislative assembly of forty: nineteen elected members; eight official members, five of whom would be nominated; and thirteen nominated unofficial members selected by the governor and by specified organizations such as the Chinese Chamber of Commerce).[20] There were to be no reserved seats. Every male with either a school certificate or a minimum amount of property would be eligible to vote. The existing five constituencies would be maintained, returning three to six members each.

Soon after the proposals were published, Mackenzie-Kennedy convened the second consultative committee and asked its members to accept these proposals or to suggest a reasonable alternative. This committee was larger than the first. All elected and unofficial members of the Council of Government were included, as well as twenty additional people. Among these twenty were seven Indo-Mauritians, including Ramnarain, Seeneevassen, and Aunauth Beejadhur, the editor of *Advance*; six Franco-Mauritians, including Koenig as well as representatives of the planters; and seven members of the Creole community, including Curé and Anquetil. Bissoondoyal was not appointed, but he helped Ramnarain and a representative of the small planters write their speeches.[21]

The reaction to the proposals was mixed. Laurent and Curé found them suitable. The Franco-Mauritians thought they were radical, but were prepared to accept them on the assumption that there would be no further change for many years. Anquetil, Ramgoolam, and the

other Indians rejected them, claiming "we have been presented with
the same old Council of Government in a new shape."[22] They objected strongly to the fact that the proposed constitution did not give
a majority in the Council to the elected members. The victory of the
Labour party in London and the appointment of Creech-Jones to the
Colonial Office had led them to expect support for more radical reforms than those proposed.

For the Indians, franchise was the most crucial question.
Seeneevassen had made the Indian position clear during the meetings
of the first consultative committee when he advocated universal male
adult suffrage:

> At this stage of our evolution I think it is imperative that we should
> extend the franchise to the masses who are dissatisfied, and if we
> don't do it now, we may not have that opportunity later and we
> shall always have trouble.[23]

By 1947 the Indians knew that universal suffrage was being introduced in Trinidad, and they took it for granted that similar actions
would occur in Mauritius. The Franco-Mauritians and the Creoles,
however, adamantly opposed such an extension of the franchise,
claiming that "the backward classes would suffer if pushed ahead too
rapidly." It was clear to them that a council elected by universal suffrage would not represent the "rights and the interests of the communities of Western civilization in Mauritius."[24] When they realized
that universal suffrage might be accepted by the Colonial Office, the
Franco-Mauritian and Creole elites presented a memorandum to the
governor: universal suffrage—the demand of the Hindu community
exclusively—would mean "dissention and would aggravate class and
racial antagonism." Specifically, "given the Indian nationalistic ten-
dencies which have become apparent, universal suffrage might open
the door to external interference in the affairs of the Colony."[25]
Mauritius, in other words, might become an Indian colony.

Franco-Mauritians knew that a radical change in the franchise
would undermine their control of the political structure. They feared
that the Indians, with no experience in government, would promote
irrational economic policies. But even more than economic crisis,
they felt threatened by the challenge to two centuries of Franco-
Mauritian hegemony.

While the Muslim representatives to the committee vacillated, the

Hindus stood firm in their demand for male adult suffrage. In a lucid memorandum, they objected to the proposed educational requirement by saying that not everyone in the country was able to obtain primary school education. But behind the argument lay a threat: if the Indians were deprived of the vote, they would form a militant and nationalistic group. To gather support for male adult suffrage, Indian leaders held meetings throughout the country and passed resolutions demanding the vote.

Tied to the franchise issue was the question of female suffrage. Paradoxically, Indians objected to giving women the vote, while Franco-Mauritians insisted that women who could meet the qualifications be registered. The Indians quite resented the fact that Franco-Mauritians, so strongly opposed to widening the franchise, should favor such an "experiment." But why did the Indians, so adamant in wanting to extend the franchise, oppose female suffrage? Arguments about women's ability to make political decisions were carried on at a high plane, but it was evident that on a more practical level each community had its own interests at heart. If literacy tests were retained as a minimum requirement, few Indian women would qualify—but nearly every Franco-Mauritian woman would.

No agreement about the franchise was reached in the consultative committee, but all sides gave ground. More important than producing pages of incompatible suggestions, the committee provided a meeting ground for Mauritian leaders. For the first time in the island's history, leaders of all classes and all communities were assembled in one room to discuss a common problem. In the Council of Government, the Franco-Mauritians had met the Indian elite—such as Ramgoolam and Atchia—but they had never met Ramnarain or the representative of the small planters, Sookdeo Balgobin. In an official forum, politeness forced each member to listen to others, to treat others with at least a minimum of respect, and to talk together about the future of Mauritius.

But if a sense of common ground was one result of these discussions, greater awareness of both community and class was another. Each community acted as a unit in discussing major issues, such as the franchise and the composition of the Legislative Council. With each group approaching the issues in its own cohesive way, together the constituencies laid a foundation for the communal politics that was to come.

The New Constitution

Fully informed on local opinion, Mackenzie-Kennedy went again to London in 1947, only to be frustrated once more by Colonial Office bureaucracy. So he himself undertook the work of drafting sections of a new constitution. His part in the process is an interesting one. Had it not been for his commitment to a post he so disliked, constitutional reform in Mauritius would undoubtedly have been delayed another two years. Proposals that might have been accepted in 1945, however, were by 1947 unworkable. The Indo-Mauritian community was better organized and sharply demanded meaningful change. As Mackenzie-Kennedy explained, the Mauritian dilemma was that the "bulk of the population was unprepared for democratic institutions" and yet at the same time would feel "defrauded" if deprived of the right to select those who would govern them. He wrote to Creech-Jones with remarkable sensitivity:

> This then is the problem, how to bring the diverse elements of this heterogeneous population into the proper channels of political development without at the same time running the risk of political domination of the colony by representatives of an ignorant and illiterate electorate, forming a particularly attractive hunting ground for unscrupulous and subversive demagogues. The exclusion of the bulk of the labouring classes will foster resentment in all sections of those classes and will inevitably tend to drive them into the arms of mischievous and disloyal political opportunists. Feeling that they have nobody to speak for them directly elected by them, they will tend more and more to rely on intemperate and unconstitutional action. I have come to the conclusion that, given adequate safeguards such as complete discretion in the Governor in the nomination of unofficial members, the power of veto, the retention in the hands of HMG of the power of disallowance, a risk should be taken now and not a few years hence when it may be difficult to resist the impression that political rights can be obtained by subversive activity.[26]

This time Mackenzie-Kennedy returned with a constitution that provided for nineteen elected members from five multimember constituencies, twelve nominated members, and three official members (rather than the eight proposed a year earlier). Men and women over twenty-one able to prove they could write simple sentences in any one of the languages used on the island would be permitted to vote.[27] On December 19, 1947, King George VI signed the Order in Council putting the new constitution into effect.

The Franco-Mauritians were furious: the Colonial Office had virtually ignored their suggestions; the new constitution was clearly a victory for the Indians. True, universal suffrage had not been granted, but property requirements had been dropped and formal schooling was not required. Most important, elected members, not nominated or official, would constitute the majority in the new Legislative Council.

Viewed from the vantage point of any but the Franco-Mauritians, the new constitution was neither innovative nor imaginative. Elements—such as the wide franchise, the unofficial majority, and the election of some members of the Legislative Council to the Executive Council—reflected changes taking place throughout the colonies. The reforms, if not as far-reaching as those in Jamaica, did give Mauritians a greater role in government than did the constitutions introduced in the Gambia or Tanganyika in the 1940s.[28]

The constitution forced a complete realignment in Mauritian politics. Franco-Mauritians could no longer control the new Legislative Council as they had the Council of Government. Uncertain of the results, but fully aware that things would never be the same now that the Indians were a majority of the electorate, the Franco-Mauritians withdrew into their community to look for means other than election of maintaining their influence. Although there were Franco-Mauritian candidates in the elections, none of the old guard stood as candidates. The melée of elective politics was not for them. And the Creole elite, represented by Laurent and Rivet, allied themselves with the Franco-Mauritians, for both groups feared Indian domination.

Rozemont's compelling personality held the enfeebled Labour party together. But the Indians, skeptical of the men Rozemont proposed as party candidates, were not sure that their interests still coincided with those of the Labour party. In the past few years, many laborers had become aware of their communal as well as their class interests. Given the factions and divisions within the island, and an electorate that had increased sixfold overnight, Mauritians could only be certain of one thing: the 1947 constitution had permanently and drastically altered the politics of the island. The precise nature of the

change and its impact on communalism in Mauritius would be revealed in the coming years.

CONSTITUTIONAL PROPOSALS

	Members	Official	Unofficial	Elected	Nominated
Clifford, 1939	42	21	21	21[a]	21
Mackenzie- Kennedy, 1945	32	8	24	16	16
Mackenzie- Kennedy, 1946	40	8	32	19	21
	Franchise limited by education (school certificate) or property.				
Mackenzie- Kennedy, 1947	34	3	31	19	15[b]
	Franchise: basic literacy.				

[a]Includes seven Franco-Mauritians, seven Creoles, seven Indians.
[b]Includes three officials.

7. Growing Communalism
1948–1956

IN THE DECADE following the 1948 elections, the Indo-Mauritian community consolidated its newly acquired political strength, while the Creole elite and the Franco-Mauritians, for the most part, looked on with disbelief and then with active alarm. For all communities, the new Legislative Council was a learning experience. The Indians and the Labour party Creoles were learning how a parliamentary system actually worked. The Franco-Mauritians and their supporters were learning a new form of politics. The changed size and composition of the Council required new tactics, even for those who had gathered experience during the old Council of Government.

In Mauritius, as elsewhere, incorporating a sizable portion of the island's population into the political system required new mechanisms for channeling opinion to the government. Interest groups and political parties developed to fill the gap, and as they did so, Mauritians became increasingly aware of their differences. Gradually each group came to understand that it must learn how to use the political system to protect and promote its own interests and its own concept of what Mauritius should and could be. The learning process was a slow one, but by 1956 political parties clearly emerged and different viewpoints among these parties were sharpened.

Although the 1948 constitution suddenly altered the political balance on the island, subsequent change in the economic and social structure came more gradually. Still, the progress of the Indian community was marked. Franco-Mauritians managed to maintain their control over the sugar factories and the most productive land. Even so, by 1948 over half the land planted in cane, as well as most tea and tobacco estates, belonged to Indians. In 1901, only 2 percent of the island's doctors and 1 percent of its lawyers were Indian; by 1944, the percentages had risen to 14 and 15 percent respectively, and by 1954 they reached 29 and 25 percent.[1] Indian professionals served the Indo-Mauritian community. Their growing numbers meant better services for Indians, but had no impact on the daily lives of the Franco-Mauritians. For the most part, the Franco-Mauritians remained ignorant of and aloof from the changing communities around them, and it was through the political process rather than any daily contact that new relationships first began to develop between individuals in these two groups.

In any plural society, the nature of the electoral process and the elections themselves take on an unusual intensity. Because voting patterns and ethnicity coincided to a certain extent in 1948, politicians could predict how most voters would respond at the polls. The registration process, the method of representation, the boundaries and sizes of constituencies, and the system of counting votes all became crucial to the outcome of an election, as the events of 1948 demonstrated.

The 1948 Campaign

In Mauritius, registration at first was poorly organized and somewhat haphazard. Although forms were distributed to the sugar estates, they did not always reach the workers, and few government registrars actively canvassed to register voters. More significant, the party organizations that in many countries bring voters to the registration centers were nonexistent in Mauritius in 1948. The candidates themselves, all relatively inexperienced, were not aware of the determining influence registration can have on an election, even before the election takes place.[2] An active registration campaign in the press failed to do the job, and many voters were never registered.

Even so, the size of the electorate increased sixfold. Before 1948, fewer than 12,000 people were qualified to vote in a national election. When the books closed that year, the number of registered voters totaled 71,806.[3] In spite of the fact that many Indians were unable to meet the literacy or property requirements, most of the new voters were Indian; 23 percent were women.

Perhaps the most active registration agent was Basdeo Bissoondoyal, not himself a candidate. His goal was to enlarge the Indian percentage of the electorate. Believing that within two months he could teach illiterate laborers and their wives to read and write well enough to satisfy the registration officer, he extended his network of schools. Armed with a blackboard and infinite patience, he and his teachers prepared thousands of voters. And as before, Bissoondoyal did more for the Indian community than improve literacy rates. While learning to write and to vote, the Indian laborers began to gain self-confidence. Bissoondoyal convinced them that their vote could matter and that they could actually participate in shaping Mauritius's future.

Political parties that were later to dominate Mauritian politics were not a factor in the 1948 election, for only the Labour party presented candidates committed to a common program. As defined at the Labor Day meeting in 1948, this program included social security, old-age pensions, compulsory education, low-cost housing, cooperatives for small planters, and nationalization of certain industries.[4] Rozemont, still the party leader, drew his major support from Creole artisans who belonged to his union, but Creoles and Indians alike flocked to hear him speak. The campaign kept the Labour leader on the estates and mingling with the people, where he was happiest and most convincing. The force of his personality was reviving the floundering organization from which Curé had resigned.

But the campaign also revealed Rozemont's weaknesses. Rozemont selected and placed in constituencies Labour candidates, both Indian and Creole. But he did not choose the most experienced members of the party, who were also the most independent-minded. Perhaps fearing competition and wanting to hold on to his role as leader, Rozemont picked second-rate candidates — men with little education, no experience in the Municipal Council or in the consultative committees, and little understanding of the complex problems that would face the legislature. They idolized Rozemont, drank rum with him, and flattered him, but they were unable to command the support of party members. To make matters worse, Rozemont was a poor organizer. Because of the quality of his candidates and his lack of organization, Creoles and Indians who were loyal to Rozemont voted for him personally but not for the other party candidates, and several of the most distinguished members of the party resigned to stand as independents.

With the exception of Jules Koenig, the Franco-Mauritian candi-

dates were newcomers to politics. They were often members of establishment families, but had no previous experience in the Council of
Government. For example, André Nairac, long-time member of the
Council of Government, did not stand as a candidate, although his
younger brother, Paul, did. Franco-Mauritians who had been active
in politics before 1948, and who were used to being nominated by the
governor or elected in a safe constituency, did not want to face the
demands of a political campaign or the anxiety of a possible defeat.
Despite their real fear of Hindu hegemony, they remained aloof.

Most of the 104 candidates in the 1948 election were from the
Hindu educated elite. Most stood as independents, but in a few cases
small groups of friends published joint manifestos. Neither of the two
wartime Indian leaders—Ramnarain or Bissoondoyal—stood for
election. Bissoondoyal's brother, Sookdeo, who had at last resigned
his post as a school teacher, represented the family. "The Professor"
said he was not a candidate because working in the villages was more
important than debating in Council—but others charged that he was
afraid of losing.[5]

The communalism that so conspicuously marked subsequent
Mauritian elections was rarely discussed openly in 1948. Franco-
Mauritians, in spite of their general anxieties, had not fully recognized the threat to their position, and the goals of the Indo-Mauritian
community, which had never before elected its own candidates, were
still unclear. Then, too, most candidates stood as independents.
Holding individual meetings in their own constituencies, they only
rarely ventured into neighboring districts to speak for a friend. There
were no large groups of candidates of one ethnic or class background
making charges against another.

For candidates and voters, the campaign was a new experience.
Uncertain of the exact nature of the electorate, candidates made few
bold proposals. Poorly organized and inexperienced, they spent little
money on publicity and none had the complex network of paid agents
that became a feature of later elections. The lack of party machinery
turned the election into a popularity contest. Voters of the five constituencies selected those who were best known and most successful,
and therefore often best educated. If these leaders came from their
own community, so much the better. If not, they would vote for
members of another community who were respected leaders.

The 1948 campaign was fought as much in the newspapers as in the villages. Due to the high price of paper, now being imported from Canada, *Advance*, *Le Mauricien*, and *Le Cerneen* still appeared on a shared single sheet with separate editorial columns. On some occasions, voters were urged by the same morning newspaper to vote for three different sets of candidates. *Advance* supported the Indian intellectuals; *Le Mauricien*, still edited by Rivet, backed the Creole elite and some Franco-Mauritians; and *Le Cerneen* backed the Franco-Mauritian elite.

Voters went to the polls on Monday and Tuesday, August 9 and 10, 1948. Rozemont, worried that many estate workers would stay home rather than risk reprisals for voting, soon saw that his fears had been unfounded: over 90 percent of the registered electors voted.

The results, reflecting the new composition of the electorate, confirmed the worst fears of those who had wanted to preserve the old constitution. Only one Franco-Mauritian was returned—Jules Koenig—and he had never been a part of the sugar oligarchy. Eleven of the nineteen elected members were Hindu; the rest were Creole. No Muslims were elected, although Muslim candidates did well in Port Louis, where there was a large Muslim population. Since the Chinese continued to remain aloof from politics, no Chinese candidates stood for election. Establishing a pattern for the future, Creole candidates were most successful in urban areas, while Hindus swept the villages.

At the celebrations in Port Louis following the elections, Rozemont spoke about the great Labour victory, but there was actually little cause for jubilation. Rozemont himself was returned by virtue of his personal popularity, but only three other Labour candidates were elected. All of Rozemont's men, including his brother, were defeated. Afterward, Rozemont complained of the tendency of rural voters to select candidates from their own community:

> It is due to the non-political education of the Indian labourers or to their desire, after all legitimate, to elect Indian representatives instead of candidates of the coloured population or any other community. Even some of the Indian candidates are more conservative than the white Franco-Mauritian conservatives. . . . Nevertheless, there is no fear that communalism will have a chance to overpower our present Legislative Council as the leaders of the workers will piteously crush any move which might make Mauritius a little India.[6]

By surrounding himself with friends rather than with men who were respected in the island, Rozemont was partly responsible for the Labour party's poor showing. At the same time, the election results demonstrated a shift in Creole leadership from the old guard to the new. For years Rivet had been considered the hero of the colored population, and before the election, predictions were that no one could move him from his usual position at the head of the poll, even though his standing in municipal elections was dropping. As it turned out, he was ranked sixth in the poll, the last candidate to be elected.

His near defeat marked the end of an era: the Creole elite had had its day in Mauritian politics, and in 1948 Rivet and Laurent were dismissed as too conservative.[7] They had dutifully defended Creole interests as they saw them, but had shown no concern for the lower-class Creoles or the Hindu laborers. As part of an elite, and as members of the Council of Government for over twenty years, they had more in common with Franco-Mauritians than with the new Creole and Hindu leaders. Catholic in religion and French in culture, Rivet represented hundreds of upper- and middle-class Creoles with wide literary interests who had for generations monopolized the majority of posts in government, trade, and commerce. Now the Creole elite was caught between two stronger groups. It had neither the economic power of the Franco-Mauritians nor the numbers of the Indian community. And unlike the Franco-Mauritians, Creoles could not flee to Natal or Australia should a real crisis develop. Their choices would become clearer during the 1950s, but in 1948 they were uncertain about the future.

If the election results sounded a warning to the Creoles, the sound heard by the Franco-Mauritians was even more ominous. Clearly, the impact of the new constitution could not be ignored. Every Franco-Mauritian except Koenig had been defeated; the Council would no longer be in the hands of men who looked after their interests. Instead, "demagogues and communalists," who had preached "class hatred and a short-sighted political philosophy," would dominate the legislature.[8] The Franco-Mauritians placed their hope for the future in the governor, for only his "reserved powers" could protect them from the feared radicalism and communalism of the new council. By the end of the month, the governor would show that their hopes had not been misplaced.

The Muslims were the most disappointed of the communities.

They claimed that voting had been entirely communal.[9] Indians voted for Indians and Creoles for Creoles. Because Muslims were scattered throughout the island and had no overall majority in any constituency, they had lost. In the consultative committee meetings, Muslim representatives had rejected proposals for reserved seats. But after the election, at a public meeting in September 1948, the Muslim community approved a petition asking for communal representation. It could not tolerate its interests being safeguarded "by elected members belonging to another community with a different culture and different religion."[10]

The real victors were the Hindus. They won every seat in the three-member "country" constituencies. Sookdeo Bissoondoyal, who headed the poll in Grand-Port Savanne, benefited from his brother's reputation. But other Bissoondoyal-supported candidates were defeated, for like the Labour party, the Bissoondoyal movement centered upon one man. Most of the Indians elected were professionals who were actually critical of Bissoondoyal, the doctors and lawyers who in 1936 had organized the Indian Cultural Society but had not participated in Curé's Labour party. This group included the five candidates in an informal alliance organized by Ramgoolam. Articulate and ambitious, these men had served on the constitutional consultative committees and had earned reputations in their professions. In the Legislative Council, they soon replaced Laurent, Rivet, Le Clezio, and Raffray as the principal elected figures in Mauritian politics.

But although the Indo-Mauritians were at last incorporated into the political system, their victory was shortlived. The governor, on whom the Franco-Mauritians' last hopes rested, still had a move to make. On August 30 Mackenzie-Kennedy made public his twelve nominations to the Legislative Council. None of his selections had supported the new constitution; six were members of the old Council of Government who represented the Creole and Franco-Mauritian establishment. Curé—whose political career everyone, except the governor and Curé himself, thought was over—was also appointed. The nominations drew criticism from all sides. Even *Le Cerneen* denounced the choice because the governor had chosen to reward the old guard who did not even participate in the elections. Younger, more adventurous Franco-Mauritians who had stood as candidates were overlooked. *Advance* and Millien's radical *L'Oeuvre* were outraged for another reason: the appointment of twelve conservatives nullified the election results. The two conservative elected members, Koenig and Rivet, could combine with the nominated members and the three official members to stop any measure supported by the remaining seventeen elected members.

The psychological effect of the nominations was as great as their impact on the voting strength in council. A productive Legislative Council depended on a certain amount of trust between the government and the elected members. The nominations destroyed whatever goodwill had been built up during the constitutional negotiations. The elected members, convinced now that the government did not want to cooperate with them, began to oppose it at every turn. The deep suspicion that resulted disrupted even routine business.[11]

Donald Mackenzie-Kennedy opened the first session of the new Council with a series of warnings. He warned that the constitution would not work unless the members cooperated in establishing, "among other essentials, a fundamental loyalty and a unity of purpose, which will impel Mauritians to work together as Mauritians for the general good of Mauritius and the Commonwealth." Further, he warned members to recognize the limitations of the Council and not to "read anything into the constitution which is not there." But his most serious warning was about the danger of communism, a threat he saw emanating from Malaya. "Defeated, or only partially successful on one hand, they [communists] will look for other areas into which to penetrate and we must be continually on the alert. . . . If the mass of peasantry is led to believe that they lead such a miserable life that any change is for the better, they might well become fifth-column recruits."[12] Mackenzie-Kennedy's fears, though ill-founded, would seriously divide the island later on. At the opening session of the Council, however, these fears only gave the Labour members new reason to distrust the government.

The first session of the Council lasted fifteen and a half months; during this time new members with little or no previous parliamentary experience began to learn about politics and procedure. Lengthy and repetitive speeches drastically delayed government business, as did time squandered unnecessarily on minor issues. Road construction nearly came to a standstill in 1949 because approval of the public works budget was delayed. Foreign experts, crucial to the success of a campaign to eradicate malaria, almost had to pack their bags and leave the island because of the delay in voting their salaries. Labour party members, caught between a desire to pass social measures and an equally strong desire to balance the budget, often blocked legislation because it was incomplete or inadequate.

In its first session the Council met seventy-nine times, and disposed of seventy bills and twenty-two private members' motions, with over one hundred divisions. The new members asked over four hundred parliamentary questions.[13] Even the Indian representatives felt that more than half of the debates and practically all of the questions could have been eliminated. By the next year, the members had learned that the simplest way to obtain information was to request it privately from the department concerned. In forty-four meetings of the second session, the Council members decided on eighty-four bills and asked only one hundred and twenty-five questions.[14] By then, they were more seasoned.

Parliamentary discipline was another problem in the first session. In November 1948, only two months after the Council first met, Sookdeo Bissoondoyal was suspended for openly insulting the governor.[15] As the session wore on, his constant and irresponsible criticism of the government and its departments, his lengthy speeches, his unorthodox behavior, and his refusal to learn the art of compromise antagonized elected and nominated members alike. But Bissoondoyal was tempered neither by suspension nor by open criticism; his speeches did not change in tone or length. He was removed bodily from the Council in 1949, suspended again in 1952, and sent to prison three times for disorderly conduct.[16]

Dr. Edgar Millien, too, acquired a record with the law, as a result of several libel suits. But the member of Council most often in court was Rozemont. His volatile temper provoked his enemies and at the same time urged his henchmen on to action. In 1950 he was arrested for illegal picketing; in 1951 he spent six weeks in jail for criticizing three magistrates; and in 1953 he was sentenced to three months in prison for "breach of peace."

Prison sentences usually had little overall effect on a politician's popularity, however. In the Legislative Council a motion that Rozemont's 1951 sentence was "harsh and unfair" was defeated, but only after considerable debate. To many people, the government was the enemy, and those who violated its regulations, courageous.

Nevertheless, evidence that members of the Council were not always law-abiding did set an unfortunate precedent.

In spite of procedural difficulties and the misdemeanors of its members, the Council approved a good deal of legislation during its first session. Much of it provided for improvements in the island's embryonic social welfare programs. Details of many of the programs had been worked out by the 1947 Economic Commission, which had been appointed by the governor to make recommendations for the effective use of money made available by the Colonial Development and Welfare Act of 1946.[17] Whatever their origins, malaria eradication schemes, public works programs, minimum wage laws, social security provisions, agricultural extension projects, and village government ordinances were long overdue.

Politics and Parties

During the early stages of national politics in Mauritius, as in other colonies, parliamentary groups and factions were formed after rather than before elections. The Labour party was formed to provide an organized base from which to respond to attacks from the Franco-Mauritian community, and to promote social and economic reform as well as constitutional change. The *Parti Mauricien*, in turn, emerged as a direct response to the Labour party. The Muslim community was not a particularly organized or powerful political force at first. But colonial officials encouraged the formation of political interest groups. Indeed, many colonial civil servants measured their success in terms of the establishment of a viable two-party or multiparty system. According to Robert Newton, colonial secretary in Mauritius between 1954 and 1960, colonial officials "were well aware that, since few governments are composed of the wisest and the best, they should avoid, if possible, entrenching one party or another without hope of change or effective criticism."[18] Newton, like other officials, recognized the dangers of communal politics, but hoped that individuals could be persuaded to join a party for reasons of policy rather than community. Instead, as it turned out, the encouragement of party politics accentuated the communal nature of politics.

When the Mauritius Legislative Council first met in 1948, most nominated and elected officers were independents. What few alignments there were, even within the Labour party, were based on friendship. Five years later, when new elections were held, a rudimentary party system had developed. The Labour party had undergone a considerable metamorphosis, and the changes gave it strength as well as a new form. At the same time, Franco-Mauritian and Creole conservatives, as well as some Muslims, formed a new political alliance, the *Ralliement Mauricien*, to combat the Hindus.

The Labour party was going to change from a loose association of Rozemont's followers into a disciplined party dominated by Hindu intellectuals and the evolution began soon after the Council met in 1948. Rozemont himself, still very popular among young Creole dockworkers and Indian laborers on the estates, had no particular liking for legislative procedure. He really was not suited for that kind of methodical undertaking, and, as was to be expected, was neither an effective nor a conscientious member. More at home in informal gatherings on the estates than in Government House, he took little interest in what was happening in Council and rarely attended its sessions.

Of the members friendly to Labour, only Ramgoolam had previous legislative experience. He had already earned respect and a sound reputation by defending the interests of the Indian community in the Council of Government, and new members naturally looked to him for advice. Unlike Rozemont, he was neither flamboyant nor charismatic, but he had a gift for compromise and negotiation. From the beginning, Ramgoolam was assured the support of all Indians, with the exception of Bissoondoyal. It was natural, then, that as Rozemont faded into the background, the Creoles who had supported Rozemont would turn to Ramgoolam for leadership; and for his part, Ramgoolam was careful to court the Creoles and Rozemont, for he hoped to inherit Rozemont's following. Besides having such contrasting personalities, the two men approached the party differently. Rozemont had built his Labour party from the bottom up, starting first with mass support; Ramgoolam, however, would build from the top down, starting with support in the Legislative Council and then seeking popular backing. But it was the power of the newspaper *Le Cerneen*, as well as Ramgoolam's own political abilities, that ensured his position as leader of the parliamentary Labour party—a goal just about the opposite of the one the paper had set for itself.

Always afraid of Hindu domination, *Le Cerneen* began to attack

Ramgoolam in 1949. When the paper shortage ended in 1949 and *Le Cerneen*, *Le Mauricien*, and *Advance* again published separately, a group of Franco-Mauritians asked a Mauritian-born journalist, Noel Marrier d'Unienville, to return from France and use his pen to attack the Hindus. N.M.U., as he was casually called, obliged. Beginning his attacks on Ramgoolam shortly after the governor had warned the Council against the danger of communist influence spreading from Malaya, N.M.U. went on to suggest that ever since India's independence, Indian "expansionists" had looked on Mauritius as an "advanced base of pan-Indianism on the flank of Africa."[19] In an article including a picture of Ramgoolam with the caption "L'homme de Kremlin," N.M.U. called Ramgoolam "the figure of the communist movement in Mauritius," and talked of "his complex of hatred, and his frantic sectarianism."[20]

In fact, communism posed no real threat to Mauritius. Labour party leaders looked to India and the Fabian Society for guidance, not to the Soviet Union or Marx. But in the Cold War context that prevailed at the end of the 1940s, the Franco-Mauritians misinterpreted the Labour party program as being communist-inspired, confusing communism (in a pattern that would repeat itself around the globe) with the desire of the Indians to participate in the political and economic system of Mauritius.

In the 1953 election, N.M.U. openly charged that the Labour party was instilling fear of the white man in every Hindu voter by repeating the slogan "khoonism," a Hindi term for blood and race, and in Mauritius a synonym for racial hatred. N.M.U. also preached that each racial and religious group in Mauritius should live as separately as possible from the others to avoid the amorality and skepticism that were inevitable in a mixed population. As N.M.U. slandered Ramgoolam, Indo-Mauritian and Creole elected members, with the exception of Rivet, grouped themselves around the Indian in defense. Since their programs coincided, Rozemont's Labour party and the elected members sympathetic to Ramgoolam often voted together during the first session of the Legislative Council. Slowly they were drawn into the Labour party, the only existing party organization. Among the Indian intellectuals, only Seeneevassen had been associated with the party since the 1930s. Ramgoolam had shown cautious interest in 1946, but did not associate his name with the party until 1950, when he became its undisputed leader in the Legislative Council. The party's most pressing goals were increased benefits for workers, universal adult suffrage, and "responsible government," which would augment the power of the elected members of the Council by placing elected members in cabinet-level positions as ministers, responsible for the management of departments. In the 1953 elections, for example, their program proposed nationalization of the sugar industry, health insurance, food subsidies, improved roads, and more schools and hospitals.[21] In those elections the party, under the leadership of Rozemont and Ramgoolam, won thirteen of the nineteen seats.

In spite of N.M.U.'s charges, the Labour party was still primarily a party of the working classes, Creole and Hindu. Communalism was not part of its program. The nature of government, however, was communal, and when the new governor, Sir Hilary Blood, who replaced Mackenzie-Kennedy in 1949, followed his predecessor's pattern by nominating twelve conservatives to the Council in order to offset the Labour victory, the party reacted intensely, becoming more insistent than ever in its demands for constitutional reform.

The governor's nominations ended any chance of cooperation between the Labour party and the government. According to *Advance*, "Those who had some confidence in the impartiality of the Governor and his sense of reality find their hope has been shattered to pieces. Reaction has been installed for the next few years."[22] To the Labour party, the reforms made possible by the 1948 constitution now seemed meaningless. Labour party leaders were not satisfied that in five short years they had built a relatively united and disciplined political party that could win nearly 70 percent of the elected seats. Nor did it seem enough that its leading members were members of the Executive Council with quasi-ministerial responsibilities, and that once unheard of social programs, such as old-age pensions and a social security system, were now law. Their consuming ambition was to remove the restraints imposed by the governor's nominations. This left one course of action: immediate constitutional change.

With Labour party support, the Legislative Council passed a motion in 1953 demanding constitutional talks. The secretary of state, however, called the motion premature and asked Blood's successor, Sir Robert Scott, to sound out opinion in Mauritius and send proposals to London for the consideration of the secretary of state.

In the early 1950s, any chance for a two-party system in Mauritius depended on developing an effective opposition to the Labour party.

Stirred by the growing strength of Labour and stimulated by N.M.U.'s journalism, a group of Mauritians formed a loose political organization to counter Ramgoolam's group. Franco-Mauritian and Creole conservatives were aware that they alone could not block the Hindus; they needed to persuade other groups to join them. The Muslims were willing. Most Muslim candidates in the 1948 election had been defeated by Hindus, and Razack Mohammed, a member of the Municipal Council since 1943 and the most outspoken of the community's leaders, believed that the only chance for political success was through an alliance. In December 1952, the *Ralliement Mauricien* was formed to prevent one community from dominating another and to create instead a "Mauritian unity" by guaranteeing each community the right to participate in Mauritian politics.[23] The *Ralliement* was not a political party, but an informal *groupement* opposed to the Labour party program, universal suffrage, and a shift of power from the colonial government to local officials. It had no membership lists and collected no dues.

Jules Koenig emerged as the *Ralliement* spokesman. Leaning heavily on Koenig's liberal background, *Ralliement* organizers hoped to avoid being seen as stooges of the estate owners, but it was a label they could not escape. When the *Ralliement* was first formed, Koenig was vehemently opposed to creating a disciplined political party, resenting the obligations imposed by a formal party structure. His individualistic approach to politics made it difficult for the *Ralliement* to build a political base.

By 1953, both the *Ralliement* and the estate owners were looking to the government for support. While most estate owners did not actively participate in elective politics, they did give financial support and advice when asked. While they may have found the *Ralliement* more progressive than they liked, they were beginning to realize that modest changes would be required in Mauritius. The *Ralliement*, if not the estate owners, favored reforms, but insisted that they be limited and within the bounds of the budget. Working with the government, members of the alliance diluted and then voted for some Labour party proposals. In Labour's view, however, the *Ralliement* was formed exclusively to protect the estate owners' interests and to promote communal divisions. Distinctions among the views of N.M.U., the estate owners, and the more moderate *Ralliement* were blurred, and soon those wealthy Indians who shared economic interests with the members of the *Ralliement* began to join the party of the Indians. Communalism was replacing class as the determining factor in Mauritian politics.

Although *Ralliement* members insisted that they were not a formal political party, they did organize voters for the 1953 election. Their opposition to a ministerial system of government was staunch. Even Jules Koenig equated responsible government with Hindu domination and claimed that majority rule would "be the end of Western Civilization and Christian tolerance in Mauritius."[24] For Koenig, the 1953 election was a referendum and a chance for voters to denounce the Labour party's unrealistic and irresponsible demands. The *Ralliement* somewhat naively believed that voters of all races would grasp the logic of their arguments against a ministerial system of government and nationalization of the sugar industry. Thus, except in N.M.U.'s columns, their campaign was neither communal, as it would become after 1960, nor particularly aggressive.

It is therefore not surprising that only two *Ralliement* candidates, Razack Mohammed and Jules Koenig, were returned, along with thirteen Labour candidates. Koenig lost his referendum. He believed that Mauritians had lost sight of the issue and had voted communally, although it was apparent from the election results that Creoles and Muslims had divided their votes. The election proved to Koenig that the issues needed to be separated from the politicians. He advocated a special island-wide referendum solely to address the question of a ministerial system of government, so that the constitution, not the candidates, would be the issue. This was the first time since its founding that the *Ralliement* had made a demand for a referendum separate from a general election; it would not, however, be the last.

Since the governor's nominations ensured that the *Ralliement* would have a considerable voice in the Legislative Council between 1953 and 1959, its leaders saw their position as stable. They did not fully understand that the Colonial Office would not support them indefinitely.

To put their position in perspective, one must remember that in 1953 the Mau Mau terror was reaching its peak in Kenya, a state of emergency was still in force in Malaya, and the Soviet Union and the United States were deadlocked in the Cold War. But it was events in British Guiana that most terrified the minority groups and alarmed the civil servants of Mauritius. In the Guyanan election of April 1953,

Cheddi Jagan's predominantly Indian People's Progressive party won 51 percent of the popular vote and eighteen of twenty-four Legislative Council seats. In October 1953, two months before Mauritians began debating constitutional change, the governor of British Guiana suspended the constitution because of evidence of communist subversion of the government and the threat of a breakdown of public order. Similarities between British Guiana and Mauritius were obvious; both countries were sugar colonies and both had multiracial populations, including a large Indian population descended from indentured immigrant laborers. Reform of the Mauritian constitution, it was feared, might lead to a disaster like the one in Guiana.

In this context, it was not surprising that the nominated members, backed by Koenig and Mohammed, firmly opposed further constitutional talks, which they knew would lead inevitably to more change. At the same time, they had to recognize that as a loose *groupement*, the *Ralliement* was ineffective in combating Labour policies. To be a positive alternative to Labour, British officials had told them, they needed a strong leader, a structured party, and a carefully developed program with defined goals. On a visit to Mauritius in 1952, Lord Munster, then parliamentary undersecretary of state for the Colonial Office, had explained that Koenig had an obligation to turn the *Ralliement* into a formal party, and Munster had promised that once this step was taken, the *Ralliement* would carry more weight in London.[25] The governor, Sir Robert Scott, concurred: "It is time that those elements in Mauritius who cannot find representation in the Labour Party should, in their own interests and in the wider interest of the island, cease to hold themselves aloof from politics or to lean too heavily upon representation by nomination."[26] Scott, slowly becoming exasperated by conservatives who refused to participate in politics but expected their interests to be defended, made his feelings known to Koenig on several occasions.

The announcement that the constitutional conference would take place in the summer of 1955 finally forced the *Ralliement* into action: in April 1955 it became the *Parti Mauricien*, with Koenig as president.[27] Koenig had a love for detail that made him a superb lawyer and an excellent speaker in council, but he was unwilling to delegate responsibility, so that party decisions were often held up for several weeks on his desk.[28] Since he and Razack Mohammed were the only members of the party executive committee in the Legislative Council, they automatically became its leading party spokesmen. The Labour party, watching these developments, viewed the *Parti Mauricien* as an officially sponsored party of minorities, and its suspicion of the government mounted.

The impasse seemed insurmountable. Divisions between the Franco-Mauritian and Indian communities, minimized in 1948, had by 1955 been solidified and institutionalized through the formation of political parties. The Mau Mau emergency in Kenya and Marxist Cheddi Jagan's rise to power in British Guiana had fueled the fears of Mauritius's white ruling elite—people unused to sharing power and lacking both flexibility and imagination. The political newcomers, both Indian and Creole, were still learning about the processes of government. Their awkward mistakes and naive excesses only aggravated the fears of the Franco-Mauritians during the first session of the Legislative Council. For both groups, the process of learning about members of other communities was a slow one. Suspicions were aroused when members of one group defied the century-old codified behavior patterns. The newcomers could not feel secure with their new power; the old guard could not see the inevitability of change, nor could they imagine sharing their responsibility with others. When the British governor reinforced the old guard's views, their confidence grew. In the next decade, as Mauritians debated the very nature of their system of government, the differences between the old and the new would become even sharper.

8. Responsible Government

WHEN THE NEW Legislative Council met in 1953, the members of the Labour party were frustrated and bitter. The governor had, for all practical purposes, cancelled out their elected majority. On top of that, preoccupied with the financial difficulties of the island, he was ignoring the impending political crisis. But by 1959, the Labour party had had six years to consolidate its power and recoup its strength enough to dictate the terms of a new constitutional and electoral system. Although the "winds of change," long felt, had not been officially acknowledged, Secretary of State Oliver Lyttelton saw that "the dominant theme of Colonial policy had to be the careful and if possible orderly progress of the colonies toward self-government within the Commonwealth."[1] Means for transferring power needed to be devised. In its efforts to devise such means, the Colonial Office, concerned with the legalities of constitutional change, often failed to consider the realities of the social structure of individual colonies.[2]

The British system of government, one obvious model to consider, itself enjoyed a mixed press. Not everyone agreed on how effective it would be if applied to the colonies. Many colonial officials were dedicated to transferring the Westminster model to the colonies, but others, such as Mauritius's governor, Hilary Blood, were concerned about the political and economic "burden" the Westminster system might impose on small territories.[3] But in Mauritius, as elsewhere, whenever colonial servants tried to develop new techniques of government for the colonies, local leaders were apt to complain loudly that these were just new attempts to maintain colonialism. "If it isn't good enough for Britain," the response went, "then it isn't going to happen here."

In Mauritius, attitudes toward the British system of government varied according to the self-interest of the community involved, and proposals for constitutional changes fueled bitter and heated debates among political groups and sharpened communal tensions.

Local and National Changes

To keep pace with developments on the national level, changes were also made in the system of local government. British officials thought that participating in local government offered colonists good training for work in national representative institutions. To provide this "training program," in the 1940s and 1950s officials developed elaborate pyramids of district and village councils throughout the colonies. In Mauritius, Donald Mackenzie-Kennedy took the first steps to provide a system of local government in the island. In 1946 and 1947 he appointed three civil commissioners and gave them responsibility for local administration in three sections of the island. Forming a personal link between the government and the governed, the civil commissioners were seen as the solution to all problems:

> We shall see a real progress towards the removal of grievances, forced or real, and the elimination of the dishonest, the irresponsible and the subversive. The interest in public affairs of sober and responsible men will be quickened, the establishment of local government will be hastened in areas which have at the moment no proper guidance, the diverse activities of the Government will be coordinated to give effect to the Government's policy and deputies will have in their constituencies men whose task it is to perform the administrative duties which are at present imperfectly performed or not performed at all.[4]

Soon after the civil commissioners were appointed, village councils were established, in many cases growing out of an already existing village body, the antimalaria committees. By the end of 1947, forty village councils were functioning throughout the country, and by 1951, eighty-six.

The first councils had little real responsibility, and the members, since they were appointed by the civil commissions rather than elected by the people, won little respect. Problems of administration, arising from everything from personal rivalry to insufficient finance, dampened the initial enthusiasm for the councils. The situation began to improve in 1951, however, when the Village Councils Ordinance was changed so that eight members out of the twelve were elected to the councils. The new ordinance also revised village boundaries, and gave the councils increased responsibilities, including the building of schools, health centers, and marketplaces.[5] Still, until they were empowered to tax in 1956, the councils were totally dependent on the government for financing.

The first village council elections were held in 1952, taking place at public meetings in small villages and by secret balloting in larger villages. Every villager over twenty-one could vote, but the candidates themselves had to own property valued at two thousand rupees or more or be government employees. Because being a council member meant having power over expenditures and patronage, prominent village leaders naturally tried to get elected. Like an echo of the approach to national politics, six or eight candidates in a village often joined together in a *groupement*. Generally these alliances reflected ongoing conflicts among traditional leaders, sirdars and contractors, and more educated leaders, school teachers and government employees.[6] Religion and personal factors also entered into these alliances, and the *groupements* seldom survived more than three years of village politics, if that. As national parties developed in Mauritius in the 1950s, they solicited village council support, but rarely did the parties themselves become involved in local elections until the 1960s.

When the Legislative Council provided for village council elections, it also enlarged the Municipal Council of Port Louis to sixteen and provided for election of two-thirds of the members of the three town councils: Curépipe, Beau Bassin–Rose Hill, and Quatre Bornes. Unlike village elections, which pivoted on local issues and people, town and municipal elections were related to national politics. Control over the urban councils brought opportunities for patronage and publicity and strengthened a political party. As party rivalries took shape, Curépipe and Rose Hill became reliable sources of support for the *Parti Mauricien*. Quatre Bornes, originally a *Parti Mauricien* town, switched to Labour. The Port Louis municipality changed hands from *Parti Mauricien* to Labour control in 1956, but after 1959 it had a large *Parti* majority.

Town and municipal elections, particularly those in Port Louis, served as a bellwether for Legislative Council elections: Rozemont's poor showing in the 1950 municipal council elections, for example, was a signal to Ramgoolam that Rozemont's popularity was beginning to fade. Conversely, the respectable showing of Verasamy Ringadoo, a Tamil who had just returned from London with a law degree, earned him Labour backing and, as a result, victory in a 1951 Legislative Council by-election.

On the national level, the nature of the constitution profoundly influenced the behavior of many members of the Legislative Council. Along with many other colonial constitutions of the 1940s, the Mauritius constitution had one principal drawback: it bestowed upon the newly created Legislative Council considerable power and little responsibility. As the Donoughmore Commission pointed out in Ceylon, "denied of all prospects of office, the unofficial members were in no danger of being called upon to translate their criticism into action and to execute in practice the measures which they advocated."[7] Since powers once given to the legislatures could not be withdrawn, colonial governors came to believe that the only way to encourage unofficial members to change their ways was to incorporate them more fully in the decision-making process.

In Mauritius, the first step was to include unofficial members on the Executive Council, as provided for in the 1947 constitution. But these members did not respond as expected. Presumably a link between the Executive Council and the Legislative Council, the unofficial members were to explain to their colleagues in the Legislative Council the reasons for Executive Council decisions. But it was hard for them to break their old habit of opposing the government. While they often supported unpopular but necessary measures in the privacy of the Executive Council, they could not be trusted to defend them openly in the Legislative Council, for by cooperating with the government too regularly, they could compromise their futures as political leaders.

One way to alter this automatic, seemingly indiscriminate opposition was to give the unofficial members specific responsibilities for specific departments. And in 1950 the governor of Mauritius did just that: he assigned each unofficial member on the Executive Council to a department. Once these "liaison officers" were familiar with the workings of their departments, including finances, they were expected to make suggestions for modifying and executing policy, and also to support their department head in the Legislative Council. But this system was inadequate. Because the liaison officers had no ex-

plicit responsibility for the department, the civil servants responded to
the department head rather than to the liaison officers. Until the
unofficial members had full responsibility for their departments, they
were unwilling to act as if they had such responsibility. And as long as
the Executive Council included an official majority, the concept of
collective responsibility was repugnant.

It was not until 1957 that members of the Mauritius Executive
Council were given responsibility for their departments. In 1961 the
leader of the majority party became chief minister, and the governor
was required to consult him about the appointment of members of
the Executive Council and the allocation of portfolios. A full
ministerial system was introduced in 1964. During this period of
transition, however, membership on and composition of the Executive Council were sources of political debate.

Constitutional Reform: Round One

Although the 1953 Legislative Council elections were a clear victory for the Labour party, the results were once again virtually nullified by the governor, who nominated twelve conservatives to the
council. Only the far-sighted members of the *Ralliement* realized
that the nominations would ultimately harm their position. Thanks to
the governor, they were guaranteed control of the Council for another session, but compromise with Labour became impossible.
Whatever tentative rapport had existed between the members of the
Labour party and the other members of the Council had broken
down by 1953. N.M.U. had aggravated the tension between the two
groups. The governor, by openly supporting the conservative elements, had given reason for further distrust.

Indeed, Blood's policies, as much as anything else, strengthened
the Labour party's belief that the status quo could not last. Colonial
historians may remember Blood as a governor who took special interest in the problems of small colonies, but Mauritians remember him
as a man who served weak drinks at Le Reduit. Franco-Mauritians
had a special liking for him, but the Labour party found his open
support for the island's conservatives intolerable. In the face of his
policies, Labour leaders became uncompromising and impatient.
They deplored the opposition to constitutional change on the ground

that the 1948 constitution had not had a fair period of trial; and they never forgave Blood for his choice of nominated members on the Council, although it was these nominations that in fact drove Labour to force the issue of constitutional change before either the *Rallie-ment* or the Colonial Office thought it necessary.

Soon after the first meeting of the new Council in 1953, the Labour party asked the secretary of state to invite a delegation of Mauritians to London to discuss constitutional change "which would satisfy the legitimate aspirations of the people of this country."[8] During the debate in the Legislative Council, Labour's goals became clear: believing that it represented the Mauritian population better than any other party, Labour wanted to increase its influence in the government through constitutional change.

The appointment of a new governor in 1954 gave the party some hope. A modest and thoughtful man from Exeter, Robert Scott brought with him twenty years of experience as a colonial civil servant, mostly in Uganda, Palestine, and the African Gold Coast. Lacking Hilary Blood's style, perhaps, he at least did not share his predecessor's arrogance and affinity for the life of the Mauritian elite. As governor of Mauritius from 1954 to 1959, Scott sat through conference after conference trying to resolve the constitutional crisis he had inherited from his predecessor. He found that "the most daunting obstacle in the way of healthy political development in Mauritius is the manner in which the political and social structure is pervaded through and through by fear and suspicions, jealousies, and dislikes."[9] No community trusted another, and suspicions within communities further complicated the matter. As it had in its early days, the island's small size still influenced its political life, and, in Scott's view, only made matters worse. Every politician knew too much about every other politician, and the personal lives of Mauritian politicians were no different from the personal lives of politicians in most countries. It was simply harder to keep one's public and private life separate in Port Louis than it was in London.

The new governor's first hope was to create conditions for closer working relationships among the communities.[10] In this effort he was aided by a particularly astute colonial secretary, Robert Newton, who had served with Scott in Palestine, and was one of the few colonial officers admired and respected by all politicians in Mauritius.[11] He was, for instance, among the first colonial officers to entertain Indians in his home, and his reputation as a fair and concerned administrator was still intact a decade later—a remarkable feat in a colony as fraught with tension, gossip, and rumor as Mauritius.

Scott and Newton together represented an important transition for
Mauritius. They clearly took the Indian politicians seriously, and
Franco-Mauritians could no longer expect to work out an informal
deal with the government over drinks at the governor's home.

Scott and Newton felt it was essential to eliminate the hostility of
the unofficial members of the Legislative Council toward the government. Some of the responsibility for the division lay with former
governors, who had given the Labour party little reason to trust
them. Scott blamed the constitution itself, since it gave the Legislative Council great power and no responsibility. At the same time,
Scott recognized the Labour party as a major political force and grew
to believe that the more responsibility Labour leaders had for government decisions, the more reasoned their words and actions would
become.[12] According to Newton, Scott "saw clearly that the problem
was how to facilitate an acceptable system of representative government which was also reasonably efficient." More was required than
"patching up" the constitution; "fundamental" change was necessary.[13]

A cautious Colonial Office asked Scott to learn more about the
changes sought by those who favored reform. Through meetings with
Labour party leaders, representatives of the *Ralliement*, and representatives of other interest groups, Scott became even more convinced of the necessity for change. In August 1954 he met with the
leaders of each community and party to ask them to consider a
council of twelve nominated and twenty-four elected members, chosen from eight three-member constituencies. This Legislative Council would then elect two-thirds of the members of the executive
council; the governor would nominate the remaining third. Convinced that the existing electoral system did not provide adequate
safeguards for minorities, Scott suggested that an electoral commission from Britain redraw the boundaries of the constituencies.

The Labour party backed his proposals; the Muslim community
demurred, arguing that the proposals did not provide for adequate
Muslim representation; and the *Ralliement* flatly opposed them. According to Koenig, the existing constitution was still sound; a constitution like the one Scott outlined, on the other hand, would ensure
Hindu domination of Mauritius.

The governor sent his proposals, along with the comments of the various political groups, to the secretary of state, Alan Lennox-Boyd. Four months later, in April 1955, Lennox-Boyd suggested that a discussion with representatives of all community and interest groups from Mauritius would be useful. No date was set for the conference, but the statement mobilized the parties. The Labour party and the *Ralliement* sought support both at home and in London. Labour was the more effective in generating support among members of Parliament, particularly from James Johnson, Labour M.P. for Rugby, who became known as the "first Member for Mauritius."

The *Ralliement* response to Labour's publicity campaign was feeble. In a four-year period, between 1953 and 1956, while Labour party representatives asked eighteen questions in the House of Commons, people sympathetic to the *Ralliement* asked only two. At heart it seems that *Ralliement* leaders doubted the Colonial Office would ever do anything so rash as to grant Mauritius independence and give political power to the Indians, believing that the arguments against it were so compelling that they did not even need to be publicized. Furthermore, the leaders of the parties had different kinds of relationships with the power bases in Britian. While the leaders of the Mauritius Labour party had been in close communication with the British Labour party since the 1930s, the *Ralliement* and later the *Parti Mauricien* had no such long-standing political connections with political groups in England. What the forerunners of the *Parti Mauricien* did have was access to Colonial Office officials, and in the 1950s the *Parti* tried to maintain its influence on policy through these officials rather than through parliamentary questions. Of course, the Mauritius Chamber of Agriculture, with permanent offices in London, continued to represent both the economic and the political interests of the Franco-Mauritians and, therefore, of the *Parti Mauricien*.

In July 1955, the secretary of state met in London with eight Mauritian politicians. No communiqué followed the end of the 1955 London meetings. Rather, the delegates reached an informal agreement that the number of elected members be increased from nineteen to twenty-five, while the number of nominated members would remain at twelve. The Legislative Council would no longer elect members of the Executive Council. Instead, the unofficial members of the Executive Council, increased from four to nine, would be appointed by the government in consultation with the leader of the majority, a system already in effect in a number of colonies. The impasse arose, from the electoral system: the delegates could not agree on the mechanics of voting and the number of constituencies to be formed, and the secretary of state promised to make a recommendation based on the conference discussions.

Lennox-Boyd's proposals were not made public in Mauritius until March 1956, eight months after the conference. The secretary of state began his dispatch by explaining that the Colonial Office ideal was a constitution patterned on the Westminster model, which required a second, opposition party which had a reasonable opportunity for election, and that the party in power should "not achieve such a preponderant position" that it could disregard minorities. Because the chances of fulfilling these conditions in Mauritius seemed remote, Lennox-Boyd concluded that the constitution must at least ensure "the most adequate reflection possible of the main elements of responsible opinion."[14] In his view this could best be done with an electoral system of proportional representation, a single transferable vote, and universal suffrage.

Publication of the Lennox-Boyd proposals marked the end of the preliminary discussions about constitutional reform. The concept of a majority leader, an increase in the number of elected members of council, and universal adult suffrage constituted a significant gain for Ramgoolam and his party. That left the question of the electoral system, and for the next three years all attention would focus on that.

Constitutional Reform: Round Two

Discussions about voting in the 1946–47 consultative committees had been but a prelude to those to come. In 1946 the issue had been eligibility to vote; between 1955 and 1958 and again between 1965 and 1966, it was the system of voting and the boundaries of the constituencies. But each time, underneath each issue, the basic question was the same: how to ensure the fair representation of the major political parties and communities (or, conversely, how to ensure that one party or one community was not given an "unfair" advantage by the electoral system). Lennox-Boyd's proposal of proportional representation and the single transferable vote triggered a long and heated debate about the electoral process. It was confused even further by the fact that what the Colonial Office was recommending was an extremely complicated electoral system. Since so few people could understand the system, everyone became more anxious about it.

What would be the effect of proportional representation and the single transferable vote? The goal is to ensure the majority party majority representation, but only in proportion to the total number of votes received. Thus proportional representation is designed to avoid the defeat of the party with the majority of popular votes, overrepresentation of the majority, or underrepresentation of strong minorities.

In an election under this system, each party presents a list of candidates in a multimember constituency, and voters select candidates in order of preference. The total number of votes is added up; this total is divided by the number of seats vacant, plus one: the result is the quota necessary for election. Candidates receiving this quota of first-choice votes are automatically elected; "surplus votes" are distributed according to the voters' second preference listed on the ballot. This redistribution should then give another candidate the election quota. Redistribution of ballots continues until all vacant seats are filled.

The *Parti Mauricien* was ready to accept proportional representation, but Labour rejected it, appeased neither by the grant of universal suffrage nor by the immediate introduction of the ministerial system, which the secretary of state proposed at the same time. For six days, members of the Legislative Council debated Lennox-Boyd's proposals, and debated with more emotion than realism. The Labour party claimed proportional representation was a gimmick London was imposing on Mauritians to deprive them of their true choice. First, they feared that proportional representation would destroy the party system: candidates who should be working together for a common party goal would instead be competing with one another for preference. On top of that, because minority groups were assured of representation, a number of splinter groups would be formed instead of two strong parties. That was not all: by guaranteeing an accurate reflection of the electorate's opinions, a situation could easily arise in which the council would be deadlocked; it was often politically useful to have the wishes of the electorate exaggerated, giving the majority party a clear majority. And the single transferable vote was too complicated. How could illiterate voters possibly understand the system?

Each candidate, rather than each party, would have to have a symbol, and the procedure for ranking candidates according to preference was difficult. Finally, if proportional representation was such an effective system, why did the secretary of state retain any nominated members? And why had proportional representation not been adopted in England?[15] In short, as the majority party, Labour was willing to "placate minorities," but it was convinced that another electoral system had to be found.

By contrast (and Mauritius, as usual, was nothing if not an island of contrasts), both the nominated members and the *Parti Mauricien* elected members defended proportional representation as adamantly as Labour attacked it. Answering Labour's specific charges, Guy Sauzier, a stalwart of the Mauritian Chamber of Agriculture, claimed that the system itself was perfectly easy to understand. In Malta, where a large portion of the electorate was illiterate, proportional representation had been introduced without any trouble. But it became clear that the *Parti Mauricien* was afraid of majority rule. Koenig explained that minority groups could never have the party discipline of the predominantly Hindu Labour party. Yet at the same time they should not have to accept the dictatorship of the majority party.[16] André Nairac continued:

> We must also remember that it is not only fear of what has been called "Hindu domination" but also fear that in the delicate economic fabric of the island of Mauritius, in view of the times which every thinking man knows to be ahead, complete power given to politicians, many of whom have proven their complete lack of capacity to grasp economic problems . . . might very quickly play havoc in the economic fabric of Mauritius.[17]

When the vote was taken on May 11, 1956, nominated members combined with *Parti Mauricien* and official members to adopt the secretary of state's recommendations by fifteen to fourteen. The Labour party was outraged that the Legislative Council could approve a motion opposed by 90 percent of the elected members, taking it as proof that the existing constitution was unworkable. To prevent the implementation of proportional representation, Labour agreed to boycott the elections for the executive council in September.

Rational or not, opposition to proportional representation was now so widespread that Robert Scott quickly saw the dangers of imposing it, and the possibility that it could destroy his careful work of building confidence between the Labour party and the government. Subtly, Scott had changed the role and image of the colonial governor; while maintaining an appearance of neutrality, it was his responsibility to cooperate as much as possible with the elected majority in the legislature. The failure of the colonial government in British Guiana to destroy a nationalist party through open attack made it clear that to denounce the Labour party and impose proportional representation in Mauritius would be unwise. At best it might lead to organized civil disobedience; at worst, to violence.

Unprepared to take these risks, Scott flew to London to confer with Lennox-Boyd and consider alternative electoral systems. He was joined there by eight Mauritian legislators, four from the *Parti Mauricien* and four from the Labour party.[18] Proportional representation was abandoned, but the size of the constituencies became a source of major conflict. Unable to break the deadlock, British officials proposed that a commission be appointed to devise an electoral system. The commission would go to Mauritius to determine whether it was possible to follow Labour's suggestion of dividing the island up into "forty single member constituencies, with opportunity to secure representation in the Legislative Council corresponding to its own number in the community as a whole." If this were not possible, the commission would choose the *Parti Mauricien* alternative and divide the island into eleven three-member constituencies, thus enhancing the chance of returning Creole and Franco-Mauritian candidates from urban and suburban areas.[19] Small Indian population pockets in or near urban areas that could make up a single small constituency would be out-voted in a large constituency.

The Electoral Commission

The *Parti Mauricien*'s opposition to the commission, specifically to the alternative of single-member constituencies, was allayed by informal conversations. Colonial officials stated privately that it would be impossible to divide the island into forty constituencies which ensured just representation for each community. By accepting the commission, the Colonial Office assured the *Parti Mauricien*, they would lose nothing; in the end, the Labour party would have to ac-

cept the eleven three-member constituencies.[20] Labour welcomed
the idea of the commission, its spokesmen confident they could bring
the commissioners around to their view.

Appointed in July 1957, the commission was chaired by Sir Mal-
colm Trustram-Eve, later Lord Silsoe.[21] It heard evidence from any
groups or individuals who wished to depose, including special interest
groups and language groups such as the Tamils and Telegus. But the
main evidence came from the Labour party, the *Parti Mauricien*, and
Razack Mohammed.

The testimony may have been considerable, but it was hardly re-
freshing. Neither Labour nor the *Parti* contributed any new ideas.
Labour continued to believe that forty single-member constituencies
would ensure an accurate reflection of the feelings of the electorate
in the new council. The *Parti Mauricien* maintained that strong
minorities would be unable to return candidates. *Parti* leaders were
convinced that the Labour party would be able to win a majority in
most of the constituencies, and that the minority would, therefore
not be represented. The *Parti* proposed a modified version of proportional representation.

Only Razack Mohammed's testimony was startling. Although he
had agreed to the Colonial Office alternatives in London, when the
time came for him to speak up, he denounced them before the
commission. He had been persuaded by other Muslim leaders that
both systems were unacceptable. Speaking for the Muslim Constitutional Reform Committee, Mohammed demanded instead separate
electoral rolls and reserved seats, saying that a party system could
only spring from the initial communal satisfaction of the various
groups.[22] In taking this independent position, Mohammed said he
had been advised by his "Central Committee of Action," a group of
twenty selected by four hundred Muslims from rural and urban areas
of Mauritius. Mohammed's committee had decided that Muslims
would have more influence as an independent political group than as
a reliable ally of the *Parti Mauricien*. Mohammed's turnabout was
significant not only for this issue; it was also the first real sign that the
Muslims had been establishing their own political organization.

The Trustram-Eve Commission did not report until early 1958, a
year after the Colonial Office, the Labour party, and the *Parti
Mauricien* had agreed to its appointment. The conclusions were a
surprising victory for the Labour party. The commissioners believed

that the main sections of the population, the Hindus, the Muslims, and the general population (comprising the Creole and Franco-Mauritian communities) *could* be adequately represented by members selected from forty single-member constituencies, if just after the elections the governor would nominate "best losers"—candidates who failed to be elected but who had a reasonable following. In addition, all voting requirements would be dropped; any Mauritian over the age of twenty-one could vote.

Koenig was furious, charging that the commissioners had exceeded their explicit terms of reference. Since the suggested system depended upon nominations by the governor, the commission had in fact been unable to demarcate forty constituencies that in themselves ensured adequate representation. In this case, according to commissioners' terms of reference, they should have demarcated eleven three-member constituencies. The Colonial Office, in approving the commission report, had, in Koenig's view, betrayed him.[23]

In the debate on the motion to approve the Trustram-Eve Report, the *Parti Mauricien* had its chance to object, their principal objection being that the smaller constituencies would foster communalism and exhibit cooperation among candidates.[24] Seeneevassen responded for the Labour party. Answering charges that the Trustram-Eve recommendations would lead to Hindu domination, he told the *Parti Mauricien*:

> Do not point to the Hindu alone. He [the Hindu] is not worse than anybody else. I repeat: Learn to treat him like you treat yourselves and your own; you who talk of Mauritianism, learn to know he is a Mauritian too.[25]

Razack Mohammed, speaking for the Muslims, accepted the Trustram-Eve Report. He had been persuaded that separate communal roles would never be adopted and so he went along with the Colonial Office proposals.[26] This fact alone diminished the impact of the *Parti Mauricien* claim that the proposals would not give minorities adequate representation.

After nineteen hours of debate in three days, the government withdrew the motion to approve the Trustram-Eve Report. No vote was taken, for the governor, despite *Parti Mauricien* opposition, had decided to impose the recommendations. Two out of three major factions, the Labour party and the Muslims, were satisfied.

The support of the Muslims had been crucial to the government's decision. Once Muslim backing was assured, only one significant voice of opposition remained—that of the *Parti Mauricien*. A defeated *Parti Mauricien* would be easier to placate and would pose no threat to the island's internal security. An angered Labour party could, theoretically, arouse thousands of Hindus and possibly even Creole laborers.

Parties under the New Constitution

The new constitution was promulgated in 1958, and elections were scheduled for March 1959. Even so, the political parties and organizations were uncertain of their own strength; the effects of universal adult suffrage and the new electoral system were unknown. But more important, each party had undergone significant change since the last Legislative Council elections.

Between 1953 and 1959, the Labour party shifted dramatically from being a class party to reflecting a communal alliance between the Hindus and the Muslims. Guy Rozemont's death in March 1956 was the turning point. The party had already changed considerably from the one Rozemont had created, and Indian intellectuals, who had been on the periphery in 1948, were now dominant. While Rozemont was alive, the Creoles had remained loyal to their leader. After, they knew that they would never have the same special understanding with Ramgoolam and Seeneevassen that they had had with Rozemont, yet they remained as marginal members of the party for a few more years. Not until the 1960s, under Gaetan Duval's leadership of the *Parti Mauricien*, would the Creoles return to mainstream politics.

On Rozemont's death, Labour elected another Creole, Guy Forget, as its president, in part because the Indians believed a Creole president was needed to keep the Creoles in the party. Seeneevassen, the leading Indian candidate and Ramgoolam's closest friend, would probably have been a more effective leader, but he was a Tamil, and his election would have left Labour open to accusations that it was becoming an Indian party.[27] Nor did it seem appropriate for Ramgoolam, the *de facto* parliamentary leader of the Labour party, to assume responsibility for party organization: not only was he fully occupied with his ministry, but he, too, was clearly identified as an active member of the Hindu community.

Forget was an intellectual, with neither the time nor the temperament to spend hours on the sugar estates or at the docks as Rozemont had. His time and attention were taken up with Council debates on the constitution and the ministerial system, and with strengthening internal party organization. His duties as minister of health, and as deputy mayor and then mayor of Port Louis, made additional demands on his time.

The first dissatisfaction with the party occurred among unions. At first Forget was not aware of the weakening ties between the two. The unions had a quota on the executive committee of the party, ostensibly enough to keep them involved.[28] But it was not. No longer courted by the leadership, many artisans and dockers, mostly Creoles, thought about sitting out the 1959 election. Hanging in limbo, they felt removed from the Labour party, yet not attracted to the *Parti Mauricien*.

Creole apathy was only one of Labour's problems; the party was also increasingly open to attack from radical Indian groups. By 1958, members of the Labour party had served as ministers in the government, and while they could and did blame the colonial administration for failure to act, they themselves had to share in the responsibility. The vulnerability of the Labour party seemed to be increasing dramatically in 1958 and 1959.

The most vehement criticism of the Labour party came from Sookdeo Bissoondoyal, on the left. Of the Indians in the council, only Bissoondoyal remained apart. He accused the intellectuals of being latecomers and opportunists who had joined the struggle for constitutional rights, schools, and wages only after it had become acceptable. He pointed out that Labour leaders were doctors and lawyers who had assumed European manners and customs and had almost no contact with workers in the fields. Furthermore, they were ready to compromise in the Legislative Council. Although his speeches were boring, his techniques had a definite effect, for no one was particularly anxious to be marked down in Bissoondoyal's black book. Zealous and persistent, he was continuously investigating the activities of departments and ministries, particularly those related to food, finance, and supplies, and could be counted on regularly to refer to the "60,000 people who are not getting two meals per day."[29] The mere knowledge that Bissoondoyal could expose malpractices in a department must have substantially cut down on their actual number.

Undaunted by increasing criticism from his colleagues in Council about his disruptive personal style, Bissoondoyal claimed he had considerable popular support, and as early as 1951 he was referring to his "party," the Independent Forward Bloc. In 1953 Bissoondoyal and one of his supporters, Satcam Boolell, were returned to the Legislative Council. By 1958 it was clear that they had gained still more ground in rural areas at the expense of Labour. In April 1958 Bissoondoyal officially announced the formation of the Independent Forward Bloc (IFB) as a political party, in direct opposition to Labour. His criticisms of the police and the education system and his demands for social reform appealed to many villagers, as did his attacks on the unpopular civil commissioner in the south. Since all the ministers responsible for education, social welfare, and labor were from the Labour party, Bissoondoyal's criticisms were direct attacks on the party. And although the extent of his support was not clear, Labour had reason to fear he would form an alliance of convenience with the party of the Franco-Mauritians, the *Parti Mauricien*. In these circumstances, the position of the Muslims, with control of a swing vote, became increasingly important.

The Muslim community emerged as a political force during the 1950s. Ten years earlier, in 1940, A. H. Osman, a planter and a Muslim, had been appointed to the Council of Government. But the most outspoken Muslim politician was Razack Mohammed, a merchant. When the Muslims failed to win any seats in the 1948 election, Mohammed became keenly aware of the need to find political allies and to advocate communal representation. Since Muslim fear of the Hindus was nearly as great as the Franco-Mauritians', it was not surprising that Mohammed allied himself with the *Ralliement Mauricien* and was returned in the 1953 elections as a *Ralliement* candidate.

Mohammed was an astute politician—and an opportunist. As mayor of Port Louis in 1953, he gained a wider following, and his personal prestige continued to grow despite his being linked to electoral fraud regarding the registration of voters in 1956. His association with the *Ralliement* promised to help him in Port Louis politics. But by the late 1950s it was clear that the conservative policies of the *Parti Mauricien* were not sympathetically received in the Colonial Office. Yet the Muslim community was not large enough to command a majority in any house. During the 1957 discussions about the electoral system, Mohammed made it clear that his allegiance to the *Parti*

Mauricien was not permanent. Before the members of the electoral commission arrived, he held public meetings without including *Parti* leaders. At one of these he openly criticized both Labour and the *Parti Mauricien*, thus suggesting a role for the Muslims as an independent political force. The *Parti Mauricien*, Mohammed implied, had been using the Muslims as a tool and looking after Muslim concerns only for its own interests.[30] This was not a real partnership. On the other hand, in spite of his long friendship with Ramgoolam, he could not support Labour, because of his feuds with some of its leaders. Like a young woman playing off two suitors against each other, Mohammed made the most of whatever uncertainty he could generate. As long as his political affiliation was in doubt, both parties would try to woo him, and he could choose the one that offered him the most power and his community the most seats in Council. In loosening his ties with the *Parti Mauricien*, he was greatly increasing his strength.

At the time Mohammed's allegiance became an issue, Labour's need for more support was becoming apparent. Party leaders began to court Mohammed and his central committee with remarkable persistence. Some committee members were reluctant to reach any agreement with Labour, for they doubted whether a Hindu-dominated party could ever be trusted to defend Muslim interests. Furthermore, there were rumors that Labour's final goal was independence, and this the Muslims did not want. But Mohammed also knew that the Muslims would never be strong enough to protect their own interests and that they had the most to gain through political alliance with the winning side. In the autumn of 1958 an agreement was made. The Labour party promised to back Mohammed's candidates in selected constituencies and not to present Muslim candidates of its own. In turn, the Muslim committee, then called the *Comité d'Action Muselman* (CAM), agreed to encourage Muslim voters to vote for Labour. Even though Mohammed's reputation for corruption was widespread, his power and influence meant that his allegiance could be counted as an important gain for the Labour party.

The *Parti Mauricien* itself was in a weak position in late 1958. Surprised by the desertion of the Muslims, the party looked elsewhere for support. Jules Koenig understood the need to develop a popular base, but his personality and style ruled him out as a leader with an island-wide following. The *Parti Mauricien* lacked charismatic leaders; while Koenig knew this was a drawback, he still hoped that his arguments about the need to grapple with the island's economic problems would fall on sympathetic ears. Unfortunately, this was little more than wishful thinking. However much Koenig struggled to identify with the major social problems of the island, he could not overcome the fact that his was the party that attracted Franco-Mauritian support. What had once been an asset had in 1958 turned into a liability, since the other groups on the island, with the exception of some Creoles, could not overcome decades of suspicion and mistrust and throw their lot in with the party of the sugar barons. As the 1959 elections approached, the *Parti Mauricien's* chief goal was to defeat the Labour party, and to do this it was willing to make strange alliances. The Independent Forward Bloc shared the *Parti Mauricien's* desire to defeat the Labour party, and Koenig reached an understanding. *Parti* officials agreed to urge their supporters living in country constituencies that the *Parti Mauricien* would not contest the vote for IFB candidates, and IFB members in towns were asked to vote for the *Parti Mauricien*.[31]

The 1959 Elections

Extended suffrage enhanced the importance of the registration process; now the government had to compile new registers and inscribe the names of thousands of illiterates who had never before voted. Both parties urged their supporters to register. Labour had the most to gain by a countrywide registration campaign, since the majority of the newly enfranchised voters were Indian laborers on the sugar estates. Many, especially women, were reluctant to come forward. When the deadline approached, the Labour party estimated that only 60 percent of those eligible had registered. At Labour's request, and in spite of Koenig's objections, the governor extended the registration period for five days to permit more voters to register.

In the February heat, 159 candidates toured their constituencies. One of the unknown factors in the election was the influence of the new voters. Another was the effect of the change from five multimember constituencies to single members, a change which doubled the number of people elected but seriously restricted the breadth of the candidate's constituency. Most candidates campaigned only in their own constituencies. Since these were smaller than in previous elections, it was easier to establish close contact with influential village leaders. In addition, smaller constituencies enabled candidates to organize a more effective network of paid agents, who kept committed voters from changing sides and bribed or threatened other voters, a form of corruption that became widespread in later elections.

The elections themselves were held on March 9. Although the Labour party was expected to maintain its strength in the Council, few people predicted the extent of its victory. Labour won twenty-three of the forty seats, a clear majority in the expanded Council. The voters returned only three *Parti Mauricien* candidates. Bissoon-doyal's IFB, proving that it had significant support in the countryside, won six seats. Three independent candidates were returned, but sixty-two of the seventy independents failed to attract the required minimum number of votes and therefore forfeited the money required as deposit from all candidates, a fact that discouraged independents from standing in subsequent elections.[32] Five election petitions resulted in two by-elections, and as a result Labour lost one seat to the *Parti Mauricien*.

The surprise of the election was the success of the *Comité d'Action Muselman*. Five of Mohammed's candidates were returned, the first Muslims to be elected in a general election since the 1947 constitution was introduced. The CAM's success was clearly a result of its alliance with Labour. In Port Louis Maritime, there were three Muslim candidates, one CAM and two independents. Labour party orders to its supporters to vote for the CAM candidate ensured his return. Similarly, Ramgoolam urged Hindu voters in Rivière des Anguillies to vote for the CAM president, Ajin Dahal. Left to their own discretion, they might have chosen the IFB candidate. The benefits of the CAM-Labour alliance were mutual. In Port Louis West, Muslim voters followed the CAM's orders and returned a Labour candidate; and in Curépipe, Muslims voting for the Labour party defeated Gaetan Duval.[33]

The effectiveness of the CAM-Labour alliance was evidence that for the first time since 1948, voters were willing to accept a degree of party discipline. The 1959 elections were not as much a popularity contest as previous elections had been. Although few of the electors could discuss the policies of the candidates in meaningful terms, more voters than before understood that each candidate was standing with a group of others, and that this larger group had a program it would follow if elected. There was some sense that one party was "good" and another "bad," a sense of identification with a party as a whole, generally because it represented communal rather than class interests.

Also, for the first time in an election, caste was a significant factor. Hindus, constituting a majority of the electorate, could be assured of winning a majority of the seats. The question became, which Hindus? Bissoondoyal, aided by the *Parti Mauricien*, exploited the antagonism of the low-caste estate workers toward the higher-caste intellectuals who had dominated politics since the war. In Grand Baie, an established Labour representative was defeated by a low-caste Hindu who had gained notoriety as a village council president. Caste also narrowed Ramgoolam's margin of victory in Triolet, with its majority of low-caste Hindus. Ramgoolam's prestige was enormous, but his low-caste opponent, who had little personal popularity, was able to win 40 percent of the votes.[34]

And this governor, unlike the last two, was careful not to upset the decision of the electorate when making his nominations. Following the "best loser" system, Scott's nominations slightly improved the position of the *Parti Mauricien* in the Council and provided the Chinese with some representation, but the Labour majority was not endangered. For the first time since its formation, the Labour party did not disapprove of the governor's choice of nominated members. Scott and Newton had succeeded in gaining the confidence of Labour politicians and in convincing them that the colonial officials were not in league with the *Parti Mauricien* to block change in Mauritius.

Two important newcomers to Mauritian politics emerged in the 1959 elections: Harold Walter and Gaetan Duval, both young and clever Creole barristers. Walter, the son of a Protestant minister, had served in the Mauritius Regiment during the war. Embittered by the policy that only Europeans could become officers, he had made up his mind to be the first colored officer, and by the end of the war had been commissioned as a captain. Afterward he went to England to study law. He returned to Mauritius in 1951 and, after establishing himself, joined the Labour party, despite Rivet's urging that he join the *Parti Mauricien*. Quick and determined, an able and efficient administrator, Walter was to become a powerful Labour leader, han-

dling well the tasks given him by the party. Strong-minded and sometimes ruthless, Walter did not tolerate laziness; however, he was sensitive to criticism and susceptible to flattery. Behind his ambition was
a hatred of the long-established Franco-Mauritian power in
Mauritius, a power which he intended to destroy.[35] In 1959 he was
elected to the Council as a Labour representative from the southern
constituency of Mahébourg.

The second newcomer, Gaetan Duval, had returned from studies
in England and France two months before Rozemont's death in 1956.
Duval was then twenty-six. Through his contacts in London he had
become interested in politics, and on his return went immediately to
see Raoul Rivet, still considered the wise man of Mauritian politics.
On Rivet's advice, Duval interviewed the leaders of each party. He
found Forget full of grand words, but Koenig impressed him by his
detailed grasp of the Mauritian economic and political situation.
Koenig also had a reputation for defending Creoles in court. And so
in the spring of 1956, Duval joined the *Parti Mauricien*. He was defeated in the municipal elections of that year, but he had been home
only six months and was not well known.

In 1959 he stood in Curépipe and was defeated by a narrow margin.
But an electoral petition charging that the Labour party victor had his
popular name rather than his legal name on the ballot paper was
upheld by the Supreme Court, and a by-election was scheduled for
January 1960. Like Rozemont, Duval began spending his afternoons
with the voters. Duval's personality became as much a political issue
as his ideas. Bright, articulate, and charming, he enjoyed the company of people who were also bright, articulate, and charming. In
addition, he drew around him groups of people whose principal attri-
bute was that they were totally devoted to Duval. They savored his
every word and action and were blindly loyal to their leader, supporting and idolizing him. He in turn was devoted to these close followers, whom he later tried to launch in the political arena. Duval's difficulties came later on when the boundaries between his personal life
and his political life began to crumble. But in 1959 his political career
was just beginning, and his intelligence, his charm, and his fresh
views on the island's problems appealed to large numbers of Mauritian Creoles who were looking for a leader. Duval fought the by-
election on a communal basis, talking of the dangers of Hindu
hegemony and the need for the general population to protect its in-

terests. Since over 50 percent of the Curépipe electorate belonged to the general population, he won easily—the first step toward building his reputation as "King of the Creoles" and as a rival of Harold Walter.

How well did the electoral system devised by the Trustram-Eve Commission ensure "representation of each section of opinion"? There are two main considerations in assessing the results: first, the proportion of seats obtained by each *party* in relation to the proportion of votes obtained, and second, the proportion of seats obtained by each *communal group* in relation to its proportion of the population as a whole. In the first instance, the system benefited Labour at the expense of the *Parti Mauricien*. Labour won 41.4 percent of the votes and 57 percent of the seats, whereas the *Parti Mauricien* won 15 percent of the votes and 7.5 percent of the seats. The IFB obtained 18 percent of the votes and 15 percent of the seats; the CAM received 8.55 percent of the votes and 12.5 percent of the seats.

Judged by communal standards, the Muslims, with five seats, were underrepresented by only one member, while the Hindus, with 62.5 percent of the members of the Council and 51 percent of the population, were overrepresented by four. The general population, however, was exactly represented—approximately 25 percent of the population received 25 percent of the seats. The Chinese, with no elected members, were underrepresented by one.

The Trustram-Eve Commission, aided by a realignment of parties, had succeeded in providing a system whereby Muslims could be elected to the Legislative Council without communal rolls, and essentially every main segment of the population had adequate representation. The electoral system did not, however, permit the parties to be represented precisely according to strength. In trying to protect each community, the commission tended to neglect the party system.

Between 1953 and 1959 Mauritius advanced considerably on the road to responsible government. Universal adult suffrage, the ministerial system, and clear limitations on the governor's powers were the most significant constitutional changes. The Labour party's dogged opposition had diminished. The *Parti Mauricien*, however, had become increasingly suspicious of the government. For its part, the Colonial Office had clearly opted for constitutional progress and for internal self-government as the next step. Ramgoolam and the Labour party were to be the beneficiaries.

At the same time, a two-party system, albeit a somewhat weak one, had been established. The *Parti Mauricien* was hardly an immediate threat to Labour, but it was an outspoken and organized opposition. It had not, however, been able to attract Hindus, although its economic policy was more in line with the interests of wealthy Hindu planters than was that of Labour. Communal politics were already too well entrenched.

The political negotiations of the 1950s had also demonstrated that all communities and all parties recognized the need for finding a *modus vivendi*, an accomplishment due to some extent to the tact and patience of Robert Scott and Robert Newton. Credit for this accomplishment is also due the Franco-Mauritians, although in a somewhat uncomplimentary way: As they had in the past, Franco-Mauritians—as a group—tended to turn a blind eye to the political realities of life on the island. This time they could not yet believe Britain would actually grant independence.

Nevertheless, a new cohesiveness was emerging. As Newton wrote, there was in 1959 in Mauritius "a mutual trust, transcending differences. And I think that my prevailing feeling on leaving Mauritius was not only sober confidence but above all gratitude to those who had come to give trust and confidence when so much in their environment, past and present, discouraged it."[36] In 1959, Mauritius's problems were great, but they seemed by no means hopeless.

9. Independence or Association

1959–1967

BETWEEN 1959 AND 1967, Mauritius made steady, but hardly smooth, progress toward self-government and independence. The competition for influence, an inevitable part of the transition, aggravated communalism. Increasingly, conscious of communal interests, minority groups demanded safeguards, while the majority demanded immediate power with majority rule. The *Parti Mauricien* threatened violence; the Labour party accused the Colonial Office of moving too slowly and of trying to sabotage independence. The Colonial Office had approved the principle of self-government for Mauritius before 1960. But that was not good enough for the Labour party. The granting of independence in 1959 to the French colonies, some nearly as small and seemingly nonviable as Mauritius, had combined with United Nations pressure to make independence an immediate goal. The problem for colonial officials in London and in Mauritius was to mediate between the two parties and to create workable institutions that would provide a basis for democracy and stability following British withdrawal.

During this period, the Colonial Office held two constitutional conferences in London. In Mauritius the *Parti Mauricien*, under the leadership of Gaetan Duval, acquired a new image and gained new support at the expense of Labour. The two-party system was strengthened, but divisions were increasingly on communal lines. As Mauritians faced one political crisis after another, the economic problems identified in the 1950s became acute.

In 1959, Sir Robert Scott, who had served as governor in Mauritius for five crucial years, was replaced by Sir Colville Deverell. Although

Colonial Office policy was to encourage self-government everywhere,
Deverell saw that Mauritius, because of its size, its dense multiracial
population, and its massive economic problems, differed from most
other colonies, and he believed that the best program would be to
delay political progress while the island coped with these other challenges. With this in mind, he asked James Meade, a Cambridge
economist, and Richard Titmuss, a sociologist from the London
School of Economics, to come to Mauritius and report. But even as
Deverell was planning for economic and social reform, the winds of
the Indian Ocean added to the island's troubles: two cyclones devas-
tated Mauritius.

Cyclone Alix left six dead and £3 million damage on January 19,
1960. But Alix was only a forerunner of the more formidable Carol.
On Feburary 28, Carol's 160-mile-an-hour winds swept Mauritius,
leaving 42 dead and 1,772 injured. At least ten thousand buildings
were destroyed; thousands more were damaged. Over seventy
thousand Mauritians flocked to refugee centers, and the whole country looked with despair at the ruined sugar crop.[1] Carol's bill was £30
million worth of destruction to sugar and buildings. The financial
secretary estimated that Carol would reduce earnings for the 1960–61
financial year by Rs 6.2 million, while increasing expenditures by Rs
6.8 million.[2] To meet the crisis, the Mauritian government turned to
Great Britain. In London, in March and again in June 1960, Ramgoolam, then leader of the majority party, made repeated pleas for
assistance, and eventually Britain promised £6.33 million in loans and
grants.[3] The five-year plan for 1957–1962 was dropped, and another
emphasizing cyclone repair was approved in its place. Cyclone-proof
villages were built, although sites were often selected without consideration for availability of water, transport, and other essentials.
Carol's scars still mark Mauritius.

Economic and social problems, aggravated by Alix and Carol,
reached crisis proportions in the early 1960s. Overpopulation was
acute. The Mauritian population explosion can be traced back to the
late 1940s and the successful eradication of malaria. Death rates
dropped; fertility rates rose; and the population increased at 3 percent
a year. Between 1944 and 1958, the population expanded from
419,000 to 614,000, an increase of 46 percent. In 1957, 44 percent of
the population was under fifteen years of age.[4] By 1960 Mauritius was
one of the most densely populated countries in the world, and conditions were getting worse.

As early as 1948 the government recognized that overpopulation was a potential problem, but little was done until 1960, when Deverell determined that the time had come for action.[5] On April 12, the financial secretary, George Wilson, introduced in the Council a plan designed to encourage families to have no more than three children. Wilson's timing was unfortunate. His announcement, coming at the beginning of Holy Week, gave the Catholic clergy more opportunities than usual to attack the plan—Palm Sunday, Maundy Thursday, Good Friday, and Easter Sunday. The same week, council members from all parties and all communities criticized Wilson's motion.[6] Koenig said, "Dieu bénit les nombreuses familles." Bissoondoyal provided an impressive list of famous fourth children and promised to oppose the motion "in the country throughout its length and breadth." According to Ajin Dahal, a prominent spokesman for the *Comité d'Action Muselman*, Muslims were "definitely against any form of birth control."

These reactions masked communal tensions, never far under the surface. If, in good faith, one community limited its population growth, what assurances could there be that others would do the same? The community that took the lead in family planning could in fact lose political influence if, over time, it became a smaller portion of the population.

Taken aback by the intransigence of the opposition to a birth control program, Colonial Secretary Robert Newton adjourned the debate. The government decided to put family planning aside until Professors Meade and Titmuss had published their reports. The Titmuss Report, issued in early 1961, predicted disaster unless the government acted immediately to limit population growth.[7] Titmuss believed that both family planning and emigration warranted urgent government support. In the debate on the report, Ramgoolam urged that "Government should provide all facilities which will enable the population to adopt the methods they like," concluding somewhat appropriately that "this is a question of life and death." But the Legislative Council only took "note" of the Titmuss Report.[8] It was not until 1965 that the Ministry of Health openly supported the two family planning associations in Mauritius, and not until 1966 did the government give any financial assistance.[9]

Unemployment was a corollary to the population problem. To stop the rapid increase of unemployment, Meade recommended stabiliz-

ing wages as well as restructuring methods of recruitment and training. He outlined steps to promote investment in industry and to halt
expansion of the sugar crop in favor of diversification in agriculture.
Unless the government implemented his recommendations immediately and as a whole, Meade foresaw that the standard of living
would steadily decline.[10] The recommendations were stated clearly,
but the Labour party was not yet sufficiently convinced of their
urgency to implement them. In spite of Deverell's urgings, Labour
politicians failed to recognize economic realities. They feared that the
governor's pleas for attention to economic matters were little more
than diversionary tactics intended to postpone independence.[11]

Party Problems and Interest Groups

The fears were unfounded, for Labour had a powerful ally in the
person of Ian Macleod, secretary of state for the colonies. In April
1960, Macleod visited Mauritius at the end of a tour of Central Africa
and Kenya. In Northern Rhodesia and Nyasaland, Macleod had
promised constitutional talks, and he did not change his speech for
Mauritius.[12] Deverell, however, believed that once the prospect of
constitutional reform became clear, the Labour party would neglect
the island's basic problems.[13] To Macleod, it seemed that Deverell
was trying to halt the "winds of change," and plans were made for a
constitutional conference in mid-1961. As one observer wrote, "by
the spring of 1959, the Secretary of State was in no mood to stand on
ceremony with the sensitive feelings of governors."[14] In 1960 the initiative in policy formation had been transferred from Mauritius to
London. The effect on the civil servants in the colony was, as to be
expected, depressing, for London was more concerned with pressures
for rapid decolonization coming from the United Nations, the United
States, and France than with particular circumstances in a specific
colony.

Divisions within Labour and the CAM distracted both parties following the 1959 elections. Guy Forget resigned as president of the
Labour party, and although Ramgoolam remained its nominal head,
custom dictated that the president be a Creole. Raymond Rault,
neither an astute nor a powerful politician, was selected and shortly
became embroiled in a bitter feud with another of the party's outspo-

ken Creole leaders, Harold Walter. Rault made up his mind to throw Walter's supporters out of the party. Ramgoolam, who did not support Rault, arranged a special meeting of the party at which Dr. Regis Chaperon, a mild-mannered and not particularly ambitious person, was elected president. Rault then formed his own party, which was soundly defeated in the 1963 elections.[15] But divisions and disputes within the Labour party did not help. Creoles in particular, skeptical of Indian leadership, became increasingly disaffected by the feuding. Some left to join Rault's splinter party, taking their first step away from Labour.

Labour was not the only party with internal problems; a number of Muslims were anxious to leave the CAM. Mohammed and Dahal were feuding, and it was clear that they could not continue to share leadership. When they agreed to let the party executive committee choose between them, the committee refused; Dahal resigned from his office and was eventually expelled from the party. He was convinced that Labour was taking advantage of the CAM as the *Parti Mauricien* had done earlier. As soon as independence was obtained, Labour would ignore Muslim demands.[16] On the eve of the municipal elections in December 1960, Dahal made his final break with the CAM and with Mohammed. In June 1961 he formed his own party, the Muslim Democratic League. Determined to block constitutional advance leading to independence, the League entered into a loose alliance with the *Parti Mauricien*.[17] But since Dahal had neither the political organization nor the influence of Mohammed, most Muslims remained within the CAM.

While the Labour party and the CAM were resolving their own crises of leadership, a number of smaller communal groups were exploring the need to safeguard their interests by political action. The formation of the CAM had increased the bargaining power of the Muslim community in its dealings with the government. Neither the Labour party nor the *Parti Mauricien* had shown any special interest in the Tamils or the Telegus, the other large minorities within the Indian community. Tamil and Telegu customs and languages had survived the indenture system, and there was a strong community feeling in both groups.[18] Labour leadership had included two distinguished Tamil lawyers, Seeneevassen and Ringadoo, but both were committed to building a Mauritian nation rather than to protecting Tamil interests. Young and ambitious Tamils and Telegus, unable to find a place in Labour, hoped to gain political power by forming their own parties. The Tamil United Party and the Telegu League were born in 1961.[19]

Ramgoolam actively opposed the splintering of the Indian community into special interest parties. The *Parti Mauricien*, on the other hand, knowing that divisions within the Indian community would effectively diminish Ramgoolam's power, reportedly went so far as to bribe the Tamil and Telegu leaders to break away from Labour.

By 1961 the usually apolitical Chinese community was showing a new interest in politics. Jean Ah-Chuen, an influential businessman and the only Chinese member of the Legislative Council, was the principal spokesman. Ah-Chuen recognized that the *Parti Mauricien* and Labour would be vying for Chinese votes in Port Louis, and he wanted to keep the Chinese uncommitted for as long as possible. Before 1965, and particularly at the constitutional conferences of 1961 and 1965, Ah-Chuen's main concern was to avoid becoming embroiled in party politics and at the same time to make sure that adequate safeguards for minorities were incorporated in any constitutional revision. Finally, in 1965, he allied his community with the *Parti Mauricien* in an effort to block independence. But even then, the *Parti Mauricien* could not count on him; he became known as the "Chinese puzzle."

Each of the new special interest parties, factions, or cliques represented a communal or a religious interest group. Each was formed because its founders believed enough members of their group were sufficiently disenchanted with the Labour party or the CAM to provide an adequate following. After the establishment of the ministerial system in 1957, the association of Labour with the government left the Labour leaders vulnerable to attack. Once Raymond Rault had shown the way, other aspiring leaders, hoping to enhance their careers as politicians, followed.

Constitutional Reform: London 1961

In this climate of shifting alliances and growing factionalism, Mauritian politicians assembled once again in London in June 1961 to discuss their constitution. Formation of two Hindu communal parties and the leadership disputes had clearly weakened the Labour party. It was evident that both the Independent Forward Block and the *Parti Mauricien* had gained popular support at Labour's expense, but no one knew how much. With only three members in the Legislative Council, the *Parti Mauricien's* power was considerably less than the economic power of its members. Because the *Parti* represented the largest communal minority, the general population, as well as the powerful sugar interests, both Deverell and the Colonial Office considered it the principal opposition party. Labour delegates to the conference resented the fact that a party with only three out of forty elected seats should have been given a serious hearing and considered a major opposition party.

Apart from the official delegation, there were the hangers-on— those who felt that as a result of political developments since 1959 they deserved a place at the conference: Tangavel Narianen, from the Tamil United Party; Jean Ah-Chuen, of the Chinese community; and Raymond Rault, who was making a bid for Colonial Office support by arguing that the Labour party had communist connections.[20] Macleod received each of the unofficial delegations in his office, but refused to admit them to the conference. By refusing officially to recognize the new parties and special interest groups that had been at the center of Mauritian politics in April and May 1961, Macleod consciously minimized their significance to the benefit of the established parties, and the Labour party in particular.

When the conference opened, each party reviewed its own position. Koenig, speaking for the *Parti Mauricien*, said that the island was not ready for independence and instead favored integration with the United Kingdom: "Only when the various communities can transcend their communal loyalties and feel a higher allegiance to a Mauritian community, can Mauritius be able to face independence with no problem."[21] The chaos that was bound to accompany independence, Koenig explained, would provide a wonderful opportunity for communist expansion.[22] To win Muslim support, Koenig asked that separate communal rolls be provided for minority communities. But he remained opposed to any other change in the constitution. Razack Mohammed was also opposed to independence, but less adamantly than Koenig, for he wanted to maintain the CAM's electoral alliance with Labour, tenuous as it was. For the Muslims, the issue of independence was secondary to that of separate electoral rolls.

The Independent Forward Bloc, too, was more concerned about safeguards than independence. Bissoondoyal proposed the creation of a tribunal composed of three members named by the Queen to protect the rights of individuals; his suggestion led to the appointment of an ombudsman in 1968. In addition, Bissoondoyal, anxious to take advantage of the weakness of the Labour party, urged immediate elections without major constitutional reform.[23]

As the conference opened, it was apparent that Labour, representing 42 percent of the popular vote in the 1959 election, was the only party pressing for independence. But the Colonial Office, and Macleod in particular, were committed to constitutional change throughout the colonies and saw no reason to make Mauritius an exception. Halfway through the conference, on June 30, Macleod presented the Colonial Office proposals for constitutional change. In face of strong opposition from the IFB, the CAM, and the *Parti Mauricien*, the Colonial Office agreed to minor revisions and presented them to the closing session of the conference on July 7.

Macleod explained that the proposals were to provide the basis for progress toward internal self-government. Two stages of constitutional advance would correspond to the first steps toward a ministerial system of government that had been taken in other colonies. In the first stage, to be implemented immediately, the leader of the majority party (Ramgoolam) would become the chief minister, and the colonial secretary would be called the chief secretary. The governor would be obliged to consult the chief minister before appointing or removing members of the executive council and in allocating portfolios.[24]

Following the 1963 elections, the chief minister would be given the title of premier; the executive council would become the council of ministers and would include representatives from all parties that accepted an invitation to join the government on a basis of collective responsibility. The Legislative Council would be renamed the Legislative Assembly and the speaker, when the incumbent retired, would be elected by the assembly from among its members. External affairs, defense, and internal security would remain the governor's responsibility, although he would consult with the premier before making decisions. The constitution would safeguard human rights, but no details about these safeguards were given.

In presenting these proposals, Macleod explained that it was unrealistic to expect unanimous support for any constitutional change in Mauritius, but in his view a "sufficient measure of acceptance" had been indicated to justify recommending adoption.[25] Actually, that was overstating the case. In fact, only the Labour party and the CAM approved the proposals, and then with reservations. Labour claimed the proposals did not mention the prospect of independence; the CAM complained that all requests for protection of minority interests by separate electoral rolls had "fallen on deaf ears."[26]

Both Bissoondoyal and Koenig rejected the proposals, Bissoondoyal charging that they opened the way for dictatorship by the Labour party (he felt that the Colonial Office had decided to back Labor even before the conference began), Koenig objecting to the move toward internal self-government and to the tactic of imposing a constitution in the face of objections by two of the major parties.

The extent of agreement between the Independent Forward Bloc and the *Parti Mauricien* at the London conference suggests that the informal arrangement made for the 1959 elections had been maintained. In 1961 the IFB went so far as to back the *Parti Mauricien*'s demand for separate electoral rolls, while the *Parti* approved the IFB's requests for a special court to protect individual rights. This underground "alliance" between the IFB, reputedly the defender of Hindu interests, and the *Parti Mauricien*, with its Franco-Mauritian and Creole support, led one of Bissoondoyal's more energetic supporters to leave the IFB and join Labour in October 1961.[27]

For the Labour party, the 1961 conference was a victory. It looked as if the colonial secretary and his senior advisors had decided Ramgoolam was the politician to support in Mauritius, at a time when Ramgoolam himself was nervous about the strength of his party.[28] By minimizing the role of new parties, Macleod had ensured that the focus of Mauritian politics would be the competition among the four parties with representation in the Legislative Council at the time. On that basis Ramgoolam could win. Although all his requests were not granted, he left London more satisfied than any other party leader. Most significant, the Colonial Office had not yielded to *Parti Mauricien* and IFB pressure to call an immediate election, which left Ramgoolam time to rebuild his party.

The 1963 Campaign

As Deverell had predicted, the 1961 constitutional conference placed a premium on political maneuverings at the expense of economic planning. The warnings of Titmuss and Meade, combined with those of the development economist, Dr. Thomas Balogh, who visited Mauritius in 1961, went unheeded.[29] Governor Deverell became increasingly frustrated and, before he had spent two years in Mauritius, retired from the Colonial Service. His successor was John Shaw Rennie, a social anthropologist and an intellectual, who had served in Mauritius as deputy colonial secretary between 1951 and 1955.

While guiding the island toward internal self-government and independence, Rennie did his best to see that certain standards of practice and procedure were maintained, and that all sides had a fair hearing. Anxious to avoid violence at any cost, however, he followed a short-term policy of least resistance and interfered as little as possible in politics. During these final years the governor had little power, and Rennie's job was more that of arbitrator and conciliator than decision maker. To his credit it was a task he performed with considerable understanding and sensitivity.

Rennie would weather many political storms. He spent well over a year in Mauritius before encountering the first, the 1963 elections, important because they would show exactly how much the Labour party had lost and how much the *Parti Mauricien* had gained since Mauritian voters last went to the polls in 1959. Moreover, they would be followed by the implementation of the second stage of the 1961 London agreement.

Registration began in July, and the government machinery to handle it, almost unchanged since 1948, was cumbersome and by no means foolproof. Parties organized registration drives and provided transportation, but there is little doubt that many qualified voters were not registered and that others were falsely registered. As the campaign unfolded, it also became apparent that some candidates—Mohammed, Walter, and Duval in particular—employed habitual criminals as agents. These "protection gangs" spent much of their time keeping an eye on one another, but they also intimidated ordinary voters, and fear became a factor in the election. To what extent these thugs influenced the outcome of elections is impossible to know.

The 1963 campaign presented Ramgoolam with problems he had not faced in 1959; now he had considerable difficulty in selecting and allocating his forty candidates to the forty districts. First, he was forced to accomodate minority groups who had not previously asked for political representation. Second, frightened by the possibility of a

secret IFB–*Parti Mauricien* alliance, he did not want to leave himself
open to Bissoondoyal's charges that Labour was a high-caste party, a
party for the Indian elite. Responding to pressures from within, Ramgoolam dropped four of his high-caste deputies from the nomination
lists, replacing them with newcomers associated, for the most part,
with lower castes. One of those dropped was promised the post of
Mauritian representative in London, but the others were left to fend
for themselves.

The candidates had a complex network of agents, most of whom
were paid out of their own funds. The *Parti Mauricien*, endowed with
money from the sugar estates, was accused of attempting to buy
Labour votes and agents. But the Labour party, with a number of
wealthy Indian planters and traders contributing to its treasury, was
hardly poverty-stricken, and when a final tally was taken, it appeared
that the sugar interests had contributed, although not equally, to
both parties.

The *Parti Mauricien* conducted a communal campaign. Duval, by
now the recognized party vote-getter, urged Creoles to vote for him
and the *Parti* to save Mauritius from Hindu domination. Koenig's
speeches were milder, but there was no doubt that the *Parti Mauricien* was not an all-Mauritian party, though the Tamil United Party
cooperated with it. With general population (Creole and Franco-
Mauritian) majorities in urban areas, the *Parti* hoped to return candidates from the three towns and Port Louis. It had controlled the
municipal council and the three town councils since 1960, and in
most cases had used them as a base from which to widen its political
support. In 1963 Labour had tried to counter *Parti Mauricien* control
of the councils and had extended the boundaries of the municipality
as well as the towns to include more Hindu voters.[30] This gerryman-
dering (a blatantly political move over which the thirty-four *Parti
Mauricien* members of the town and municipal councils resigned)
had antagonized the urban population to the benefit of the *Parti
Mauricien*. It provided proof of the "dictatorial" attitude of the
Labour party.

In the countryside, the *Parti Mauricien* left the task of defeating
Labour to the IFB. Bissoondoyal revived his usual themes of extravagant and unjust government expenditure—which, since the introduction of the ministerial system in 1959, were direct attacks on
Labour Ministers. Ramgoolam, as a result, had to face organized op-

position from the IFB in the rural areas and from the *Parti Mauricien* in the cities. With twenty-two out of forty seats in the assembly, Labour could afford to lose only three seats. Ramgoolam would under nearly every contingency retain a plurality; the possibility of a *Parti Mauricien*-IFB coalition government was remote, but he did not wish to have to rely on CAM votes in the council for a majority. His agreement with Mohammed was already breaking down, for in four constituencies both CAM and Labour candidates stood for election.

Ramgoolam was naturally worried. The 1963 election was the first national election in which one of the major parties—the *Parti Mauricien*—had set out deliberately and openly to stir up communal fears. How many Creoles would respond to Duval? Although some of his candidates were not above communal campaigning, it is significant and in character that Ramgoolam did not himself launch a communal campaign. In view of Duval's communalism, it was unlikely that Indians would vote for the *Parti Mauricien* anyway, and it was to his benefit not to alienate whatever Creole followers he had. A number of Creoles in prominent leadership positions in the party gave the appearance of some national appeal. If Ramgoolam had succumbed to communalism, these men would have been placed in an embarrassing position. Furthermore, Ramgoolam must have sensed that the British government would have been disappointed if he had turned the election into an openly communal campaign that could lead to civil disorders. In private meetings some of his candidates did appeal to their constituencies on communal grounds, but except in areas with large Creole populations, this had little effect. Ramgoolam's general campaign emphasized issues, not communities— the need to wrest economic power from the Franco-Mauritians, and the government's record in helping the people, such as the recent large increase in wages that had been recommended by a wages council. He advocated independence, but did not make it a major issue.

The elections took place on October 21, 1963. Only 84.3 percent of the registered voters went to the polls, compared to 91.3 percent in 1959. When the votes were counted, the Labour party had lost four seats and was just two short of a majority. Under Ramgoolam's leadership, the party had held its own, with 42.3 percent of the vote. Its erstwhile ally, the *Comité d'Action Muselman*, won 7 percent of the vote and four seats, losing one seat. The Independent Forward Bloc, with 19 percent of the vote, gained one seat, bringing its total to seven. The greatest gain was registered by the *Parti Mauricien*, which secured 19 percent of the total vote and returned eight members to the Legislative Assembly—a gain of five seats. With 20 percent of the seats in the new Assembly, the *Parti* became the strongest opposition group, particularly since it could count on the regular support of one of the two independents elected. Partly as a result of the split in the CAM leadership in 1960, Razack Mohammed was not able to deliver the Muslim vote for the Labour party candidates. The sizable Muslim population in Port Louis West, for example, failed to return the Labour candidate. In the rural areas, a number of seats changed hands between the IFB and Labour, although the strength of the parties remained the same. These contests between the IFB and Labour may have been decided by personal popularity rather than by voter support for one program or party.

The communal balance of the new council was slightly altered. The Muslims retained five members but only twenty Hindus were elected (fourteen Labour and six IFB), while fourteen members of the general population were victorious, three as Labour candidates in Hindu constituencies. As a result, the general population was over-represented. In 1963, the Muslims voted more independently than in 1959.[31]

The governor's nominations retained the electoral balance between the two parties, increasing Labour membership in the Legislative Assembly from nineteen to twenty-five and *Parti Mauricien* membership from eight to eleven. Labour had lost ground between 1959 and 1963, but since it was still by far the largest parliamentary party, and only two seats short of a majority, Ramgoolam had little cause to worry. His party had survived a crisis of leadership, and with the record high sugar prices of 1963, it seemed that Labour would benefit from the coming prosperity. Ramgoolam would be able to dominate Mauritian politics until the next election; Labour would establish its claim as heir to the British government.

For the *Parti Mauricien*, the 1963 elections were hardly a victory, but they were, in the governor's words, a sign of "the crystallisation, after some hesitation, of General Population opinion in their favour. . . . The reasons for this crystallisation are to be found in persistent fears of Indian domination under self-government, and eventually independence, and of undemocratic methods."[32] Some credit must also be given to Duval's popular appeal. Energetic and imaginative, Duval had persuaded young Creoles that they could effectively participate in Mauritian politics. He talked with them for hours, exchanging ideas, painting a picture of a prosperous Mauritius with Creoles playing a leading role, and overcoming their qualms about being associated with the party of the sugar barons. The *Parti Mauricien's* communal appeal had been successful, but only in a limited way. Without support from other elements within Mauritius, it could never form a government. The demographic realities could never be overcome. More concerned with gaining support from traditional *Parti* members, Duval was unable to see the need for non-Creole support. In 1963 he was content with his new title, "King of the Creoles," and with the allegedly handsome salary supplied by the sugar estates.

At the first meeting of the new council, now called the Legislative Assembly, the second stage of the 1961 London agreement (providing for a premier and a council of ministers) was due to be implemented. To show their continued discontent, *Parti Mauricien* representatives boycotted the opening session on November 19, 1963. Several thousand supporters surrounded Government House and joined in the protest. As the demonstration grew, the police ordered the crowd to disperse. Koenig cooperated with the police, but Duval, standing at a window out of Koenig's sight, motioned to the crowd to stay. They remained until the police used tear gas. This moment symbolized the transfer of effective party leadership from the aging Koenig to the more volatile Duval. Duval knew that his popularity was assured, and from his new position of strength he could increasingly influence party decisions. Without him the *Parti* would lose most of its popular following. It was in the interest of those who opposed independence and who financed the party, mainly people in the sugar industry, to keep Duval.

Coalition—and Violence

The secretary of state had urged that the implementation of the second stage of the 1961 agreement be accompanied by the formation of a coalition, including ministers from all parties willing to accept the principle of collective responsibility.[33] Ideally, this "coalition" should include representatives of every party. The governor's task, therefore, was to persuade all to participate. The negotiations were bitter, but finally an agreement between the Labour party, the CAM, the IFB, and the *Parti Mauricien* was reached, ministries were allocated, and Duval was named deputy speaker. Early in November the governor came from Le Reduit to install the new government, but when he arrived in Port Louis he found that the fragile accord had broken down. The day before, Duval had made a speech that the Labour party interpreted as anti-Hindu.[34] Under such circumstances, Ramgoolam said, he could not ask his party to elect Duval deputy speaker. Out of party loyalty, Koenig then refused to accept his portfolio as minister of education. The carefully constructed coalition collapsed without holding a single meeting.

Despite the breakdown, both parties did have an interest in the eventual formation of such a coalition. Labour hoped that a coalition would encourage the Colonial Office to grant independence without further delay. *Parti Mauricien* leaders recognized that as ministers they would have more influence over decisions and be in a better position to moderate legislation. They must have also been aware of the patronage that comes with nearly every ministry, and the prospect of rewarding loyal supporters with jobs was pleasing.

Attempts to renegotiate the coalition failed in Mauritius, but the Colonial Office hoped they might succeed in London, since Mauritians seemed more willing to compromise away from home. On February 28, 1964, following a special meeting of leaders in London, the coalition was formed. The new government included six ministers from the Labour party, three from the *Parti Mauricien*, two from the IFB, and two from the CAM. One ministry was reserved for an independent.[35]

Sometime after October 1965, Mauritians were scheduled to meet again in London to consider the future status of the island. As long as it was unclear whether Mauritius would remain a colony or become an independent state, it was difficult to make decisions about the island's future.[36] Normal tensions within the all-party government were aggravated by this uncertainty and by personal differences among the ministers. Duval was still on excellent terms with Ramgoolam, but other Labour ministers found his manner intolerable. He was young, and his informal approach differed considerably from the more correct behavior of most of the Indian ministers. Duval continued to surround himself with young, second-rate men, just as Rozemont had done. A cult grew up around the young leader; his followers began to copy his dress and his mannerisms. Just as Duval's men were loyal to Duval, so he was loyal to them, giving them jobs and money. In terms of this much valued loyalty, Duval did not appear to regard patronage or interference with the law as dishonorable. Housing was well known as the patronage ministry, and Duval did not hesitate to replace Razack Mohammed's Muslim staff with his Creole friends. He was following an established precedent, but such behavior hardly suited the new mood that the Colonial Office hoped would accompany the "all-party government."

The major difficulty was the personal antagonism between Duval and Harold Walter. From the beginning, Walter had disliked the young and energetic Creole. Both men lived in Curépipe, and each stationed guards around his own house and spies around his opponent's. Walter, jealous of the young Creole who had risen so fast, was determined to drive him from power.[37] Walter and Duval were perhaps the ablest and most imaginative men in the all-party government; it was only a matter of time before one, making life intolerable for the other, would force the collapse of the coalition. Twice between March 1964 and November 1965 Duval threatened to resign. That the government remained intact for over a year and a half is much to the credit of Ramgoolam. The premier liked both Duval and Walter, and although Walter never understood the special relationship between Ramgoolam and Duval, he respected Ramgoolam and recognized the importance of remaining in his favor. Duval, for his part, had great respect for Ramgoolam, and often accepted the premier's advice.

The coalition government was intended to mark the beginning of cooperation between parties and communal groups in Mauritius. Instead, there was an increase in tensions between Labour and the *Parti Mauricien*. It is difficult to place the blame for the deteriorating situation. The imminent transfer of power from Great Britain to Mauritius created an atmosphere of fear and desperation among the minority communities, particularly the Creoles. *Parti* leaders, realizing that the prospect of economic crisis alone would not prevent the Colonial Office from granting independence, hoped that the prospect of political chaos would. Aware of the dangers of a breakdown of law and order, most likely they intended only to create an atmosphere of acute tension and a widespread fear of communal violence. As expected, the Hindus responded to the bitter Creole communalism. That the riots of May 1965 did not turn into civil war was probably because the Labour party had much to lose and little to gain by violence, for Labour was trying to prove to the Colonial Office that it could govern an independent Mauritius.

While the *Parti Mauricien* provided an outlet for Creole communalism and backed other minority interest parties, there was no strictly Hindu communal party until December 1964, when the All-Mauritius Hindu Congress was formed.[38] The Hindu Congress emerged as a direct response to the *Parti Mauricien*'s communalism. Its founder, Prenchand Dabee, had been dropped as a Labour candidate in 1963, and since then had been working as town clerk in Vacoas, a civil service post supposedly immune from political patronage. In March 1964, following a *Parti Mauricien* victory in the Vacoas town council elections, Dabee was fired and replaced by a Creole. Angry and bitter, he formed the All-Mauritius Hindu Congress, with Devendranth Varma.

First and foremost, the Congress was a Hindu party. Dabee and Varma demanded that 52 percent of government jobs be given to Hindus to reflect the proportion of Hindus in the population as recorded in the 1960 census. Next, they specified that these jobs should not be given solely to high-caste Hindus: they wanted democracy within the Hindu community. Although Dabee and Varma both came from a relatively high caste, they hoped to attract a significant low-caste following from among the workers on the sugar estates. With no ministerial responsibilities themselves, they were free to attack Ramgoolam and his ministers for "selling out" to the British. The Congress charged that Labour party leaders, seduced by official parties and travel overseas, had compromised the island's independence. The Congress's first target was Duval, but its second was Ramgoolam and all the high-caste Hindus who dominated Labour. To publicize their ideas, Dabee and Varma started a newspaper, *Congress*, and made it clear that they did not want to "substitute brown capitalistic autocracy for a white one."[39]

The Congress quickly became known throughout the countryside. Working through village councils and *baitkas*, militant Congress agents condemned the Creoles and stirred up the Hindus. Duval and

his men responded with equal militancy. In early 1965 Duval began
turning the loosely organized *Parti Mauricien* into a highly structured
party. He began using militaristic terms in his speeches, calling for
discipline and "national mobilization," and by April 1965 the south
was nearing the kindling point. Both sides predicted violence.

The catalyst was a series of demonstrations. In April 1965 *Parti
Mauricien* supporters lined the streets of Curépipe to welcome the
secretary of state for the colonies, Anthony Greenwood, who was in
Mauritius for constitutional discussions. Duval, driving in his blue
Triumph, joined the official procession from the airport on the out-
skirts of Curépipe, his own constituency, and led the governor and
the secretary of state through fifty thousand supporters wearing blue
shirts for the *Parti Mauricien* and waving Union Jacks for the principle of association. The Curépipe demonstration was a success, and a
crucial one. Larger and more enthusiastic than any previous *Parti
Mauricien* demonstration, it proved that Duval's popular support was
growing rapidly. Some Franco-Mauritians joined the demonstration,
but more remained behind the scenes as organizers. The white population of Mauritius was using the Creoles as a buffer between itself
and the Hindus. Most remarkable was the fact that a large number of
Chinese participated. Usually politically apathetic, the Chinese were
sufficiently afraid of independence to demonstrate in the streets.

The Labour party planned its major demonstration for May 1. By
that time communal tension was mounting. The criminal fringes of
all parties stepped up their activities. It was probably with the Congress's sanction that Hindu youths began looting Chinese shops in
late April in retaliation for Chinese support at the *Parti Mauricien*
demonstration. There were minor disturbances in the south of the
island in April, but May 1 is considered the day after which further
violence became inevitable.[40]

Skirmishing between thugs of the Labour party and the *Parti
Mauricien* began late in the afternoon following the Labour party
rally. Later, someone in a *Parti Mauricien* bus threw a stone from a
window, killing a Hindu boy. Rumors spread. Ramgoolam's and Satcam Boolell's houses were reported stoned. The police, whose task it
was to keep order, were ineffectual. Their already tarnished reputation had been destroyed by the Congress's repeated charges of corruption and communalism, and by now the police force was viewed
as a Creole institution.[41]

Violence began again on May 10. Three days earlier, Koenig had telephoned the commissioner of police in Port Louis to warn him that riots were imminent. Both Duval and Congress leaders were losing control over their thugs. *Parti Mauricien* agents were circulating regularly in the areas of highest tension, supposedly to keep Duval informed, but more often aggravating fears. The police were concerned, but did not act. The tension was highest in the south, particularly in the village of Trois Boutiques. On May 10 firecrackers were set off—the signal for mobilization in the Hindu areas. A Franco-Mauritian was dragged from his van and beaten to death, and a policeman on patrol was shot. Fighting continued throughout the day as armed patrols of Hindus and Creoles met in the cane fields. In a forty-eight-hour period, ninety-eight were arrested.[42] People talked of civil war. In one sense it was worse than the sugarcane riots in 1936: for the first time in Mauritius's history, members of the two major communities had taken up arms against one another.

The next day the newspapers joined in an appeal for calm, but everywhere in the island there was fear that violence would spread and that there was no place to go to escape it. Already one hundred Creoles had sought refuge in Curépipe.[43] The governor declared a state of emergency and asked for British troops. The Coldstream Guards promptly arrived from Aden, and the violence ended. Although the state of emergency was lifted in August, British troops remained in Mauritius until December 1965. The death toll was small, compared to that of riots in other countries, but the communal nature of the violence created nationwide fear. Failure to control the violence could threaten everyone on the island—rich and poor alike.

Everyone agreed on what had happened, but they could not agree on who was responsible. Labour leaders blamed Duval: his men and his cars patrolling Trois Boutiques at a time of extreme tension provoked the villagers. Duval blamed the Congress: its communal preaching had stirred up the Hindus. Others blamed the police: they had failed to dispel the mounting tension, giving support to the belief that they were inefficient. The newspapers were in part responsible: one community read and believed *Advance* and *Congress*, which created a fear of Creoles; the other read anti-Hindu statements in *Le Mauricien* and *L'Action*.

Whatever the causes, the Trois Boutiques violence had widespread repercussions. It was the first serious outbreak of clearly racial violence in Mauritian history. And since it was violence between the island's major population groups, the implications were particularly frightening. Was this the first of many such incidents? Or was the violence an exception to the usual practice of resolving conflict peacefully?

In the spring of 1965 it seemed that the efforts of many Mauritians and colonial officials to overcome communalism had failed. Trust between the communities had disappeared. In the government, the bitterness over Trois Boutiques led to a breakdown in cooperation. Labour party leaders, blaming Duval for the violence, found it impossible to work with him. The *Parti Mauricien*, believing that Trois Boutiques proved without question the need for British intervention in Mauritian communal disputes, became increasingly adamant about the dangers of independence.

London 1965: Independence or Association?

In the meantime, the Colonial Office proceeded with its plans to determine the final status of Mauritius. The six-day visit in April 1965 of the secretary of state for the colonies, Anthony Greenwood, concluded with a promise to hold a constitutional conference in the autumn to "reach an agreement on the [ultimate] status, timing of accession to it, whether such accession should be preceded by consultation with the people and, if so, in what form."[44]

Both Duval and Ramgoolam knew Greenwood, and each expected his point of view to be favored. Knowing that the Colonial Office was considering alternatives to independence for its mini-territories, Duval hoped to persuade Greenwood that Mauritius should be given a special associated status with Britain. Yet as far as Mauritius was concerned, the Colonial Office was firmly committed to granting internal self-government and had not discouraged talk of independence. No matter what his sympathies, it would have been exceedingly difficult for Greenwood to alter the trend even though the increasingly communal nature of Mauritian politics was alarming to some colonial officials. The very uncertainty of Mauritius's future was itself a source of danger. Every issue became a political one, and the economic crisis that Titmuss, Meade, and Balogh had predicted was still impending. Governor Rennie disagreed with his predecessor; he saw that until the political question was settled, economic problems would continue to be ignored by Mauritian politicians.

In preparation for the conference, each party had prepared a

memorandum outlining its demands and explaining its points of
difference with other parties. The most important issues dealt with
the final status of Mauritius, the size of the legislature, and the electoral system that should be put into effect once final status was determined.

The Labour party memorandum was an appeal for independence
within the Commonwealth. According to this memorandum, "the
overwhelming majority" of Mauritians favored independence, and
"delay [would] only encourage further appeals to communal fears and
prejudices." It concluded that "no more time can be wasted on the
playing of further variations on the theme of internal self-government
as a prelude to Independence."[45] Control over external affairs was,
according to the Labour party, an important aspect of independence.
Labour's view of the electoral system and of the legislature differed
from that of the other parties. Labour favored extending the franchise to eighteen-year-olds and proposed that this enlarged electorate
should choose sixty representatives from twenty three-member constituencies. Believing that the system should facilitate voting by political principle and party rather than by race and religion, Labour rejected the Muslim demand for separate communal rolls. At the same
time, its leaders proposed that additional representatives be selected
through a best loser system and through nomination to ensure
adequate representation of minority communities and that best losers
did not cause an imbalance in party representation. (This system of
"correctives" paralleled that which the Banwell Commission would
propose eight months after the conference.)

In addition to advocating independence and provision for minority
representation, Labour urged that the Westminster pattern be followed in establishing the relation between the Executive Council and
the Legislative Assembly and that the constitution include a "chapter
of Fundamental Human Rights, with adequate provision for their
enforcement," and provision for an ombudsman.[46]

The Independent Forward Bloc backed the Labour demand for a
system of correctives with best losers and for independence within the
Commonwealth, but asked that defense and "a large measure of
Foreign Affairs" remain the responsibility of the United Kingdom.[47]
When pressed, Bissoondoyal said he would support that arrangement
even if it meant giving up United Nations' recognition of Mauritius as
an independent state. According to the IFB, "the drawbacks of the

present constitution, which are responsible for principles of taxation favoring the very rich," were more fundamental than the electoral system and legislature. Claiming that large constituencies tended to diminish corruption and at the same time that Mauritius could not afford an assembly larger than forty-six members, the IFB outlined specific proposals for seven four-member constituencies and six three-member constituencies. Bissoondoyal had openly supported Labour in its demand for independence, but by presenting his own proposals for an electoral system he made it clear that he could not be counted on to support Labour at the constitutional conference.

The Muslim Committee of Action memorandum was a masterpiece of neutrality, carefully constructed to avoid supporting or offending either the *Parti Mauricien* or Labour. Mohammed knew that both parties would want to claim Muslim support, and that the longer he refrained from supporting one or the other, the better his chance of having his demands met at the conference table. The CAM statement about the final status of Mauritius was, then, equivocal:

> The Muslim Committee of Action being not desirous of hampering constitutional progress and at the same time being not in favour of rapid or hasty constitutional reforms take the view that there should be a transitional period of ten to fifteen years between full internal self-government and any ultimate status that may be agreed upon.[48]

Referring to the conclusions of the Trustram-Eve Commission, the CAM memorandum pointed out that in view of the "geographical spread" of the Muslims in Mauritius, they would have trouble securing "by their own votes alone representation proportionate to their strength in the total electorate," unless a quota system was established.[49] Mohammed proposed that eleven seats in a house of sixty be set aside for Muslims. While all parties were prepared to support the principle of reserved seats, only the *Parti Mauricien* was prepared to support the request for a separate electoral roll.

Speaking for the Chinese, Jean Ah-Chuen urged further constitutional advance, but pointed out the need for close economic ties with and continued emigration to Britain.[50] Further, the fears of the Chinese community could be allayed only if Britain remained responsible for internal security and external affairs. By not mentioning either independence or association, Ah-Chuen also avoided taking sides between Labour and the *Parti Mauricien*, at least theoretically, but in fact his demands were most compatible with those of the *Parti Mauricien*.

The *Parti Mauricien* memorandum was the most elaborate. Pointing to the increasing population and the falling sugar prices, the *Parti* argued:

> the basic ailment of Mauritius is economic though its symptoms have largely been racial and political. The remedy is therefore in a Constitution which will primarily ensure jobs locally and elsewhere, and a long-term market for the whole of our sugar production at a remunerative price.[51]

Association with Great Britain was the best alternative. If Mauritius maintained a relationship with Britain comparable to that of Puerto Rico to the United States, the Cook Islands to New Zealand, or the Overseas Territories to France, Mauritius would continue to have an outlet for its growing labor force,[52] an outside power to guarantee constitutional safeguards for minorities, and a long-term marketing agreement for the disposal of sugar at a good price.[53] In August 1965 the prospects of Great Britain joining the Common Market seemed good. As a colony of Britain, Mauritius would, under article 221 of the Treaty of Rome, automatically be entitled to benefits resulting from Britain's entry. But if Mauritius were an independent state, even within the Commonwealth, it seemed that she would be excluded. For these reasons, the *Parti Mauricien* saw "Independence or any irreversible step towards Independence as fatal to the prosperity and the peaceful and harmonious development of Mauritius as part of the Free World."[54]

Koenig and Duval had chosen to emphasize the economic advantages of association, but they also made explicit the political dangers of independence. Independence could prepare the way for a one-party state, a development that was particularly undesirable in view of the communal divisions within the country. Furthermore, a Hindu-dominated government, however noble its intentions, would be subject to pressures from "extremist communal parties" such as the Congress.

The memorandum went on to present detailed proposals for the way in which association should work (the principles were used several months later in establishing the ill-fated association of the Windward and Leeward Islands). Internal security, defense, and external affairs should be left exclusively to Britain. Mauritius and Britain would share responsibility for justice, police, education, external trade and communications, social legislation, and economic and social development. Finance, health, agriculture, and housing were among the remaining local affairs for which the Mauritian government would have exclusive responsibility. These local affairs would be directed by a council of ministers and a territorial assembly composed of members elected from party lists. In London, Mauritius would be represented by one nonvoting member of the House of Commons or two members of the House of Lords.

Most important, the *Parti Mauricien* opposed holding a general election to determine final status. Instead, the leaders demanded a referendum:

> The question of Mauritius' future status is of such fundamental importance to all our people that it must be resolved by a system of consultation which focuses public attention on this issue alone.[55]

In a general election, it was feared, party loyalties would blur that issue; voters would be electing those who would govern them for the next five years, not simply deciding on final status. Other issues such as wages, education policy, and unemployment would inevitably intervene. For these reasons, the *Parti Mauricien* refused to consider any issue until all parties had agreed that the question of independence would be decided in a referendum.

Even before the conference, Labour had prepared a response to the *Parti Mauricien*'s proposals. Labour's objections were fundamental: "Clearly the proposals [of the *Parti*] spell dependence on the United Kingdom and a position of inferiority." Leaving the responsibility for internal security and external affairs to the United Kingdom was "pure colonialism." The Labour party paper asked, "What are two life peers in the House of Lords but window-dressing?" and pointed out that after Britain's entry into the Common Market, special negotiations would be required on behalf of Mauritius no matter what her final status. According to Labour, the *Parti Mauricien* proposal that through association "the sovereignty of Britain over Mauritius should be entrenched in the Constitution" was contrary to the United Nations requirement that a territory should be free to terminate the association at will.[56]

By the time the conference began, each party had clearly defined its position. The challenge for the twenty-eight delegates from Mauritius and the eight representatives from the Colonial Office was to find a suitable compromise. In his opening remarks on September 7, 1965, Secretary of State Anthony Greenwood made it clear that the Colonial Office had not ruled out any solutions in advance. He did not think it right that "the British Government, although it has ultimate constitutional responsibilities, should attempt to lay down in advance constitutional solutions for highly developed communities many thousands of miles away."[57]

In order to find ground for possible agreement, the Colonial Office met privately with each of the parties represented as well as with the two independents, while proindependence pickets surrounded Lancaster House. During these discussions, the electoral system remained an insurmountable problem. The *Parti Mauricien* held to its demand for a party-list system, and the Labour party still refused "to consider either proportional representation or a party-list system." Razack Mohammed remained firmly committed to reserved seats and separate electoral rolls for Muslims, adding that if the conference was prepared to concede the safeguards he was demanding, he in turn was prepared to agree to independence. Both the *Parti Mauricien* and Labour seemed to agree on combining the existing forty single-member constituencies into twenty multimember constituencies, and Ramgoolam suggested a maximum of three members from each constituency.

The question of separate communal rolls remained a major point of dissension. Ramgoolam, caught between his basic disapproval of the system and his need for Muslim support, was willing to take Mohammed up on his offer: Muslim support for independence in return for Labour party support for separate communal rolls. But Greenwood remained opposed, reflecting Colonial Office policy which had been to discourage the development of communal politics. He had grave doubts that once such a system was introduced it could easily be abolished, and agreed with Duval that "it would be difficult to confine communal rolls to only two minority groups."[58]

Anticipating Greenwood's closing remarks, *Parti Mauricien* leaders decided to boycott the final session. The conference hall was therefore half empty when Greenwood pronounced the official view that a referendum would "prolong the current uncertainty and political controversy in a way which would only harden and deepen communal divisions and rivalries."[59] On the second point of disagreement, the electoral system, the Colonial Office was unable to decide on an official view. Greenwood therefore proposed that a commission be appointed to recommend a suitable system within the principles which most parties had agreed upon: multimember constituencies, a common electoral roll, the provision for discouraging small parties, an opportunity for fair representation for all sections of Mauritius, and representation from the island of Rodrigues, a dependency of Mauritius and a reliable constituency for the *Parti Mauricien*.

On the third issue, the final status of the island, the secretary of state was straightforward: "It was right that Mauritius should be independent and take her place among the sovereign nations of the world."[60] Following the report of the electoral commission, a general election would be held and a government formed.

> In consultation with this government, Her Majesty's Government would be prepared to fix a date and take the necessary steps to declare Mauritius independent, after a period of six months full internal self-government, if a resolution for this was passed by a simple majority of the new Assembly.[61]

As some consolation to the minority parties, Greenwood presented a number of safeguards, beginning with a list of fundamental rights and freedoms, in the form of a framework for the constitution. Adopting an earlier suggestion of Bissoondoyal's, the new constitution would provide for the appointment of an ombudsman who would step in, either on his own initiative or following a complaint, to investigate the official acts of government departments and all public authorities. A public service commission and a police service commission were provided, with the goal of ensuring the impartiality of appointments to the civil service and the police. Finally, the approval of three-quarters of the Legislative Assembly was required to alter any of the entrenched provisions of the constitution—those relating to the sections on fundamental rights, the powers of the legislature, the judicial system, the public service and police commissions, the ombudsman, and the method of constitutional amendment. Amendments dealing with sections other than the entrenched clauses would require approval of only two-thirds of the Assembly.

At the conclusion of his speech, the secretary of state outlined the
steps toward independence which he thought could be accomplished
by the end of 1966; he failed to suggest even the possibility of associate status. It seemed clear that Labour would win the forthcoming
elections, given a reasonable electoral system, and independence
would naturally follow. Labour had every reason to celebrate: it had
won substantial victories in the past four elections, and there was no
reason to fear that the electorate would suddenly change its allegiance. The *Parti Mauricien* was a communal party and could hope
for the support of just over 30 percent of the population, at most,
whereas Labour had no reason to expect less than 45 percent of the
popular vote even without an alliance with Mohammed or Bissoondoyal.

The *Parti Mauricien*, firmly believing that a referendum was the
only way to ensure that people would vote exclusively on the issue of
independence rather than party or community, again felt betrayed.
No one had been able to destroy the case for a referendum effectively, and even Greenwood's final arguments were weak. *Parti
Mauricien* leaders believed they had reason on their side, and yet, as
in the past, Colonial Office officials had led them on, praised them,
but finally ignored them. In the end, political reality—the fact that
the Labour party represented 42 percent of the electorate and the
Parti Mauricien only 19 percent—had prevailed. Koenig was de-
pressed; Duval, however, was determined to win the election on Colonial Office terms.

In six years the island had overcome disaster from cyclone damage
and had progressed constitutionally from colonial status with a limited form of responsible government to near independence. Two national parties, Labour and the *Parti Mauricien*, had emerged along
the lines envisaged by those seeking a Westminster model. More
Mauritians were taking an active part in politics than before. Although tension was still high, Mauritius had survived the first outbreak of violence between the two major communities in recent history, and it appeared that once the island's status was determined, its
people would assume some sense of national identity and perhaps
channel communal energies into new directions.

In the background, however, lurked the unsolved economic problems. The population was increasing; unemployment was rising; the

budget would not balance without new taxes. None of these problems could be dealt with properly so long as politics dominated the island. But soon, it was hoped, politics would cease to be a major preoccupation once Mauritians had determined the island's final status.

10. A New Nation
1965–1967

IN 1965 MAURITIUS seemed on its way to independence. But ahead lay two turbulent years. Its last two years as a colony were fraught with unexpected tension, fear, and violence. In September 1965 it seemed that all that remained was to hold an election and—assuming the approval of the electorate—proceed to independence, a process that was scheduled to take nine months. But because of political maneuvering, the process was drawn out to twenty-three.

Both the Labour party and the *Parti Mauricien* shared responsibility for the delay: both blamed the Colonial Office. In the twenty-three months between the constitutional conference and the election, political controversy focused upon unemployment, the report of the electoral commission, and the timing of the elections. No party or politician responded to these issues without consciously considering the implications for the coming election campaign. Nothing mattered so much as what voters would do on election day.

The significance of these elections extended beyond Mauritius. The issue was not simply which party and community would govern the island, but whether Mauritius would remain a colony. The British government was giving Mauritius a chance, through these elections, to decide whether to remain a colony or become independent. Such an election was unique in British experience and differed considerably from referenda about continued association held in former French territories, where the French government was explicit about economic sanctions for those who voted no.

In the background of the London negotiations over constitutions and electoral systems was another issue, never actually discussed in conference but presumably the subject of the two meetings between Prime Minister Harold Wilson and Ramgoolam. This was the question of the island of Diego Garcia. The British administered from Mauritius four archipelagoes—including the sizable but virtually uninhabited island of Diego Garcia—although they were thousands of miles north of Port Louis in the Indian Ocean. With colonies disappearing rapidly, both the United States and Great Britain were anxious to maintain some kind of foothold in the Indian Ocean which would give them access to South Asia as well as Africa. The British talked to the Mauritians about a communications center, a refueling station, and possibly an air strip; the United States was developing more elaborate plans for a defense base.

Speculation about British interests in Diego Garcia was encouraged in the House of Commons on May 27, 1965, when Greenwood confirmed that Britain, "in conjunction with Americans," was considering "the possibility of establishing certain limited facilities in the Indian Ocean."[1] Throughout the summer, Mauritian newspapers tried to guess what Greenwood actually meant. Secret negotiations began in London in September. As the constitutional conference ended, Ramgoolam agreed in private to transfer the archipelagoes to Great Britain in return for £3 million, which the British government would pay in installments. In fact, the bill was paid by the United States on the understanding that some of the money would be used to relocate the existing inhabitants of the island—approximately 1,200 people. No Mauritian took notes during the negotiations, and there was no exchange of documents, hence exactly what was said and what was meant during these negotiations is open for debate.

Although the agreement remained a secret until November 10, nearly six weeks after the constitutional conference, it was easy for the *Parti Mauricien* to link the sale of the archipelagoes, and particularly Diego Garcia, to the Colonial Office acceptance of independence.[2] The *Parti* charged that the British government, desperate for a defense base, had offered independence in return for a commitment to sell the islands. They criticized Ramgoolam for helping Britain to turn the Indian Ocean into a center for nuclear weapons—and at the same time criticized the price, feeling that better financial terms could have been made.[3] In the Diego Garcia issue, the *Parti Mauricien* found the scapegoat for the denial of their requested referendum.

Duval and Koenig took full advantage of the crisis. On November 12 the three *Parti Mauricien* ministers resigned from the government, forcing a collapse of the fragile coalition of which the Colonial Office had been so proud. A month later, on December 5, the *Parti Mauricien* organized the largest popular meeting it had ever had. Calling the British "Anglo-Saxon robbers" because the islands in question were worth more than £3 million, the *Parti* wildly accused the Labour party, the British, and the Americans of encouraging another Hiroshima by permitting the installation of a military base on the island.

Diego Garcia was only an excuse for the meeting, which Duval hoped would bring new people into the *Parti Mauricien* to support his ultimate goal, preventing independence under Labour. The demonstration, even larger than the one Duval had organized six months earlier for Greenwood, was another proof of Duval's popularity.[4] Franco-Mauritians who had never before attended a political meeting wore blue shirts (the symbol of the *Parti Mauricien*) and cheered for Duval and Koenig. Desperate to stop independence, they knew that only Duval could bring opposition voters to the polls. In their heart of hearts, the Franco-Mauritians were probably also pleased with the anti-British tone of the meeting. No one questioned the contradiction between the accusations Duval was making *against* the British and the fact that the *Parti* alternative to independence was association *with* Britain—an inconsistency which reflected in part Duval's own ambivalence. On the one hand, association was the only plausible alternative; on the other, Duval had little admiration for most of the British officials with whom he had been dealing for the past five years.

Confident of the Creole, Chinese, and Franco-Mauritian vote, Duval used the December 5 meeting to announce a major change in *Parti Mauricien* policy. To win a general election, he had to win Hindu votes. In a complete about-face, he gave the *Parti* a new slogan, "Hindoo, mon frère." Communalism was out, and he promised that any members of his party whom he heard being communal in conversation or action would be properly punished.[5] "Hindoo, mon frère" was a distasteful phrase for the Franco-Mauritians from Curépipe and for the Creole dockers from Port Louis, but they remained committed to Duval as the only alternative to independence and Hindu domination.

Immediately after the meeting, Duval began talking openly with

Indo-Mauritians—Tamils, low-caste Hindus, Muslims—any Indians who would associate themselves with the man who only a few months earlier had been a Creole communalist. The Labour party became increasingly concerned as reports of Indian defections to the *Parti Mauricien* appeared in the press. In June 1966, a group of low-caste Hindus formed the People's Socialist party and allied themselves with the *Parti Mauricien*. At the same time, the first of a number of prominent Muslims resigned from the *Comité d'Action Muselman* and announced his support for the *Parti Mauricien*.

Labour was also under pressure from the Hindu radicals. Near the end of 1962, the Independent Forward Bloc and the All-Mauritian Hindu Congress entered into an alliance and announced plans to contest the coming elections together. Since, in the past, both parties had strongly criticized Labour for not pursuing socialist policies far enough and for excluding lower-caste Hindus, Labour leaders viewed the new alliance with considerable dismay. Afraid of being squeezed between the *Parti Mauricien* and the IFB-Congress alliance, Ramgoolam decided to persuade Bissoondoyal and Dabee to join Labour and the CAM to maintain a united front in the campaign. Ramgoolam made quite a number of concessions, even promising to include the IFB and the Congress in discussions regarding the placing of candidates. For the moderate Ramgoolam, who disliked communal politics, the alliance was particularly distasteful.

The Banwell Commission

In 1956 the London conference had left the choice of an electoral system to a commission. At first Labour had hoped that the commission could make its recommendations quickly so that elections could be held in June 1966 and the way cleared for independence by December, as suggested by the Colonial Office. The *Parti Mauricien* was less committed to an early election. Duval wanted time to build up an Indian following, to show that he really meant to turn the *Parti Mauricien* into a national rather than a communal party. He also realized that uncertainty was causing economic difficulties for Ramgoolam's government, and he hoped to benefit from growing unemployment and the resulting disillusion. When the electoral commissioners arrived in early January 1966, delay was to Duval's advantage.

The commission, chaired by Sir Harold Banwell, heard evidence from everyone who wished to give it.[6] But the most important testimony was presented by Labour, the *Parti Mauricien*, the CAM, and the IFB. Keeping in mind the conditions established in London—multimember constituencies, a common electoral roll, and no nominated members—each party proposed an election method that would ensure "that main sections of the population had an opportunity of securing fair representation of their interests."[7]

Labour advocated the formation of twenty constituencies with four members each—doubling the size of the Legislative Assembly. In proposing such a large house, Ramgoolam was responding to pressures from many interest groups within his party and to the need to reserve places for IFB and Congress candidates. Consistent with his position in London, Ramgoolam asked for reserved seats for Muslim and Chinese minorities.

Mohammed supported the Labour party position, though he placed more emphasis on the need for reserved seats. The IFB and its new supporter, the Hindu Congress, did not substantially change the position it took in London.

The *Parti Mauricien* revived the demand made in London for an assembly of not more than forty-two members elected by a party-list system, which would make reserved seats unnecessary. *Parti* leaders pointed out that the system was working well in British Guiana, although they agreed with Bissoondoyal that such a system tended to diminish contact between the voters and the elected members and denied the voter any influence in selecting candidates.

It was clear to the commissioners that no system would satisfy everyone. In preparing their report, their main goals were to discourage the development of a number of small special-interest parties, to force the main parties to seek support from all communities, and to prevent the electoral system from so magnifying the power of the majority as to jeopardize entrenched constitutional rights.[8] The commissioners wanted the method of voting and allocating seats to be easy to understand.

By the end of February the Banwell Commission Report had reached the Colonial Office, but it was not released until May 28, a costly delay caused initially by cabinet changes in Britain.[9] During this period, rumors about its contents circulated wildly. All parties reacted emotionally and promised various forms of action should any rumor be shown to be true.

The commissioners had reached their conclusions through a process of elimination. They dismissed proportional representation and the single transferable vote quickly. Instead, they designated twenty three-member constituencies formed by pairing two old constituencies into one. In addition, Rodrigues was given two seats, and up to eight "corrective seats" were to be allocated after the election, according to an elaborate system designed to assist underrepresented communities and parties. Each voter was required to cast three votes. On the assumption that in many constituencies each party would have a "national" ticket and present candidates of more than one community, this block vote would force voters to cross either party or communal lines. The voter could select candidates belonging to one party but, most likely, representing two or more communities, or cross party lines and vote for candidates from his own community.

The day the Banwell Report was released the Labour party rejected it and later threatened to resign from the government if changes were not made. Ramgoolam called the report an imperialistic plot designed to put the *Parti Mauricien* in power—a "political rape of democracy"—and, accordingly, introduced a motion denouncing the report in the Legislative Assembly on June 7.[10] He objected to the pairing of the constituencies, to the complicated corrective, and to the modest size of the Assembly. To outsiders, Ramgoolam's reactions were difficult to understand. The Banwell Report seemed a careful effort to meet the difficult situation in Mauritius, and it incorporated nearly all of Ramgoolam's initial suggestions and few of Duval's. The report became a nationwide issue which few Mauritians could understand—a rallying point for both parties to demonstrate their new strength. Shortly after the report's release, the newly formed alliance of Labour, the IFB, the CAM, and the Hindu Congress organized a mass meeting in Port Louis. For the first time, leaders from the four parties spoke from the same platform; Mauritians were shown that cooperation was possible. For the year during which the alliance lasted, each party maintained its own executive and administration and published its own newspaper. But Ramgoolam knew that if he could hold the alliance together in any form, his chances of an election victory would be enhanced. The Banwell Report provided the first rallying point—an issue on which all four members of the alliance agreed to oppose the *Parti Mauricien*.

The *Parti Mauricien* accepted the Banwell Report, although the commissioners had ignored most of the party's proposals. Duval now wanted to get on with the election. To counter the Labour meeting, the *Parti* organized a mass demonstration in defense of the Banwell Report on June 26. Instead of the anti-British slogans of the December meeting, there were placards of support for the Queen, Sir Harold Banwell, and Duval. In addition to providing party leaders a chance to defend the Banwell Report, the demonstration was the first opportunity Duval had to prove that he meant what he had said in December: the *Parti Mauricien* was to become a national party. Earlier in June, Duval had promised to nominate eleven Muslim candidates for the *Parti Mauricien*.[11] Speakers at his June 26 meeting included Muslims, Tamils, low-caste Hindus, and Chinese, as well as members of the general population. But the audience was mostly Creole.

The governor and the Colonial Office were in a dilemma. It had been agreed in London that the recommendations of the commission would provide the basis for the coming elections. The Banwell Report had been accepted by the secretary of state for the colonies. But the Labour party was intransigent; if the Colonial Office should decide to impose the recommendations, more violence might result. Furthermore, over two-thirds of the Legislative Assembly had voted to reject it. The problem was to appease Ramgoolam without upsetting Duval.

The Colonial Office sent John Stonehouse, parliamentary undersecretary for the colonies, to Mauritius. Stonehouse had visited Mauritius twice previously and knew Duval, Ramgoolam, and Walter well. After a week of conferences between June 27 and July 4 with all parties, he proposed amendments which both sides accepted.[12] The pairing of the constituencies was not changed, but the system of correctives was altered slightly. The changes were hardly substantial, but Ramgoolam, able to save face, accepted them. Duval, anxious to proceed with elections, was ready to agree to nearly any change. He accepted the modifications with the clear understanding that the election would be held immediately.

Elections—At Last

The way had been cleared, but Ramgoolam was not confident enough to proceed with the election, and the governor was unwilling to use his authority to call an election without Ramgoolam's approval. In the summer of 1966 many Mauritians felt that things were getting worse rather than better, and disillusionment with the Labour government was growing daily. Corruption and patronage were flagrant. Political criteria determined economic decisions. And the poorer Mauritius became, the more time ministers seemed to spend on business trips abroad, collecting handsome per diem allowances. Ramgoolam knew that Labour's popularity was at low ebb. His government was blamed for new taxes, which many felt could have been avoided with sound economic planning several years earlier, and for unemployment. The new taxes were directed at the sugar estates, already suffering from the low world price of sugar, and at the urban middle class, mostly the general population. Although the taxes affected *Parti Mauricien* followers most seriously, a hue and cry against them went up throughout the country. The nineteen thousand relief workers who spent four days a week supposedly working on roads earning a suitable minimum wage for their trouble were as controversial as the new taxes.[13] The large-scale unemployment forecast by Meade, Titmuss, and Brian Hopkin, a representative of the Ministry of Overseas Development, had occurred. The government had done little to encourage emigration, and was still unwilling to provide much financial support for family planning.

Duval, with his slogan "Hindoo, mon frère," was gathering support. He talked of the future with an idealism and a dynamism that contrasted favorably with the speeches of Labour, CAM, IFB, and Congress alliance leaders. He was still regarded as the puppet of the sugar industry, despite daily statements that he alone would decide policy if elected, but he had new and fresh ideas and succeeded in convincing a number of voters that he had matured. The Duval who employed thugs to drive through Trois Boutiques in 1965 had disappeared. The new Duval, serious and devoted to building a Mauritian nation, was hard to resist. He knew he was gathering momentum and did everything possible to force early elections, but he could not hurry the process of registration, which began in September and took two months.

During the entire period, a team of commonwealth observers was in Mauritius preparing a report for the secretary of state on the conduct of the campaign.[14] The presence of the observers did much to limit corruption and fraud. Since any irregularities would be reported directly to the observers and become public information, most politicians tried to follow the regulations about registration of voters. The principal problem during registration was "dumping": political parties taking voters out of safe constituencies and registering them in marginal ones to swing an election.[15] At the close of registration, in fact, the electoral commissioner noted that in eight constituencies the number of claimants exceeded the number of people found in the house-to-house canvass. A fresh canvass was carried out in one district in Port Louis and in parts of five others. In the end, the commonwealth observers concluded that the administrative arrangements were adequate and were conducted in a fair and proper manner.

REGISTRATION IN MAURITIUS, 1967

	Towns	Countryside	Total
General Population	65,908	32,914	98,822
Muslims	26,216	19,860	46,076
Hindus	40,731	82,541	123,272
Tamils	13,716	17,579	31,295
Chinese	6,966	1,252	8,218
Total	153,537	154,146	307,683

Source: The M.E.F. [Mauritius Employers Federation] Newsletter, March 1967.

Once registration was over, the elections were expected to take place quickly. The law required six weeks' notice; but someone had to call the elections. The Labour party claimed that the responsibility for the decision lay with Ramgoolam as premier. The *Parti Mauricien* felt Governor Rennie should take the official step, since the constitution said that the governor, "acting in his discretion," had the power to call the elections.[16] Rennie, however, did not want to upset Ramgoolam by forcing him to call an election. The *Parti Mauricien* was enraged. They were fully aware that it was to Ramgoolam's advantage to delay the election until the crop season began in July and the government could find jobs for some of the fifty thousand unemployed.

On April 25, 1967, just after Ramgoolam had left to open the Mauritius Pavilion at the Montreal Exposition, the *Parti Mauricien* members of the Legislative Assembly all resigned in protest against "maladministration, the duplicity of the British people and the government and an indifference to poverty."[17] It was evident that they would make more trouble if the delays continued. On June 20, Ramgoolam announced that the elections would be held on August 7.

In the twelve months between June 1966 and June 1967, Ramgoolam had had a chance to consolidate his position. The memory of the 1966 taxes had faded. Britain's bid to enter the Common Market had been turned down, detracting from Duval's claim that Mauritius would be able to ride into the Common Market on Britain's coattails if the island remained a colony. And a number of voters found Duval's attempts to force the election irresponsible. Time was on Ramgoolam's side, and clearly by mid-1967 he was in a better position than he had been a year earlier.

Ramgoolam's major worry was choosing candidates and placing them in constituencies. Well before the election date was announced, the maneuvering for places had begun. Ramgoolam had sixty nominations to make; he had the IFB, the CAM, the Hindu Congress, and his own party to placate, as well as special interests within each party. He promised to consult every party involved before making decisions, but inevitably there would be many unhappy people. While the parties combined under the name of the Independence party, they in fact remained separate interest groups. Sookdeo Bissoondoyal was the cleverest. In April he had placed twelve IFB candidates in constituencies, presenting Ramgoolam with a *fait accompli*. The Labour leader was more successful in his negotiations with Razack Mohammed. The two agreed on how many candidates the CAM would be represented with in the Independence party, and then Mohammed selected them after consulting with party leaders. Surprising many observers (and departing from the pattern set by Rozemont and Duval over the years), Mohammed selected young and imaginative followers, showing a remarkable sensitivity to the desire for new faces in Mauritian politics. The Hindu Congress, with its militant but inexperienced leadership, was a major problem. Ramgoolam, aware of local discontent, did not dare to alienate it. But the Congress, annoyed that IFB candidates had already been placed, withdrew from the alliance to fight the election alone. Dabee was convinced that in some constituencies many Hindus would vote for one Congress candidate and two Labour candidates and that if the results were close, the Congress would hold the balance in the new council. Five days after the nominations were filed, Ramgoolam again offered the Congress five seats, but the Congress remained firm in its intention to stand alone, ignoring the evidence offered by Mauritian history that third parties generally do not do well.

Duval was also having increasing difficulty placing his candidates. In November 1966, Koenig had resigned as head of the *Parti Mauricien* for reasons of health, and Duval had taken his place. He had promised that several Hindus and at least eleven Muslims would stand with *Parti* backing. As a result of his new noncommunal policy, several prominent Muslims had joined the *Parti Mauricien*. Foremost among them was the influential businessman Ibrahim Dawood. In addition to these newcomers, Duval had the backing of a number of Muslims and a few Hindus who had joined him much earlier. These people lacked stature, but Duval felt they had to be rewarded for their loyalty. To whom should he give the safe seats? Could he really expect the Creoles of Curépipe to vote for a Hindu in order to make a reality of "Hindoo, mon frère"? Duval's decision was an "all or nothing" policy. He could count on eight constituencies, but to win the election he had to carry eleven. For these reasons, he put his best men in the marginal constituencies, hoping that their personal strength would carry the constituencies or that at least one or two of them would be returned on a split vote. He himself left Curépipe and fought the election in Port Louis, the stronghold of earlier Creole leaders.

In preparation for the elections, *Parti Mauricien* officers went to Réunion to study campaign techniques. All *Parti* agents were paid and organized by party officers. Fund raising was centralized. The *Parti Mauricien* rented small rooms in many villages and from there distributed pamphlets and sample ballots, and sold *Parti Mauricien* key rings, hats, and shirts. A youth center was opened in Port Louis. A pirate radio, scheduled to broadcast music and *Parti* messages, was planned but never functioned as expected.

The *Parti Mauricien* campaign was centered upon Duval. Candidates from every constituency asked their followers to vote for Duval and thus for association with Great Britain. Mauritians would then be able to emigrate to Great Britain without restriction, for a Mauritian passport would continue to be a British passport. That emigration restrictions would eventually be imposed on citizens of the independent states within the Commonwealth seemed obvious to Duval, although he tried to convince voters that such restrictions would not apply to Mauritians as long as Mauritius remained a colony. He argued that passports issued while Mauritius remained a colony were in effect issued by the British government and therefore were not subject to the regulations of the Commonwealth Immigrants Act of 1967. But passports issued by the independent government of Mauritius would be.[18] Furthermore, association would bring benefits when Britain joined the Common Market. After twenty years in power, Labour had brought only problems—overpopulation, unemployment, and debt. The imaginative economic policies of the *Parti Mauricien* would remedy the situation. The Labour party sought to redivide the national cake; the *Parti Mauricien* would make the cake larger.

While the *Parti Mauricien* undertook to meet the campaign expenses of most of its candidates and had a massive central organization in Port Louis, Labour was far more decentralized and informal. Twenty national meetings (one in each constituency), at which Ramgoolam and the main party leaders would speak, were scheduled. In addition, there were daily meetings in every village for which individual candidates were responsible. Much of the campaign was conducted in private meetings. Voters, bored with the usual public meetings and repeated platitudes, were flattered to be invited to a private gathering and recruited as agents. Although attended by the police, private meetings were not reported in the press, and candidates could gear their speeches to suit the small audiences. Accusations could not be countered by opposition. Communalism could dominate these discussions without attracting island-wide attention.

The major issue was, of course, independence versus association. Ramgoolam argued that with independence Mauritius would be free to accept money from the World Bank without having to apply through Great Britain. In addition, France and the United States would help the island with its economic problems. Ramgoolam based his claim to office on the achievements of government since 1948: under the leadership of his party much had been accomplished, and what failures or omissions there had been were simply the fault of the Colonial Office. He charged that association meant a continued tie between the Colonial Office and the sugar estates, to the benefit of the Franco-Mauritians. Besides, the *Parti Mauricien* was corrupt and was spending thousands of rupees to bribe innocent voters. "Take their money," the Independence party said, "but vote for us."[19] Labour, however, had its own form of bribery. Between March 1967 and August 1967, the number of relief workers rose from 19,290 to 30,887.[20]

Polling day, August 7, 1967, began quietly. Both parties, knowing that misrepresentation was a favorite trick, told their members to "vote early, be the first to vote in your name." By eight in the morning crowds surrounded the polling stations. By noon, over 65 percent of the electorate had voted.

In Quatre Bornes there had been a minor scuffle, but local police restored order. The real trouble was in the third district in Port Louis, where the Muslim leadership was being disputed. There, the Independence party had five candidates. Mohammed and his Muslims were standing along with two Chinese, who were expected to draw Chinese votes away from the *Parti Mauricien* ticket, led by Ibrahim Dawood. It was expected that both Mohammed and Duval would have thugs in their pay in Port Louis 3 watching for trouble. By noon Mohammed's men reported that the vote was going against him. Counting the cars bringing voters to the polls, they saw that they were outnumbered. Shortly after noon, thugs stopped *Parti Mauricien* cars before they could reach the polling station. Mohammed's men blocked the road, and at the same time started a rumor that Dawood had withdrawn from the election. By midafternoon Independence party Muslims were destroying *Parti Mauricien* cars with sticks and batons in the Muslim section of Port Louis. The *Parti Mauricien* retaliated; one house was set on fire, and several people were admitted to the hospital.[21] Soon the riots had taken on a communal nature: Mohammed's Muslims against Ah-Chuen's Chinese and Duval's Creoles, many of whom had come from Curépipe to help with the voting and polling in Port Louis. The police dispersed the crowd several times with tear gas, and by evening the Special Mobile Force was in control of the streets. On election night the governor appeared on television and appealed for calm, and early the next morning the votes were counted.

Mohammed's premonition was correct. He had alienated too many Muslims by his heavy-handed dealing in the past, and Port Louis 3 returned three *Parti Mauricien* candidates. But that was the only joy for the *Parti*. The Independence party had swept the country, making inroads in *Parti Mauricien* strongholds. The final result was thirty-nine to twenty-three.[22]

Independence was assured. Duval had lost his gamble, and some of his strongest and best candidates had been defeated. The results did reflect marked gains on the part of the *Parti Mauricien*, which now controlled one-third of the house compared with one-fifth before. Yet as long as the government coalition held together, the *Parti* would have little power over legislation in the independent state. Some in the *Parti Mauricien* feared that without the watchful eye of the Colonial Office, the government would introduce hasty and ill-considered legislation, either of a communal nature or of a sort designed to destroy the effective functioning of the sugar estates. Some began to wonder if elections would be held as required in 1972.

The greatest surprise of the election was the effectiveness of party discipline. Nonexistent in 1943, by 1967 party discipline had so developed that in every constituency people voted for three candidates of one party. Because of the overriding issue of independence and association, because of the multimember constituencies and the difficulties of voting for candidates of different parties, the 1967 election was not, like previous elections, a popularity contest. In a constituency all three candidates of the same party had the same symbol: a cock for the *Parti Mauricien*, a key for the Independence party, and a wheel for the Congress. For illiterate voters who could not read names and had to follow symbols, it would be extremely difficult to vote for three candidates of the same community but of different parties, or simply for three favorite personalities of different parties.

In the sense that voters chose to vote for members of their party no matter what the candidate's community, the voting was noncommunal. Hindus, however, voted exclusively for Labour, knowing that if there was a Muslim or Creole candidate on the list, still it was the party of the Hindus. In the same way the Chinese and the Franco-Mauritians voted for *Parti Mauricien* Hindu and Muslim candidates. The Creoles voted fairly solidly for the *Parti Mauricien*; only the Muslim allegiance was divided. The close election between Mohammed and Dawood reflected the division in Muslim opinion. Despite his electoral defeat, Mohammed remained in the assembly, for he was among the eight best losers selected.

The elections were over. The *Parti Mauricien* had lost its bid for association; would it now accept independence, or attempt to block it by extralegal means? Tension remained, and the parties did little to abate it. Mauritians watched Duval and Ramgoolam. Duval was quiet. Ramgoolam, too, was quiet, missing what many considered a natural opportunity to make an appeal for cooperation and the end of hatred.

On August 22 the Legislative Assembly voted to request the British government to grant independence. The *Parti Mauricien* Assembly members, aroused by charges Sookdeo Bissoondoyal made of bribery, walked out shortly before the vote, making the decision unanimous.[23] Ramgoolam's long-cherished dream had come true.

Independence

In the final months before independence, all the tensions of the election campaign exploded. The most serious riots since Mauritius was first populated by the French in the eighteenth century swept Port Louis. For a time it appeared that Ramgoolam's dream would be shattered, but with the help of British troops, order was restored, and Mauritius celebrated independence in March 1968, in an atmosphere of triumph, hatred, and resentment.

The first signs of trouble appeared shortly after the elections, in October 1967. Ramgoolam was preparing to leave for London to set a date for independence and to make final arrangements for the transfer of power. In Port Louis, ten thousand relief workers, many of whom had been hired in July just before the election as a form of bribery, were fired.[24] They had served their purpose: they had voted for the government, and the government could no longer afford to keep them on. In anger, they marched on Government House and rioted. The police arrested seventy-three before order was restored.

The October riots prompted rumors that Duval was preparing a disruptive demonstration for Independence Day. The government and the police were discussing the best methods of preventing the demonstration when violence suddenly exploded in the Muslim section of Port Louis. The riots were communal: Muslims and Creoles who had worked together for either the *Parti Mauricien* or the Independence party were killing each other. The fighting started between two gangs.[25] It was well known that Port Louis had a network of gangs which controlled illegal drugs and prostitution and were linked to politicians. The strongest gangs in Port Louis were the Istanbul, responsible to Razack Mohammed, and the Mafia, in the pay of a *Parti Mauricien* Legislative Assembly member. An eye for an eye was the rule, and the moment a Muslim corpse was discovered, a Creole was killed.

A state of emergency was declared on January 22. The police were unable to keep order, and Ramgoolam and Rennie agreed to call in British troops for the second time in three years.[26] Boards and barricades covered shops, and the inhabitants of Port Louis fled to the suburbs. Refugee centers were set up to house frightened Creoles and Muslims.

After ten days of rioting, the violence subsided, but hatred—far deeper than had even been suspected—remained between Creoles and Muslims.

ELECTION RESULTS 1948–1976

Party	Number of Seats						Percentage of Votes			
	1948	1953	1959	1963	1967†	1976†	1959	1963	1967	1976†
Mauritius Labour Party*	13	14	23	19	26		46.7	42.3	33.7	
Independent Forward Bloc*			6	7	12	28	19.6	19.2	15.1	38
Comité d'Action Muselman*			5	4	5		8.6	7.1	6.3	
Parti Mauricien (Ralliement)	1	2	3	8	27	8	15	18.9	43.1	17
Independents	5	3	3	2	—		8.6	8.2	—	
Others							1.5	4.3	2.7	
Mouvement Militant Mauricien						34				41
	19	19	40	40	70	70				

*Officially the Labour party, IFB, and CAM were merged in 1967 to become the Independence party. The 1976 results show only the Independence party totals.
†After the distribution of the best loser seats.

ELECTION RESULTS 1948–1967

	1948	1953	1959	1963	1967*
Hindus	11	10	25	20	35
Muslims	0	1	5	5	10
General Population	8	8	10	14	16
Chinese	0	0	0	1	1
Total	19	19	40	40	62

*Before distribution of best loser seats.

The cause of the riots lay with the island-wide malaise, a combination of the high unemployment rate, rising prices, boredom, and uncertainty. For too many Mauritians, there was little or no prospect of a future in the island in 1968. But such violent and brutal hatred between two communal groups could not have been entirely spontaneous. The *Parti Mauricien* motive would have been to stop independence, but the *Comité d'Action Muselman* also had something to gain. Angered by his election defeat and by the success of the *Parti Mauricien* in attracting Muslim votes, Razack Mohammed was desperate to restore himself as the leader of the Muslim community. If the Muslims had reason to fear the Creoles, they would leave the *Parti Mauricien* and Duval and rally behind Mohammed. This, indeed, is what happened. Muslim *Parti Mauricien* supporters went into hiding, and by the end of the riots Ramgoolam confidently claimed that Mohammed was again the leader of the Muslims. But the toll was high. More than twenty-five bodies had been found; hundreds more people were wounded, and thousands fled their homes. Any chance of using approaching independence as a basis for creating political unity vanished.

These were also the first riots in Mauritius with apparently indiscriminate killing and body mutilation. The island had never known such crude and cruel behavior. All the same, the riots had less potential for an island-wide explosion than had the Trois Boutiques riots. Fighting between the Muslims and the Creoles was bound to be limited. If, on the other hand, the Muslims and Creoles had united against the Hindus, a civil war could have resulted. In January 1968 civil war was not a danger, but Muslims and Creoles grew terrified of one another. The Muslims turned to the Hindus for support, and middle-class Creoles looked for jobs outside Mauritius.

The House of Lords approved the Mauritius Independence Bill on February 13, 1968.[27] Some observers wondered whether Mauritius would proceed with independence celebrations while British troops were stationed on the island. Ramgoolam was not deterred. He pointed to the example of Jamaica, which celebrated independence with British troops present. But the plans for the celebration were haphazard. Princess Alexandra's scheduled visit was cancelled for security reasons. Anthony Greenwood, now minister of housing, who as colonial secretary had chaired the 1965 constitutional conference, was the senior representative of the British government when the Mauritian flag replaced the Union Jack on March 12, 1968.

EPILOGUE

WHAT HAS HAPPENED on Mauritius since independence? For the first years, the country survived and even flourished. The economic chaos that was expected to follow independence did not materialize. Sugar, once considered the chief burden of Mauritius, proved a good investment for the early 1970s. Beginning in 1970, both prices and production increased dramatically. World prices, which had averaged £34 per metric ton in 1969, rose to £72 in 1972 and approached £100 in 1973.[1] At the same time, production broke an all-time record in 1973, as planters harvested over 700,000 metric tons of cane. A goal of one million metric tons was set for the early 1980s.

To complement the sugar income, the government encouraged industrial development. The Export Processing Zones Act of 1970 permitted investors to process products without paying import or export duties and helped other investors to take advantage of cheap female Mauritian labor. The only such area in the Common Market, the zone was a success. The number of tourists began to grow at a rate of 20 percent per year. Per capita income, which had been declining steadily until 1970, rose during the early 1970s, while the rate of population increase declined to 1.3 percent for the period from 1970 to 1975, and the GNP increased at an average annual rate of nearly 8 percent. Between 1972 and 1978, 67,000 new jobs were recorded. On the surface, Mauritius was doing well.

The island also had to chart a foreign policy. Acutely uncomfortable with its more radical Indian Ocean neighbors, the Malagasy Republic and the Seychelles, Mauritian foreign policy has reflected the moderate and pro-Western commitment of its present government.

Relations with South Africa are preserved because South Africans make up a significant proportion of tourists to Mauritius. Mauritian diplomats, among the few Third World diplomats who are completely bilingual, have sought and found a role for themselves in international fora out of proportion to the size of their tiny island. Ramgoolam became president of the Organization of African Unity, and in 1974 the OAU meetings were held in Mauritius.

The attention of Mauritians, however, has been focused on Diego Garcia, the coral atoll sold to the British and subsequently turned into a sophisticated naval and air base by the United States. As part of the sale agreement, the atoll's small population of roughly 1,200 was removed from the island and relocated in the Seychelles and in Mauritius. Life in Mauritius for the Ilois, as they are known, has not been easy. On one hand, the Mauritian government has been slow to distribute funds that were to help with resettlement. On the other hand, important legal questions about the right of the British to deport from Diego Garcia people who were born there are being raised in the courts. Ramgoolam has been attacked for encouraging the militarization of the Indian Ocean, and the opposition promises that once in power it will take Diego Garcia back—an unlikely possibility. From a strategic point of view, the West does not want Mauritius to have an unfriendly government, although the United States will probably never do more than use Port Louis as a rest spot—one of the few available to the American fleet in the area. For Mauritians, Diego Garcia will remain an important political issue, but from the point of view of the Americans and the British the matter is settled.

Mauritius's initial relative prosperity helped the island's politicians, but Ramgoolam—still the country's leader—has had his problems. His initial moves were, as expected, practical. After lengthy consultations in Mauritius and discussions with French officials, Duval joined the government in 1969 at Ramgoolam's request. The coalition was established on one condition—that the elections, which were scheduled for 1972, would be postponed until 1976. The coalition collapsed in December 1973.

To observers who followed the bitter debates and arguments between Ramgoolam and the Franco-Mauritians prior to independence, the coalition seemed a curious sequel to independence. In many respects, however, it was not surprising. The personal relationship between Duval and Ramgoolam, which so exasperated Harold Walter and other Labour leaders, still persisted. Ramgoolam was frustrated by Duval's erratic behavior, but he respected Duval's quick and imaginative mind. More important, once the Labour party had achieved independence for and political dominance in the island, it was able to identify areas of common interest with the Franco-Mauritians. The Labour party included a number of very wealthy traders and landowners whose economic interests directly coincided with those of the Franco-Mauritians. The economic well-being of the island was of intense concern to both parties. And the Franco-Mauritians had no choice but to work with Hindu labor leaders. Social events were still predominantly segregated on the basis of community, but there was little room for the arrogance that symbolized Franco-Mauritian behavior toward other communities in the 1950s. The coalition represented a joining of the most powerful political forces in the island.

Opposition to the coalition came from an unexpected direction. Younger, well-educated Mauritians, tired of the stranglehold that Ramgoolam and his supporters had kept on Mauritian politics since the 1950s, and frustrated by the alliance between the economically powerful Franco-Mauritians and the politically powerful governing group, began to organize. Led by Paul Beranger, a young Franco-Mauritian who had been involved in the student strikes in France in 1968, young Mauritians of all communities were attracted to a new political party, the *Mouvement Militant Mauricien* (MMM). In many ways, it seemed as if Mauritian politics had come full circle. Just as Curé hoped to unite Mauritians of all communities against the economically and politically powerful estate owners, so the goal of the MMM was to replace the communal struggle with class struggle. The MMM wanted to "wipe out twenty years of communalism, and rebuild Mauritian unity through a socialist program."[2]

Formed in 1969, the MMM flexed its muscles in 1970 in a by-election in Triolet, Ramgoolam's own constituency. An MMM candidate, Dev Virahswamy, was returned with 71.5 percent of the votes, demonstrating the party's popular appeal. Encouraged, the MMM sought and gained the support of eleven unions, including three major unions in the sugar industry, the powerful bus union, and the dock workers' union. But it pushed too far: a general strike in 1971, called by the MMM, finally provoked Ramgoolam to declare a state of emergency; he had party leaders arrested, banned the publication of the MMM newspaper, and promoted successfully a constitutional

amendment abolishing by-elections. The MMM was severely
weakened, and divisions within its leadership developed—but the
lapse was temporary.

The MMM served as a strong warning to the old guard. The government viewed the Mauritian sociopolitical situation as a fluid one
in which people could rise from relatively obscure backgrounds to
positions of power. After all, some ministers began their careers on
the sugar estates or teaching in primary schools at a time when there
was little reason to believe that they would be able to do much better
by the time they retired. But these same men were, in fact, a tiny
percentage of the population, and they have remained in power for
over thirty years. Thus it is not surprising that many Mauritians do
not share their view that Mauritian society provides new opportunities for the lower classes.

Moreover, like so many national leaders, Ramgoolam has failed to
grapple with the pressing political problem of his own succession. By
postponing elections and failing to incorporate young Mauritians into
his government, Ramgoolam made a classic management mistake
and missed the opportunity to train a generation of politicians who
will be able to take over. The government is held together largely
through the force of Ramgoolam's own personality. Ramgoolam is
over 80, and he cannot continue indefinitely.

The interests of the current political elite, which has acquired economic power in the process of obtaining political power, overlap with
the interests of the Franco-Mauritian elite. While they may be points
of tension between the two groups, both understand that political instability would destroy their own positions. Indians, Muslims, and
Franco-Mauritians who are in power want to stay there, but economic circumstances have been working against them.

The good years following independence did not last. The 8 percent
annual growth rate in the economy that marked the years between
1970 and 1975 came to a screeching halt. A third of the sugar crop
was destroyed by a devastating cyclone in 1975, sugar prices plum-
meted 75 percent, and Mauritius experienced its first trade deficit
since independence. During the good years, government expenditure
increased and consumed some of the funds that should have been
used to generate new investments. Consumption expenditure rose at
a faster rate than did GNP, and a deficit balance of payments became
a regular feature of the economy. Later, industries began leaving the

Export Processing Zone because of the difficulty in finding markets and the low productivity of Mauritian workers. European Economic Community countries began to sign bilateral trade agreements with countries in Asia. The rising price of oil has also taken its toll. And now the government is left with an expensive budget and deficits. By 1979 the situation became so serious that the government devalued the rupee by 30 percent, imposed new taxes on sugar and tourism, and increased wages across the board by 13 percent. Sugar producers claimed that it cost more to produce sugar than they could get for it. Cyclones in December 1979 and early 1980 only aggravated the situation. That boom sugar year still remains a fiction in development plans.

Unemployment continues to be a serious problem. Ten percent of the labor force was unemployed in 1978, and the Development Works Corporation was established to find public works jobs for the unemployed. In the past such work has been considered a form of political payoff, but most recently the government has begun to provide job training and supervision to these workers.

An additional economic and political problem is income distribution. In 1980, twenty-six estates continued to cultivate 57 percent of the island's arable land; another 20 percent was divided among 28,000 small planters into lots that average 1.3 arpents; most of the remainder was cultivated by medium-size planters. Since small planters are less able to take advantage of improved production techniques, and since the large owners control more land and water resources, concentration is increasing. Nearly 21 percent of the labor force remains employed in sugar. To improve income distribution, wages have been increasing at unusually high rates, both for civil servants and for agricultural laborers. Using 1962 as a base year with an index of 100, by 1971 wages has increased to 143 and the cost of living to 119. By 1977 the wage index was 507 and the cost of living 261.[3] These wage increases, accompanied by taxes and other cost increases, have been a source of considerable concern for the sugar estates. Mechanization may provide some relief to the planters, but fewer jobs for the workers. It remains unclear whether the government has found the right balance between taxing the sugar estates and keeping an important sector of the economy solvent.

Efforts at diversification have met with minimal success. Sugar is as profitable as any other crop, and yields considerably more income per acre than tea, once considered the best alternative to sugar. Even so, Mauritius's development plans call for a reduction of the island's dependence on sugar. Vegetables, litchies, and particle board made from bagasse (sugarcane residue) have replaced tea as the prime target for diversification.

As the economic downturn began, the island was preparing for the 1976 general elections—the first to be held since 1967. While 21 parties proposed candidates for election, the real contest was between the MMM, the Labour party and the *Parti Mauricien*. The issues were clear. The Labour party had been in power for too long; its leadership was old and had lost touch with the people. (In fact many Labour leaders were not chronologically old; they began their political careers at a very young age, and had been around for a long time. Walter, Ringadoo, and Boolell were 54, 56, and 57 respectively at the time of the 1976 election, but they had been central figures in the Labour party for twenty years.) The average age of Labour candidates was 50; the average age of the MMM candidates was 32.[4]

The program of each party was coherent and clear—an unusual characteristic for election campaigns in many countries. The MMM provided a Marxist critique of Mauritian society. They proposed a program of gradual nationalization in all areas, price controls, free secondary education for all, and a foreign policy of neutrality— including closer relations with the Seychelles and the Malagasy Republic, the return of Diego Garcia, and a break in relations with South Africa. The MMM was adamant in its commitment to revoke legislation that Ramgoolam had introduced between 1969 and 1972 enhancing the power of the government to declare a state of emergency and to detain dissidents. The MMM was committed to change, but not to revolution. Its constituency was the people of Mauritius; it depicted the Independence party (the coalition of the Labour party, the IFB, and the CAM that ran in 1967) as a party for the elites, and charged that it would form a coalition with the *Parti Mauricien* after the election. The MMM was a class party. It if appeared anti-white it was because most whites were capitalists.

The *Parti Mauricien* program was a stark contrast. Duval argued that market mechanisms would stimulate the economy and lead to more jobs and prosperity. The Independence party was more practical, advocating limited nationalization in the sugar industry and continued industrialization, an approach opposed by the MMM.

At the last minute, Ramgoolam himself made a commitment to free secondary education—matching the MMM platform. His principal tactic, however, was to frighten voters away from the MMM, which his party accused of having communist links and inexperienced leadership. But Mauritians, and particularly young Mauritians, were ready for change.

Ninety percent of the eligible voters turned out—and the result was a shock to the Independent party. The MMM won 30 of the 62 seats in the Legislative Assembly and 41 percent of the popular vote. The Independence party, with 38 percent of the popular vote, won 25 seats, and the *Parti Mauricien* won only 7 seats (13 percent) and 17 percent of the vote. Once the best loser seats had been awarded, the MMM had 34 seats, the Independence party had 28, and the *Parti Mauricien* had only 8. Thirty-eight sitting deputies were defeated, including ten ministers and four parliamentary secretaries, among them prominent leaders, including both Duval and Walter. While the MMM had the largest number of seats, it did not have a majority. Ramgoolam was desperate—and was forced into another alliance with the *Parti Mauricien* to form a government. Even after he formed the alliance, he had only a margin of two seats.

The MMM's general election success was repeated in April 1977, when the MMM captured control of the municipal councils of Port Louis, Beau Bassin/Rose Hill, and Vacoas/Phoenix, leaving Duval and the *Parti Mauricien* entrenched in Curépipe and with a small majority in Quatres Bournes.

Ramgoolam was not happy, and appointed a special committee, headed by Ringadoo, to investigate the reasons for his setback. Ringadoo's committee identified a number of explanations, mostly tactical, noting, however, that the party had lost significant support among trade unions. Still, many Labour members were dissatisfied. Rather than join the MMM, some of them tried to set up a reform wing of that party. Harish Boodhoo, a religious leader from the south of the island, attacked the cronyism, corruption, and elitism of the Labour party and its leaders, and attracted considerable support— even among established business interests. For Boodhoo, a reformed Labour party was a far more palpable choice than an MMM government. Ramgoolam has been slow to respond to the possible split in the party. He did not replace his old friends in the 1976 elections, but the voters threw many of them out, choosing lesser-known, younger people rather than the old, familiar, and sometimes corrupt faces.

Meanwhile, the MMM began to have its own difficulties. Beranger's defeat in the municipal elections provided encouragement to his critics. And several members of the MMM crossed the floor of the Legislative Assembly to join the majority.

A malaise continued to envelope the country. In a questionnaire that received considerable publicity on the island, Mauritians appeared on one hand anxious for change, but on the other, generally satisfied. However, half the respondents said that if they had the opportunity they would be tempted to leave Mauritius and live in another country, and 75 percent said that they would advise their children to work in another country.[5]

The economic problems facing Ramgoolam and his alliance are structural. The Export Processing Zones are not the hoped-for solution to problems of investment, employment, and balance of payments. Mauritians are consuming over 80 percent of their disposable income. The balance of payments deficit has increased each year since 1976. The price of sugar continues to fluctuate wildly; it has been rising since November 1979, but sugar prices are unlikely to increase at the same rate as those of oil and other manufactured products.[6] International organizations have helped with loans, but ironically Mauritius is too prosperous to qualify for development assistance from the Agency for International Development. Ramgoolam has much to be proud of—an electrification program, pension plans, a declining birthrate, periods of economic growth, and extraordinary educational programs. He is a remarkable man with a record of impressive accomplishments, but his government will be hard pressed to provide new jobs, reduce inflation, and return the balance of payments to Mauritius's favor.

And the Mauritian government will have to find a way of engaging the large number of professionals in the life of the island. Immigration no longer provides the solution it once did, for the doors are closing even on the well-trained bilingual Mauritian population. Currently over 700 Mauritians are pursuing medical degrees in France, and over 7,000 students are enrolled in BA programs in India. These highly skilled people provide talent for civil service, industry, and politics that few newly independent countries can claim. National examination averages are reportedly higher in Mauritius than in London; educational achievements are all the more extraordinary when one realizes that most Mauritians take these examinations in their second language. Mauritians have sacrificed a great deal to provide

their children with high-quality educations, and now they want these
sacrifices to produce rewards in terms of high pay and high-status jobs
for their children.

In other countries political tension and economic decline have fostered intense and bitter divisions that have had destructive if not violent outcomes. The next phase of Mauritian history will test the
strength of the base of Mauritian unity on which the present system
of government has been established and will demonstrate just how
effective are the existing ways of dealing with conflict.

The highly diversified, pluralistic beginnings of Mauritius are written on the faces of the people elbowing each other on the streets of
Port Louis, and in the everyday words used when individuals from
each community come together to conduct business. All land, like
the sugar estates originally, is measured in arpents because that was
how the original French planters measured land. Money, on the
other hand, is measured in rupees, as the Indians measured it before
they came to the island. The English have gone as a governing force
and, for the most part, as residents, but their language, and many of
their ideas and values, linger.

Mauritius, as a case study, demonstrates the shift from class politics
to communal politics which occurred in most plural societies. It also
suggests the circumstances that promote the current return to class
politics. A close look at the history offers some possible reasons behind the shifts and the occasional outbreaks of serious violence. And
it demonstrates how, during decolonization, the British Colonial
Office failed to cope with communal differences in the colonies.

The process of decolonization in Mauritius was not easy. But
neither was it accompanied or followed by the extreme violence
associated with decolonization in many plural societies, including
Malaysia, Guyana, Nigeria, Burundi, and Sri Lanka. Communal divisions were strongest in Mauritius before independence, for unlike
the populations of most colonies who put aside communal differences
to join the independence movement, Mauritians could not agree on
the desirability of independence itself. The communal mistrust and
anxieties that pervaded the decade preceding independence were as
strong as they had ever been. Each community felt it would suffer in
extraordinary ways if it lost the struggle.

Communal attitudes toward independence were directly tied to the
place each community could expect to have, politically and numeri-

cally, in a future independent state; minorities felt that their very
survival would be threatened if the majority came to power. Duval
threatened—and according to some, provoked—violence, believing
that the British government would not grant independence to a country that was on the verge of political chaos.

In guiding its colonies toward independence, the British Colonial
Office devoted its energies to goals which now appear naive: introducing parliamentary government to the colonies, and ensuring a noncommunal basis for politics. Failure to find such a basis for politics
was once equated with failure of the colonial administration. For
example, Drummond Shields, parliamentary undersecretary of state
for the colonies from 1929 to 1931, believed that "the only hope for
success in the working of democratic institutions . . . is the breaking
up of these old communal bodies in their political activities into individuals and groups concerned with economic and social matters
which will create other interests cutting across communal boundaries."[7]

After serving as governor of Mauritius, Hilary Blood recognized the
need for special arrangements to ensure the representation of all
communities, but even he concluded, "Heaven forbid that it should
become permanent: that would be a confession of failure, an ac-
knowledgement of a racially divided state which cannot find a national unifying principle."[8]

Blood preferred to mold Mauritian society so that it would be
amenable to a British form of government, rather than admit that the
divisions within that society were permanent and find a more appropriate form of government. Since then we have seen enough of
communal divisions and plural societies to help us understand that in
most cases intense communal conflict will impede economic development, and that in some cases it is best simply to recognize the
permanence of communal conflict. Although the content of colonial
constitutions changed with new governments in Britain and new
developments in the colonies, the Colonial Office consistently believed that the institutions of government, including the electoral system, could influence the development of noncommunal politics. But
in fact, institutions could not hold back the growth of communalism.
The self-interest of politicians, the fear of one community by another, shaped communal politics more than the Colonial Office
could.

In Mauritius, political divisions in the 1930s were based on class differences. By the late 1950s, community had become the basis for political divisions, largely as a result of the extension of the franchise. As the political system was altered to incorporate large numbers of Mauritians, the candidates began to create communal constituencies and make communal appeals. If including more people in the process of government created a communal awareness, then the promotion of a multiparty system provided the means for the political expression of communal interests. The Colonial Office hoped that party politics would be based on ideology rather than community; but in the end the new party was a communal party. The Colonial Office was disturbed by these developments, but there was little their representatives could do. It was in the self-interest of the candidates to establish a political base, and that usually was a communal one.

The challenge for Mauritius was not to find a basis for lasting unity or for ending communal conflict, but to find methods for dealing with continual conflict. Even during the most bitter election campaigns, violence was minimal; there seems to be a precedent for the nonviolent resolution of conflict. Looking back, it is safe to say that this precedent ensured that the transfer of political power in Mauritius would be accepted, even if reluctantly, at each stage by all communities. Historically, violence in one part of Mauritius has had an impact throughout the island; Mauritians fear that once violence begins, they cannot escape it. The small size of the island, as well as the organization of its economic structure, further ensures that communities regularly come into contact with one another. In spite of the social divisions that are still maintained, the isolation that permits hatred to fester does not exist. However distasteful Ramgoolam may have been to the Creoles and the Franco-Mauritians, almost all of them knew someone who knew and thought well of him. This interdependence has helped the Franco-Mauritian community to relinquish peacefully its position of dominance to the Indians, the largest community; in turn, the Franco-Mauritians rely on the Indians for the preservation of civil order and for the labor necessary to maintain the sugar estates.

Keeping reciprocal dependence in good condition is an important factor in the continuing process of resolving conflict peacefully. While the Franco-Mauritians wondered if their contribution to Mauritian society would be accepted by the Indian majority, their fears have, to this point, been unfounded.

For the moment, Mauritians of all communities understand that their current system of government represents many hours of delicate negotiations among communities, during which the British government served as a mediator. The costs of raising constitutional issues once again would undoubtedly be very great and could lead to violence. Mauritians are growing accustomed to some form of democratic government—and because Mauritius is so small, most Mauritians know someone participating at some level in the government, a contact that gives them some stake in a continuing form of government. Furthermore, in a state too small to have a military force, the prospect of a military dictatorship can be ruled out.

Mauritians have learned that political differences exacerbate communal differences, and it is generally agreed that communalism stands in the way of economic development. Contentious politics now would be at the price of economic prosperity. In a time of economic growth, to many Mauritians the risk of sparking these differences is unthinkable. But a dramatic shift in the economic climate could make these risks appear negligible. Communal loyalties, once felt intensely and articulated daily, are always just under the surface and, given the right conditions, could be easily aroused.

During the period of decolonization, Mauritians gained experience in living with these communal tensions, experience which may be of some help in the future. For the moment, Mauritians seem to be willing to compromise, to respect and live with their communal differences. There is an overall tolerance of other ethnic groups and other cultures. There is, for now, a "peace within the feud."[9]

APPENDIXES

Appendix A

Brief Chronology

8th Century	—Island appears on Arab charts.
1500-1530	—Portuguese land on Mauritius.
1598	—Dutch claim and name the island.
1710	—Dutch abandon the island to pirates.
1721	—French settlers arrive and name the island Ile de France.
1744	—First sugar factory established.
1810	—British capture the island.
1813	—Slave trade abolished.
1814	—Treaty of Paris signed ceding Mauritius to the British.
1825	—First Council of Government established.
1829	—Color bar abolished.
1835	—Emancipation of slaves; slaves given four-year apprenticeships before freedom.
183?	—Indian immigrants arrive. Immigration begins.
1871	—Indians petition government to improve labor conditions.
1872	—Commission of Inquiry into conditions for laborers on the estates.
1886	—Constitutional revisions: Legislative Council includes ten elected members.
1907	—*Action Liberale* campaign; reform campaign begins.
1909	—Commission of Inquiry into the finances of the island.
1911	—*Action Liberale* defeated in election campaign that ends in riots.
1919	—Retrocession movement begins.
1920	—Retrocessionists defeated in elections.
1936	—Founding of the Mauritius Labour Party.

1937	—Widespread riots on the sugar estates.
1943	—Riots on estates in the north.
1947	—New constitution granted.
1948	—Elections begin substantial change in political life of the island.
1953	—Significant defeat for Franco Mauritians; two-party system begins to develop.
1954	—Discussions regarding constitutional change begin.
1955	—Debate over proportional representation begins.
1956	—Ministerial system introduced.
1958	—Trustram-Eve Commission resolves debate in favor of the Labour Party.
1959	—New constitution promulgated.
1959	—Elections. CAM-Labour alliance successful.
1960	—Cyclones; government efforts to promote family planning fail.
1961	—Constitutional conference results in significant advances toward self-government.
1963	—Elections. Significantly sharpened communalism; some strengthening of *Parti Mauricien*.
1965	—Riots at Trois Boutiques; constitutional conference results in definition of terms for an election that would precede a vote on the final status of the island.
1967	—Elections. Independence Party (alliance of Labour, IFB, CAM) wins.
1968	—Independence.

Appendix B

British Governors

Sir Robert Townsend Farquhar	1810
Sir Galbraith Lowry Cole	1823
Sir Charles Colville	1828
Sir William Nicolay	1833
Sir Lionel Smith	1840
Sir William Gomm	1842
Sir George Anderson	1849
Sir James Macaulay Higginson	1851
Sir William Stevenson	1857
Sir Henry Barkly	1863
Sir Arthur Hamilton Gordon	1871
Sir Arthur Purves Phayre	1874
Sir George Ferguson Bowen	1879
Sir Frederic Napier-Broome	1880

Sir John Pope-Hennessy	1883
Sir Charles Cameron Lees	1889
Sir Hubert Edward Henry Jerringham	1892
Sir Charles Bruce	1897
Sir Cavendish Boyle	1904
Sir John Robert Chancellor	1911
Sir Hesketh Bell	1916
Sir Herbert Read	1925
Sir Wilfred Jackson	1930
Sir Bede Clifford	1937
Sir Donald Mackenzie-Kennedy	1942
Sir Hilary Blood	1949
Sir Robert Scott	1954
Sir Colville Montgomery Deverell	1959
Sir John Rennie	1962–1968

Appendix C

Selected List of Mauritian Newspapers

Advance: Paper of the Mauritius Labour Party.
Le Cerneen: Paper of the planters.
Congress: Paper of the All Mauritius Hindu Congress.
L'Express: Independent paper, supportive of lower—and middle-class interests.
Hindustani: Paper to promote interests of Indians, founded by Manilal Doctor.
Le Mauricien: Paper of the *Parti Mauricien*. Prior to the founding of the *Parti Mauricien*, represented the interests of the Creole intellectuals.
L'Oeuvre: Socialist paper of Dr. Edgar Millien.
Planters' Gazette: Paper of the planters.
Le Radical: Paper of the planters.

Appendix D

Selected List of Political Organizations

Action Liberale: Group of young Creole and Franco-Mauritians advocating reform between 1907 and 1911.
All Mauritius Hindu Congress: Party of lower-caste Hindus.
Comité d'Action Muselman: Muslim party that shifted alliances between the *Parti Mauricien* and the Labour Party. Eventually settled into alliance with the Labour Party.
Democrats: Opposed Pope-Hennessy, favored broader reform.

Independence Party: Alliance of the Labour Party, the Independent Forward Bloc, and All Mauritius Hindu Congress for the 1967 and subsequent elections.

Independent Forward Bloc: Founded by Sookdeo Bissoondoyal, political party with explicit Indian nationalist platform.

Labour Party: Party of the laborers, later became a primarily Hindu party in support of independence.

Mouvement Militant Mauricien: Multiracial party organized to oppose the Independence Party after Independence.

Oligarchs: Party of the planters, supported Pope-Hennessy reforms and the *Action Liberale*.

Parti Mauricien (Later *Parti Mauricien Social Democrat*): Party of the planters and Creoles. Later reached out to Indian community opposed to responsible government and then Independence.

Ralliement Mauricien: Preceded *Parti Mauricien*.

Retrocessionists: Group of people promoting Mauritius's return to France.

Revisionists: Group of people promoting constitutional change in the late 1920s.

Société de Bienfaisance des Travailleurs: Associated with the Labour Party, specifically to promote the well-being of the laborers in the 1930s.

Tamil United Party: Party organized in 1961 to promote Tamil interests.

Union Mauricien: Party of the Creole elite in the 1930s.

NOTES

Chapter 1

1. Nicholas Pike, *Sub-Tropical Rambles* (New York, 1873), p. 55.

2. See especially Charles Grant, *The History of Mauritius* (London, 1801); Pike, *Sub-Tropical Rambles;* Bernardin de Saint-Pierre, *Paul et Virginie* (Paris, 1838); August Toussaint, *Port Louis, Deux Siècles d'Histoire* (Port Louis, 1936).

3. I have followed the Mauritian practice of using the words "community" and "communal" to describe ethnic and/or religious groups that usually act as a political unit.

4. Governor Bruce was most scornful of the Chinese, calling them the "carpetbaggers" of the colony, because "they have always acquired a monopoly of the retail provision trade by methods which I have always regretted. They have made this branch of trade subsidiary of the retail liquor trade, of which they also have a monopoly, and profits of the trade enable them to undercut competition in the provision trade." Mauritius Archives/ S.D.156: Bruce to Chamberlain, 14 October 1901.

5. The term "Creole," which in some French colonies referred to Frenchmen born in the colonies, in Mauritius originally referred to the lower classes of the colored population. Today it is used more freely to refer to all those who are mulatto or black. I shall follow this usage.

6. *Mauritius Chamber of Agriculture, 1853–1953*, Table on Drought and Cyclone Frequency.

7. Mauritius Chamber of Agriculture, *President's Report 1973–1974*, Table 2, p. iv.

8. F. Northcoombs, *Mes Champs et Mon Moulin* (Port Louis, 1950), p. 419.

9. James Meade, *Economic and Social Structure of Mauritius* (London, 1961), p. 63.

10. *Report of the Mauritius Royal Commission, 1909*, Cd. 5185 (London, 1910), p. 8 (hereafter cited as *Swettenham Report*).

11. W. A. B. Hopkin, *Policy of Economic Development in Mauritius.* Sessional Paper No. 6 of 1966 (Port Louis, 1966).

12. Burton Benedict, *Indians in a Plural Society* (London, 1961), p. 46. More recent data by occupation and community are not available. The government believes that such information could have a divisive impact on the island.

13. The 1872 Royal Commissioners called Creole "a barbarous and corrupt jargon, utterly useless to anyone beyond the narrow limits of Mauritius." *Report of the Royal Commissioners Appointed to Enquire into the Treatment of Immigrants in Mauritius*, Cd. 1115 (London, 1875), p. 499 (hereafter cited as *Frere and Williamson*). In 1974 the Prime Minister asked Mauritian television not to use Creole and forbade the Mauritius College of the Air from using Creole as a teaching medium.

14. Albert Hourani, "Lebanon, The Development of a Political Society," in Leonard Binder, ed., *Politics in Lebanon* (New York, 1956).

15. Burton Benedict, *Problems of Smaller Territories* (London, 1967), p. 53.

16. Maurice Caperon, *Saint Pierre and Miguelon* (Paris, 1900), p. 21, quoted in William Christian, *Divided Island* (Cambridge, Mass., 1969), p. 131.

Chapter 2

1. P. J. Barnwell and A. Toussaint, *A Short History of Mauritius* (London, 1949), p. 76. "Colored" refers to those people usually of mixed race (but occasionally black) who were freed from slavery. The term is still used on Mauritius to refer to people of mixed race.

2. *Acte de Capitulation de l'Ile de France*, 3 December 1810. Twice during the nineteenth century Mauritians organized to accuse the British of violating the terms of capitulation. When slavery was abolished in the 1830s, Mauritians accused the British of unlawfully seizing their private property. Then in 1845 the government began a campaign to force the English language and Protestant religion upon the Mauritians (D. Napal, *Les Constitutions de l'Ile Maurice*, Port Louis, 1962, p. 79). The legal system is still largely French, although only the civil and commercial portions of the Napoleonic Code were applied in Mauritius. The penal code had not been introduced in France by 1810 (Anton Bertram, *The Colonial Service*, Cambridge, 1930, p. 153).

3. Under the terms of the treaty, Réunion was returned to France. Because the island lacked a good harbor, it was of little use to Britain. However, the British kept Mauritius, not wanting the island to be used again as a port for ships intent on disrupting trade in the Indian Ocean.

4. Arago, *Voyage Autour du Monde* (Paris, 1839), p. 261, quoted in Auguste Toussaint, *Port Louis, Deux Siècles d'Histoire* (Port Louis, 1936), p. 272. For a lively account of Port Louis just after the British occupation of the island, see Toussaint, *Port Louis*, pp. 267–273.

5. Toussaint, *Port Louis*, pp. 271, 273. Charles Darwin noted in his jour-

nal with amazement the number of bookstores on the island when he visited in 1836.

6. Interview with Sir Hilary Blood, London, March 1967.

7. *Report of the Committee on Immigration from India to the Crown Colonies and Protectorates, Minutes of Evidence*, Cd. 5193 (London, 1910), p. 351 (hereafter cited as *Sanderson Report, Evidence*); Sir Arthur Hamilton Gordon, *Mauritius, Records of Private and Public Life 1871-1874* (Edinburg, 1894) vol. II, p. 176. Gordon told the Sanderson Commission:

> In Mauritius the planters habitually thought they could [and they did] influence the magistrates—domineer over them. A planter would write to a magistrate and request him to punish so and so, without even going through the form of laying a complaint against him, and they were amazingly astonished, and excessively angry, when a magistrate came who summoned the planter to come and give his evidence. He said he had never been so insulted in his life, and that all friendly relations between them must cease for the future. (*Sanderson Report, Evidence*, pp. 351, 352.)

8. C.O. 882/ 11, No. 148, p. 4: Sir Hesketh Bell, Governor, to J. H. Thomas, Secretary of State, 28 February 1924.

9. This slogan was first pronounced by General Charles Gordon, who was in command of the Royal Engineers in Mauritius from April 1881 to April 1882, before he was invited to Khartoum (*Dictionary of Mauritian Biography*, p. 75).

10. To have expected the nominated members to oppose the government was unrealistic. They were appointed by the governor, and according to a circular dispatch of 1868, the secretary of state made it clear that he expected them to "cooperate with the Crown in its general policy and not to oppose the Crown on any important question without strong and substantial reason." Quoted in Martin Wight, *The Development of the Legislative Council, 1606–1945* (London, 1946), p. 112.

11. Napal, *Constitutions*, p. 96, Letters Patent Modifying the Council of Government, September 1885. The "official" members of the government were colonial civil servants who had special responsibility for the administration of an important aspect of the government; for example, the procureur-general and later the attorney general, the secretary for finance, and the colonial secretary were all official members of the legislature. The "unofficial" members were appointed by the governor and were generally wealthy and influential members of the elite. They often held their positions for long periods of time. Like the nominated members, they did not represent the people, and, since they relied on the governor for reappointment, they opposed the governor at some risk.

12. *Report of the Mauritius Royal Commission, 1909*, Cd. 5185 (London, 1910), p. 51 (hereafter cited as *Swettenham Report*; Cd. 5186, *Minutes of Evidence*, is cited as *Swettenham Report, Evidence*).

13. C.O. 882/6, No. 78, p. 7: Joseph Chamberlain, Secretary of State, to Charles Bruce, Governor, 28 February 1900.

14. Specific statistical information about the Creoles is hard to find, since census takers, aware of the difficulties of drawing a line between the Creoles and the Franco-Mauritians, lump the two together into the "General Population." This estimate is determined by subtracting those people whose forefathers spoke French and English, according to the 1972 census, from the General Population.

15. The only occupation Creoles consistently avoid is that of cane cutter. In a recent homicide case it was argued that the accused Creole could not have been guilty because the murder weapon was a *pioche*, a scythe for cutting cane. The defendant argued that a Creole would not be likely to use such a weapon.

16. In 1835 there were 24,695 freemen and 76,774 slaves. Barnwell and Toussaint, *Mauritius*, p. 159.

17. *Report of the Royal Commissioners Appointed to Enquire into the Treatment of Immigrants in Mauritius*, Cd. 1115 (London, 1875), p. 20 (hereafter cited as *Frere and Williamson*).

18. Barnwell and Toussaint, *Mauritius*, p. 255.

19. Sir Frank Swettenham, *Also and Perhaps* (London, 1912), p. 158.

20. *Report of the Commission of Enquiry into the Riots in Mauritius in January 1911* (Port Louis, 1911), p. 24.

21. Henry LeClezio, "People and Politics," in MacMillan, *Mauritius Illustrated* (1914) p. 138.

22. Retrocession to France was not a new idea. Ever since the British abolished the slave trade and finally slavery itself in Mauritius, some Franco-Mauritians had talked of returning the island to France. Sir Arthur Hamilton Gordon suggested exchanging Mauritius for French trading posts in India.

23. C.O. 822/11, No. 148, p. 4: Sir Hesketh Bell, Governor, to Thomas, 28 Feburary 1924; see also C.O. 167/826: J. Middleton, Acting Governor, to Milner, 19 April 1921.

24. C.O. 167/826: Henri LeClezio to Middleton, 21 April 1919.

25. C.O. 882/11, No. 148, p. 4: Bell to Thomas, 28 February 1924.

26. *Council of Government Debates*, 27 July 1920, p. 69; C.O. 167/833: Bell to Milner, 22 November 1920.

27. C.O. 882/11, No. 148, p. 6: Bell to Thomas, 28 February 1924. Emile Sauzier, a prominent Franco-Mauritian, provided the impetus for the movement at the inauguration of a statue of William Newton in 1922. Sauzier "expressed a strong hope that Mauritians would soon obtain a greater measure of control in the management of their affairs." But he did nothing to follow up his suggestion and took no part in the movement it sparked.

28. This phrase was taken directly from the Duke of Devonshire's statement of 1923 regarding the rights of Indians in Kenya.

29. *Debates*, 29 March 1927, p. 53.

30. C.O. 882/11, No. 148, p. 24: Amery to Grannum, Acting Governor, 24 March 1928.

Chapter 3

1. Of this total, 160,000 returned to India. (Burton Benedict, *Mauritius, Problems of a Plural Society*, London, 1965, p. 17.) See also S. B. Mookherji, *The Indenture System* (Calcutta, 1962).

2. Hugh Tinker, *A New System of Slavery* (Oxford University Press, 1974), pp. 55, 56. Tinker suggests that about one-third of the immigrants were from the low castes; another third were agriculturalists, and about one-fourth were Brahmans.

3. Roland LaMusse, "Economic Development of the Mauritius Sugar Industry," *Revue Agricole et Sucriere de l'Ile Maurice*, vol. 43, p. 115.

4. Report by John Francis Trotter, Special Commissioner appointed to enquire into the workings of the immigration agencies of Mauritius in Madras and Calcutta. *Minutes of Proceedings of the Mauritius Council of Government, 1884*, p. 27.

5. Memorandum by Gordon comparing labor laws in the West Indies and Mauritius, p. 17.

6. *Report of the Commission to Enquire into Abuses Alleged to Exist in the Export of Coolies to Mauritius and Demerera*, 1840.

7. Limited emigration continued illegally in spite of the prohibition. Tinker, *A New System of Slavery*, p. 70.

8. Governor Barkly to the Duke of Buckingham, Secretary of State, quoted in *Report of the Royal Commissioners Appointed to Enquire into the Treatment of Immigrants in Mauritius*, Cd. 1115 (London, 1875), p. 106 (hereafter cited as *Frere and Williamson*); Adolphe de Plevitz, *Petition of the Old Immigrants* (London, 1871).

9. A photograph was required to obtain a pass. In five years, the Immigration Office photographer collected £23,311 from immigrants. (Sir Arthur Hamilton Gordon, *Mauritius, Records of Private and Public Life, 1871-1874*, London, 1875, vol. I, p. 526.) Mookherji, *The Indenture System*, p. 50.

10. *Frere and Williamson*, p. 169.

11. Gordon to Kimberley, 27 June 1872, quoted in Gordon, *Mauritius*, vol. I, p. 619. Gordon felt that the system of indenture in Trinidad, where he had previously served as governor, helped the laborers in that it provided ways of obtaining wealth and property. In Mauritius, he said, the immigrants "were turned into vagrants and miserable wretches." *Report of the Committee on Immigration from India to the Crown Colonies and Protectorates, Minutes of Evidence*, Cd. 5193 (London, 1910), p. 352 (hereafter cited as *Sanderson Report, Evidence*).

12. Gordon, *Mauritius*, vol. II, p. 168.

13. There were, however, isolated incidents, as in 1904, when immigrants on Beauchamp Estate rioted to protest against inferior rice and unsatisfactory medical care and when other immigrants on Mon Desert Estate assaulted their managers and overseers before they were frightened away by police fire.

14. *Council of Government Debates*, 13 October 1908, pp. 476, 477. Edward Bateson, Stipendary Magistrate in Mauritius from 1901 to 1903, told the

Sanderson Commission, "It was difficult to see what use it was sending these people to prison, because prison fare did not appear to be any worse than what they got outside." *Sanderson Report, Evidence*, pp. 371, 372.

15. Tinker, *A New System of Slavery*, p. 200.

16. *Debates*, 5 October 1908, p. 370.

17. *Sanderson Report*, p. 31.

18. K. M. Singh, *Report on His Deputation to Mauritius* (Delhi, 1925), p. 26.

19. Nicholas Pike, *Sub-Tropical Rambles* (New York, 1873), p. 472.

20. *Frere and Williamson*, p. 507.

21. Singh, *Deputation to Mauritius*, pp. 8, 9. Education continued to be a privilege mainly for the general population. In 1944, the same number of children (18,000) from the Indo-Mauritian community and from the general population were in primary school, and yet the number of school-age Indians was nearly twice that of school-age general population children. *1944 Census*, p. 23.

22. *Debates*, 13 October 1908, pp. 476, 477.

23. *Report of the Mauritius Royal Commission, 1909, Minutes of Evidence*, Cd. 5186 (London, 1910), paras. 378, 379 (hereafter cited as *Swettenham Report, Evidence*).

24. *Swettenham Report*, pp. 58, 59.

25. C.O. 882/6, no. 78, p. 8: Bruce to Chamberlain, 25 June 1900.

26. *Bi-annual Digest of Statistics*, June 1968, p. 5.

27. Barton Schwartz, *Caste in Overseas Indian Communities* (San Francisco, 1967) p. 2.

28. *Swettenham Report*, p. 120.

29. *Hindustani*, 15 March 1908.

20. *Swettenham Report*, p. 51.

31. Marcel Cabon, *Biographie de Ramgoolam* (Port Louis, 1965), passim. Interviews with Seewoosagur Ramgoolam, April 1966.

32. R. K. Boodhun, *Indian Centenary Book* (Port Louis, 1936), p. 26.

Chapter 4

1. Answering a Colonial Office request, the acting governor, Edward Walter Evans, provided the following sketches of Rivet and Laurent:

> E. Laurent: A man of considerable vigour, both physical and mental. Tough without a touch of sensitiveness, obviously enjoys the rough and tumble of local politics and would hate to be out of it, but he is untrustworthy and he is shrewd and can hold and propound sound views when they do not interfere with his political manoeuvres. He has a big influence with the coloured element and for that reason the white element is anxious to "keep him sweet."

> Rivet: Has none of the coarse grained features of Laurent. Has a clear mind and incisive powers of expression. His 'tournure d'esprit'

is obviously French. Politically the driving force behind him is a sense of racial bitterness. He is too aloof and fastidious to become a popular leader of colour though his influence amongst the better educated Creoles is considerable.

2. C.O. 167/868, file 34607: The correspondence in this file suggests that the Colonial Office was bored with Mauritius's economic problems and annoyed that the help already provided had not placed the island's finances on a sound footing.

3. *Financial Situation of Mauritius: Report of a Commission Appointed by the Secretary of State for the Colonies* (London, 1932), Cmd. 4034, pp. 189, 190, 208.

4. D. Napal, *Les Constitutions de l'Ile Maurice* (Port Louis, 1962), p. 106. Letters Patent concerning the Council of Government, 18 April 1933.

5. *Report on Mauritius 1929*, p. 35.

6. *Le Mauricien*, 7 October 1937.

7. C.O. 167/889, file 17153: Jackson to MacDonald, 15 October 1935.

8. F. North-Coombs, *Mes Champs et Mon Moulin* (Port Louis, 1950) pp. 139, 140.

9. C.O. 167/889, file 17153: Jackson to H. R. Cowell, Assistant Secretary at the Colonial Office, 19 November 1935.

10. *Report of the Commission of Enquiry into Unrest on Sugar Estates in Mauritius, 1937* (Port Louis, 1938), p. 166 (hereafter cited as *Hooper Report*).

11. Estates with factories grew 25.9 tons per acre in 1938. *Mauritius Chamber of Agriculture President's Report 1965-1966* (Port Louis, 1966), p. iv.

12. *Le Mauricien*, 14 January 1938.

13. C.O. 854/78: Circular dispatch, 15 September 1930; C.O. 854/97: Circular dispatch, 9 November 1935.

14. C.O. 167/890, file 57027: Jackson to Thomas, 17 March 1936.

15. *Le Mauricien*, 4 July 1935.

16. *Le Nouveau Journal*, 16 December 1935; *Planters Gazette*, 20 December 1935.

17. *Le Mauricien*, 25 February 1936; Labour party manifesto, *Le Mauricien*, 20 February 1936.

18. Interview with Sir Bede Clifford, Guildford, England, February 1966.

19. C.O. 167/897, file 57227: Jackson to Ormbsy-Gore, 27 May 1937.

20. C.O. 167/890, file 57004: Minute by C. Carstairs, Assistant Principal, Colonial Office, 18 April 1936.

21. Report of a Special Committee to the Governing Body of the ILO, 1937, appendix II. Correspondence between the ILO and the Colonial Office suggests that the British officials working in the ILO Secretariat did not want to take any action without consulting the Colonial Office. C.O. 167/894, file 57004: C. W. H. Weaver to J. C. Hibbert, Principal at the Colonial Office, 23 October 1936; Hibbert to Weaver, 25 December 1936; Weaver to Hibbert, 28 December 1936.

22. Interview with Curé, London, September 1965; Mauritius Labour Party Minutes, 5 May 1937.

23. The Mauritius Chamber of Agriculture has had representatives in London nearly continuously since 1856. See *Mauritius Chamber of Agriculture, 1853-1953*, pp. 61-62.

24. Minutes of the Mauritius Labour Party, 11 August 1938; interview with Sahadeo, Mauritius, May 1966. Finding new friends in politics, Sahadeo retired from the Labour party in 1946 and founded Mauritius's only ashram.

25. *Hooper Report*, pp. 82-97. On 11 July 1937, someone in the crowd shouted in Hindi, "Let's strike." Curé did not understand him, but Pandit Sahadeo grabbed the microphone and said that "strike was not the purpose of the party." *Le Mauricien*, 23 August 1937. Under Article 341 of the penal code, advocating a strike could have brought a three-month jail sentence.

26. C.O. 167/897, file 57227: Jackson to Ormsby-Gore, 27 May 1937.

27. C.O. 167/894, file 51227: Minute by Dawe, 30 August 1937.

28. *Hooper Report*, p. 83.

29. In 1936 sugar prices reached the depression low of Rs 10.99 per 100 kilos. By 1937, prices had risen above levels of 1934, 1935, and 1936 to Rs 12.21 per 100 kilos. *Mauritius Chamber of Agriculture 1853-1953*, Appendix.

30. *Hooper Report*, p. 120.

31. This account of the riots is drawn from the *Hooper Report* and evidence before the Hooper Commission which was printed in *Le Mauricien* in 1937.

32. *Hooper Report*, p. 23.

33. Alfred Britter, *A Commentary on Facts* (Port Louis, 1938), p. viii.

34. Britter, *A Commentary on Facts*, p. 45.

35. *Le Mauricien*, 18 November 1937.

36. R. K. Boodhun, *The Philosophy of Labour and Strike* (Rose Hill, Mauritius, 1937), p. 13.

37. *Report of the Royal Commission to the West Indies, 1938* (London, 1945), Cmd. 6607 (hereafter cited as *Moyne Report*).

38. *Moyne Report*, p. 8.

39. Interview with Sir Bede and Lady Clifford, Guildford, England, February 1966.

40. C.O. 167/897, file 57172: Clifford to Ormsby-Gore, 9 November 1937.

41. *Ibid.*, Minute by P. Rogers, 13 December 1937.

Chapter 5

1. Rita Hinden, *Empire and After* (London, 1949), p. 138.

2. For an example of the planters' opposition to change, see the debates on the Industrial Associations Ordinance, April and May 1938, and on the Labour Ordinance, September, October, and November 1938. As Clifford wrote:

> Changes had to be made, but as the estate owners and their friends predominated in the Executive and Legislative Councils, it was necessary to proceed slowly with the introduction of new labour laws. . . . To have attempted anything more advanced too soon

would have led to delay and even chaos; as the legislature had to be persuaded to pass the new laws it was necessary to hasten slowly.

Clifford to author, December 1968.

3. Clifford to author, December 1968.

4. C.O. 167/897, file 57172: Clifford to Ormsby-Gore, 9 November 1938.

5. *Report on the Enquiry into the Conduct and Affairs of the Société de Bienfaisance des Travailleurs de l'Ile Maurice* (Port Louis, 1938). The enquiry was conducted by the procureur-general, S. A. Hooper, who chaired the commission investigating the 1937 riots.

6. The strike initially began over the dismissal of one docker for insubordination. For an account of the strike, see *Le Mauricien*, 2-10 September, and Bede Clifford, *Proconsul* (London, 1964), pp. 232, 233. The dockers' specific demands included the reinstatement of a dismissed man and an increase in pay that Clifford considered preposterous. (Interview with Clifford, Guildford, England, February 1966.)

7. Clifford to author, December 1968. Clifford was particularly concerned about the possibility of island-wide riots similar to those in 1937. Trouble on the estates was already brewing. On 5 September, Trianon Estate had been disrupted and laborers arrested; the cane fields at another estate had been burned.

8. *Le Mauricien*, 4 July 1938.

9. *Le Mauricien*, 3 May 1940.

10. Curé to MacDonald, n.d., Curé Papers.

11. Ridley, *Report on the Condition of Indians in Mauritius* (New Delhi, 1941), hereafter cited as *Ridley Report*; Major Granville Orde-Browne, *Labour Conditions in Ceylon, Mauritius and Malaya* (London, 1943), Cmd. 6423 (hereafter cited as *Orde-Browne Report*).

12. Interview with Ramnarain, Mauritius, August 1967.

13. *Ridley Report*, pp. 39, 40. Ridley's trip to Mauritius was prompted by articles in the Indian press about conditions in Mauritius.

14. *Orde-Browne Report*, p. 71.

15. *Ibid.*, p. 62.

16. Ramnarain Papers, Twining to Ramnarain, 16 March 1943.

17. For an account of the riot in September 1943, see *Report of the Commission of Enquiry into the Disturbances which Occurred in the North of Mauritius in 1943* (Port Louis, 1944), pp. 18-23 (hereafter cited as *Moody Report*).

18. *Le Cerneen, Le Mauricien, Advance,* 20 November 1943.

19. *Moody Report*, pp. 32-68.

20. Fabian Colonial Bureau Papers, Box 170, file 1: Report by Rita Hinden on Mauritius. (Undated but presumably Autumn 1943.)

21. Ken Baker, *Trade Unionism in Mauritius* (Port Louis, 1946), p. 1. The name Industrial Association was chosen by Clifford, who hoped that employers as well as employees would organize.

22. Burton Benedict, *Indians in a Plural Society* (London, 1961), pp. 138,

139, 145, 146. In 1954 there were 463 *baitkas* in Mauritius (*Report of a Census and Survey of Baitkas*, Port Louis, 1957).

23. Baker's ideas are clearly set forth in his lengthy correspondence with Rita Hinden, Fabian Colonial Bureau Papers, Box 170, file 1; Box 171, file 1.

24. Fabian Colonial Bureau Papers, Box 171, file 1; Baker to Hinden, 6 October 1946.

25. Mackenzie-Kennedy Diaries, 21 January 1943.

26. Fabian Colonial Bureau Papers, Box 170, file 1; Baker to Hinden, 16 May 1945.

27. Ramnarain Papers. Report of a Meeting at Goodlands, 21 January 1945. Ramnarain was not the only political leader to urge his followers to give up drinking or other habits associated with a European way of life. Strict moral codes characterized the Black Muslim movement in America, the FLN in Algeria, the Mau Mau in Kenya, and other less militant nationalist groups, such as the Neo-Destour Party in Tunisia and TANU in Tanzania.

28. *Annual Report of the Labour Department*, 1947, p. 8.

29. Mackenzie-Kennedy Diaries, 18 January 1946.

30. Among the most prominent of the independent school movements which were directly tied to nationalist parties were the Kenya Independent School Association and the Moroccan Free Schools. Some form of independent school movement was the rule rather than the exception in colonial territories.

31. *Statesman*, 12 August 1939.

32. Interview with Basdeo Bissoondoyal, Port Louis, August 1967. Bissoondoyal's father was a job contractor; his grandfather was a planter. If he had been educated in England instead of India, he would probably have been part of the professional elite.

33. Mackenzie-Kennedy Diaries, 19 January 1947.

Chapter 6

1. Minutes of the Municipal Council, 23 December 1940; *Le Mauricien*, 13 December 1940.

2. *Council of Government Debates*, 13 June 1943, pp. 862-864.

3. *Minutes of the Council of Government*, 1938, 1939, p. 3.

4. *Hansard*, 11 November 1941, vol. 374, col. 2096.

5. Fabian Colonial Bureau Papers, Box 170, file 1: *Report on Mauritius*, 1943.

6. *Hansard*, 21 July 1943, vol. 391, col. 888, 889.

7. In 1944 the governor announced that he would proceed with elections under the existing constitution. *Advance* and *L'Oeuvre* both held that elections before constitutional change would only perpetuate the existing council, which belonged "in a museum of history." Ramgoolam also protested the elections. The governor eventually changed his mind (*Advance*, 1 September 1944; *L'Oeuvre*, 1 September 1944; *Debates*, 22 August 1944, p. 1350).

8. Fabian Colonial Bureau Papers, Box 170, file 2; report of a public meeting held 4 August 1946.

9. *Debates*, 13 February 1945, pp. 1-7.

10. C.O. 882/11, No. 148: Reynolds Rohan to Amery, 30 September 1927. Amery rejected communal representation as well as any other form of constitutional reform. C.O. 882/11, No. 148: Amery to E. A. Grannum, Acting Governor, 24 March 1928.

11. Clifford to author, December 1965.

12. *Ceylon, Report of the Special Commission on the Constitution* (London, 1928), Cmd. 3131, p. 39. See also W. J. M. Mackenzie, *Free Elections* (Manchester, 1957), p. 35.

13. Mackenzie-Kennedy Papers, Jackson to Mackenzie-Kennedy, 14 February, no year, presumably 1946 or 1947. Jackson went on to say "Mauritius is *sui generis*, nearly every place is, and is really unfitted for democratic procedures, but what can one do in the present political Tower of Babel that has seized the world."

14. Chief Secretary's Office, Minutes of the First Consultative Committee, memorandum by Jules LeClezio, April 1945.

15. Chief Secretary's Office, Minutes of the First Consultative Committee, memorandum by Edgar Laurent, April 1945.

16. Clifford to author, December 1965.

17. Chief Secretary's Office, Minutes of the First Consultative Committee, memorandum by Rivet, April 1945.

18. Mackenzie-Kennedy diaries, 23 May 1945.

19. J. M. Lee, *Colonial Development and Good Government* (Oxford, 1967), p. 68.

20. *Le Cerneen, Le Mauricien, Advance*, 30 October 1946; *The Times*, 31 October 1946.

21. Mackenzie-Kennedy Diaries, 26 February 1945; interview with B. Bissoondoyal, August 1967.

22. Minutes of the Second Consultative Committee, 13 November 1946; 6 November 1946; 15 January 1947. Fabian Colonial Bureau Papers, Box 171, file 1; Ramgoolam to Hinden, 19 February 1946.

23. Chief Secretary's Office, Minutes of the First Consultative Committee, Speech by Seeneevassen, 20 April 1945.

24. Minutes of the Second Consultative Committee, 22 November 1946.

25. *Ibid.*, Memorandum to Donald Mackenzie-Kennedy from A. Gellé, R. Hein, A. Raffray, R. Rivet, E. Laurent, J. Koenig, and A. Nairac.

26. Correspondence with the Secretary of State for the Colonies (Port Louis, 1947), Mackenzie-Kennedy to Creech-Jones, 21 April 1947, p. 1.

27. *Report on Mauritius*, 1947, pp. 4, 5.

28. Martin Wight, *British Colonial Constitutions* (Oxford, 1952), p. 16. Universal suffrage was first introduced in Jamaica, Trinidad, and Barbados. It was introduced in the Gold Coast in 1949.

Chapter 7

1. Burton Benedict, *Indians in a Plural Society* (London, 1961), p. 28.

2. B. Keith Lucas, "Introduction" in T. E. Smith, *Elections in Developing*

Countries (London, 1960), p. xi. See also W. J. M. Mackenzie, *Free Elections* (Manchester, 1957).

3. *Report on Mauritius*, 1948, p. 2.

4. Mauritius Labour Party Minutes, 15 May 1948.

5. Interview with J. N. Roy, Mauritius, August 1967.

6. Fabian Colonial Bureau Papers, Box 171, file 3; Rozemont to Hinden, September 1948.

7. By 1953, J. N. Roy called Rivet "a mediaeval bourgeois freshly dropped from the moon." *Advance*, 22 August 1953.

8. *Le Cerneen, Le Mauricien, Advance*, 19 August 1948.

9. *Ibid.*, 30 September 1948.

10. *Ibid.*, a reprint of a memorandum from the Muslim community to Creech-Jones; Moomtaz Emrith, *Muslims in Mauritius* (Port Louis, 1967), p. 131.

11. Interview with Hilary Blood, March 1967.

12. *Legislative Council Debates*, 1 September 1948, pp. 5-6.

13. *Report on Mauritius*, 1949, p. 1.

14. *Report on Mauritius*, 1950, p. 2.

15. *Debates*, 23 November 1948, pp. 33-34.

16. *Debates*, 31 May 1951, p. 15; *Advance*, 15 April 1952.

17. J. H. Gorvin, *Report of the Mauritius Economic Commission, 1947-48* (Port Louis, 1948, 1949), parts I and II.

18. Newton to author, 25 May 1969.

19. *Legislative Council Debates*, 1 September 1948, pp. 5-6; *Le Cerneen*, 4 November 1955; *Advance*, 9 September 1949; *Le Cerneen*, 25 October 1951.

20. *Le Cerneen*, 17 April 1951.

21. *Advance*, 20 August 1953.

22. *Advance*, 8 September 1953.

23. *Le Mauricien*, 24 December 1952.

24. *Le Cerneen*, 12 April 1953.

25. Interview with Jules Koenig, Mauritius, July 1966; Newton to author, 25 May 1969.

26. *Constitutional Development in Mauritius*, Scott to Lennox-Boyd, 7 January 1955, p. 16.

27. In Mauritius the Labour party is referred to as either the *Parti Travaillists* or the Labour party, whereas the *Parti Mauricien*, reflecting its stronger French influence, is never called the Mauritian party. Although the founders carefully selected a name that would translate directly and easily, they themselves never used the English name, and no one else did either.

28. Newton to author, 25 May 1969.

Chapter 8

1. Lord Chandos, *Memoirs of Lord Chandos* (London, 1962), p. 352.

2. J. M. Lee, *Colonial Development and Good Government* (Oxford, 1967), p. 197.

3. Hilary Blood, "Parliament in Small Territories," in Alan Burns, *Parliament as an Export* (London, 1966), p. 249.

4. *Annual Report on District Administration*, 1947, p. 10.

5. Village Councils Ordinance, 1951 (Ordinance No. 75 of 1951).

6. Burton Benedict, *Indians in a Plural Society* (London, 1961), p. 149.

7. *Ceylon: Report of the Special Commission on the Constitution*, Cmd. 3131 (London, 1928).

8. *Council of Government Debates*, 8 December 1953, p. 12.

9. *Constitutional Development in Mauritius*, Sessional Paper No. 3 of 1956 (Port Louis, 1956), Robert Scott to Lennox-Boyd, 7 January 1955, pp. 4, 5.

10. Interview with Robert Scott, Exeter, February 1966.

11. Keith-Lucas Papers, Robert Newton to B. Keith-Lucas, 21 October 1955.

12. Interview with Robert Scott, Exeter, February 1966.

13. Newton to author, 25 May 1969.

14. *Constitutional Development in Mauritius*, Lennox-Boyd to Scott, 10 February 1956, pp. 47, 48.

15. *Debates*, 10 April 1956, Forget, p. 14; 11 May 1956, Ringadoo, p. 5; 24 April 1956, Ramgoolam, p. 24; 10 April 1956, Forget, pp. 12, 23.

16. *Debates*, 8 May 1956, pp. 15-33. Interview with Morris Abela, Advisor to the Government of Malta, Mauritius, August 1967.

17. *Debates*, 15 May 1956, p. 36.

18. Delegates to the 1957 Constitutional Conference consisted of Ramgoolam, Forget, Seeneevassen, Rault, Celestin, Nairac, Koenig, and Mohammed.

19. *Report of the Mauritius Electoral Boundary Commission*, Sessional Paper No. 1 of 1958 (Port Louis, 1958), p. 3 (hereafter cited as *Trustram-Eve Report*).

20. Interviews: Jules Koenig, Mauritius, July 1966; André Nairac, London, March 1967.

21. A barrister, Lord Silsoe served as chairman of the Local Government Boundaries Commission in England from 1945-1949.

22. *Trustram-Eve Report*, p. 18.

23. Interview with Koenig, Mauritius, July 1966; Newton later wrote, "I think in actual fact the Commission had exceeded their terms of reference. Trustram-Eve was a forceful character and determined to find a solution before his departure from Mauritius. But he found a way out of the *impasse* as later events showed." (Newton to author, 25 May 1969.)

24. *Debates*, 18 March 1958, p. 111; 25 March 1958, p. 140.

25. *Debates*, 28 March 1958, p. 272.

26. Interviews with Mohammed and Dahal, Mauritius, July 1966.

27. Seeneevassen's death in 1958 left a large void in Labour leadership, for he had been Ramgoolam's most trusted confidant.

28. Interview with Guy Forget, Mauritius, June 1966.

29. *Debates*, 21 April 1951, p. 7; 28 April 1953, p. 30.

30. Interview with Razack Mohammed, Mauritius, July 1966.
31. Interviews with Koenig and Bissoondoyal, Mauritius, July 1966.
32. *Report on Mauritius*, 1959, p. 1.
33. *Confidential Report on the Elections*, prepared in the Colonial Office, 1959.
34. *Confidential Report on the Elections*, 1959.
35. Interviews with Harold Walter, Mauritius, April 1966.
36. Newton to author, 25 May 1969.

Chapter 9

1. *The Times*, 2 March 1960.
2. *Council of Government Debates*, 12 April 1960, col. 1431.
3. *The Times*, 15 June 1960.
4. James Meade, *The Social and Economic Structure of Mauritius* (London, 1961), p. 41; see also H. C. Brookfield, "Mauritius: Demographic Upsurge and Prospects," *Population Studies*, Vol. XI, No. 2, 1957.
5. R. C. Wilkinson, *Project of Emigration from Mauritius to North Borneo* (Port Louis, 1951); *Report on a visit to Tanganyika Territory in June 1950* (Port Louis, 1950). See also: *Report of the Committee on Population, 1953-1954*, Sessional Paper No. 4 of 1955 (Port Louis, 1955); R. W. Luce, A *Time for Decision*, Sessional Paper No. 6 of 1958.
6. *Debates*, 12 April 1960, col. 427; 19 April 1960, col. 590-601.
7. Richard M. Titmuss and B. Abel-Smith, assisted by T. Lynes, *Social Policies and Population Growth in Mauritius* (London, 1961), p. 240.
8. *Debates*, 28 April 1961, col. 1396; 25 April 1961, col. 1428, 1429.
9. Action Familiale, a Catholic dominated organization founded in 1963, promoted only those methods approved by the Church. The Family Planning Association gave instruction in all contraceptive methods but emphasized the pill and later the I.U.D.
10. Meade, *Social and Economic Structure*, p. 230.
11. Interview with Harold Walter, Mauritius, April 1965.
12. J. M. Lee, *Colonial Development and Good Government* (Oxford, 1967), p. 71.
13. Interview with Deverell, London, March 1966.
14. Lee, *Good Government*, p. 71.
15. *L'Express*, 30 October 1963. Rault ran against Walter in Mahébourg in 1963 and won only 620 votes, after which he concluded that "Independents must rally to one of the national movements whose ideas are closest to theirs."
16. Interview with Ajum Dahal, Mauritius, July 1966.
17. *Advance*, 12 June 1961.
18. Burton Benedict, *Indians in a Plural Society* (London, 1961), p. 30.
19. *Advance*, 10 August 1964.
20. *Advance*, 29 July 1961.
21. *British Broadcasting Corporation Reports on the Mauritius Constitu-*

tional Review Conference, 1961, 29 June 1961 (hereafter cited as *BBC Reports*).

22. *BBC Reports*, 29 June 1961. This theme appeared often in *Parti Mauricien* speeches in 1961. *Advance*, 22 July 1961, reports Raymond Devienne as saying, "There must be no independence as long as there is a possibility of communism."

23. *BBC Reports*, 27 June 1961; 29 June 1961.

24. *Constitutional Development in Mauritius*. Sessional Paper No. 5 of 1961 (Port Louis, 1961), p. 5.

25. *Ibid.*, p. 7.

26. Mauritius Constitutional Review Conference Papers, 1961: Minutes of the 4th Plenary Session, 5 July 1961.

27. *Advance*, 24 October 1961.

28. A number of Labour party politicians disagree with this view. They argue that if the Colonial Office had really decided to back Ramgoolam, it would have outlined steps leading to independence in 1961. But in 1961 the status of small, non-self-supporting colonies was still in doubt, despite the French government's granting of independence to some small states in 1959. Independence had not yet been granted to Tanzania or Kenya, not to mention British Guiana and Trinidad, all larger countries with greater prospect of economic self-sufficiency. The policy of independence for the ministates developed after 1961, when plans for the independence of the Gambia, the Maldives, and the Southern African Protectorates were formulated.

29. T. Balogh and C. J. M. Bennett, *Commission of Inquiry, (Sugar Industry 1962)*, Sessional Paper No. 4 of 1963 (Port Louis, 1963).

30. *Report on Local Government 1968*, p. 4. Proclamation 12 of 1963.

31. Banwell Commission Papers. The General Elections, 1963. This document is a constituency by constituency report on the 1963 elections prepared by colonial officials in Mauritius for the Banwell Commission.

32. Rennie to Sandys, November 1963.

33. *Constitutional Development in Mauritius*, 1961, p. 6.

34. *L'Express*, 14 November 1963.

35. The allocation of the ministries was difficult. Labour wanted to palm off the always difficult Ministry of Labour on the *Parti Mauricien*. Koenig refused. Eventually this responsibility was given to Jomadar, whose trip to London twenty-five years earlier on behalf of the Labour party had caused Curé so much difficulty. The other Labour ministers were Ringadoo, who replaced the defeated Beejadhur as Minister of Education; Walter, who remained Minister of Works; Guy Forget, who remained Minister of Health; and Boolell, who had left the IFB to join Labour, Minister of Agriculture. Bissoondoyal became Minister of Local Government, a post from which he could easily build up his influence in the villages. For the *Parti Mauricien*, Koenig moved into the Attorney-General's chambers, and Duval took over the Ministry of Housing, a post formerly held by Mohammed.

36. Interview with Sir Seewoosagar Ramgoolam, Mauritius, July 1966.

37. Walter continually talked of threats to himself and his property by

Duval's men. In 1963 his car was attacked and overturned by five *Parti Mauricien* agents. *L'Express*, 15 March 1963.

38. It is unclear what form the "backing" took, but it seems likely that those who defected from the Labour party received money in return.

39. *Congress*, 23 February 1966.

40. This account of the Trois Boutiques incident is based on interviews and newspaper reports. It is confirmed by the "Confidential Police Report on the Disturbances at Trois Boutiques."

41. In 1964, the composition of the police was as follows: General Population 754, Hindu 427, Muslim 96, Chinese 40.

42. *L'Express*, 13 May 1965; *Mauritius Employers Federation Newsletter*, May 1965, claims that 103 were arrested.

43. *The Times*, 17 May 1965.

44. *Advance*, 12 April 1965.

45. Mauritius Constitutional Conference Papers, 1965: Memorandum of the Mauritius Labour Party, 14 August 1965.

46. *Ibid*.

47. Mauritius Constitutional Conference Papers, 1965: Proposals of the Independent Forward Bloc.

48. Mauritius Constitutional Conference Papers, 1965: Memorandum of the Muslim Committee of Action.

49. *Ibid*.

50. Mauritius Constitutional Conference Papers, 1965: Statement by Jean Ah-Chuen. Note of a meeting between Lord Taylor and the Hon. J. Ah-Chuen, 13 September 1965.

51. Mauritius Constitutional Conference Papers, 1965: Memorandum of the *Parti Mauricien Social Democrat*.

52. In 1965, Parliament had not yet considered legislation comparable to the 1968 Commonwealth Immigrants Act. But the British government was aware of and opposed to the possibility of large-scale immigration from the colonies.

53. At the time of the conference, Mauritius was selling 380,000 metric tons of sugar at the preferential price of £46 per ton and 270,000 tons at the world price of £18.25 per ton.

54. Mauritius Constitutional Conference Papers, 1965: Memorandum of the *Parti Mauricien*.

55. *Ibid*.

56. Mauritius Constitutional Conference Papers, 1965: Comment by Mauritius Labour Party on the paper by the *Parti Mauricien* on Association.

57. Mauritius Constitutional Conference Papers, 1965. Record of the 1st Meeting held in the Music Room, Lancaster House, 7 September 1965.

58. Mauritius Constitutional Conference Papers, 1965: Record of the 6th Plenary Session, 17 September 1965.

59. *Report of the Mauritius Constitutional Conference 1965*, Sessional Paper No. 6 of 1965 (Port Louis, 1965), p. 21.

60. *Ibid*., p. 4.

61. *Ibid*., p. 21.

Chapter 10

1. *Hansard*, 5th Series, 27 May 1965, vol. 713, col. 817.

2. *Financial Times*, 11 November 1965.

3. *Le Mauricien*, 6 December 1965. Evidence is inconclusive, but a number of highly placed officials suggest that Britain and the United States would have been willing to pay more than £3m. for the islands. The *Sunday Telegraph*, 14 January 1966 estimated that by closing its bases in Aden and Bahrein and using Diego Garcia, the British would be able to save £60m. per year.

4. *The Times*, 7 December 1965, estimates that between 150,000 and 200,000 people came to the meeting. Journalistic estimates of crowds were generally unreliable, and reflected the bias of the particular writer. The police, to avoid being accused of taking sides in the fierce competition between the Labour party and the *Parti Mauricien* for popular support, never published crowd estimates.

5. *Le Mauricien*, 6 December 1965.

6. The three electoral commissioners were Sir Harold Banwell, T. Randall, and Colin Leys. A member of the Parliamentary Boundaries Commission in Britain, Banwell knew the intricacies of elections, but Colin Leys was the only member of the commission who had experience in the developing countries and was familiar with the idiosyncratic behavior of politicians in new states.

7. *Report of the Banwell Commission on the Electoral System*, Sessional Paper No. 5 of 1966 (Port Louis, 1966), p. 1.

8. *Ibid.*, p. 6.

9. Between April 1965 and August 1967 five different people were in charge of the Colonial Office: Anthony Greenwood, Fred Lee, Lord Longford, Judith Hart, and Herbert Bowden. These frequent cabinet changes at such a crucial time in Mauritius's history confused constitutional and political developments. Nearly every decision regarding Mauritius in these months involved the secretary of state. No sooner had Mauritian politicians developed rapport with one than they had to deal with another. Promises one secretary of state made were often forgotten or overruled by another.

These changes also had considerable effect on the declining morale of Colonial Office officials, which the Mauritians sensed. The Colonial Office was being dismantled, and the jobs and future careers of its officials were in doubt.

10. Statement at a press conference by Ramgoolam, 31 August 1966; *Debates*, 7 June 1966, col. 991.

11. *Le Mauricien*, 2 June 1966.

12. *Agreement reached in Mauritius on the Future Electoral System on the Occasion of the Visit of Mr. John Stonehouse, M.P., Parliamentary Under-Secretary of State for the Colonies*. Sessional Paper No. 8 of 1966 (Port Louis, 1966).

13. *Mauritius Employers Federation Newsletter*, January 1967 (hereafter

cited as *M.E.F. Newsletter*). The estimated number of relief workers in November 1965 was 6,770 and in November 1966, 19,281. In July 1966 the relief workers formed a trade union. *L'Express*, 9 July 1966, estimated the daily cost of relief workers at Rs 125,000 to the government.

14. The commonwealth observers included Sir Colin MacGregor, Jamaica, chairman; Morris Abela, Malta; A. N. Kashyap, India; Charles Ross, Canada.

15. *Electoral Registration in Mauritius, Report of the Commonwealth Observers*. Sessional Paper No. 1 of 1967 (Port Louis, 1967).

16. *Mauritius (Constitutional) Order in Council 1966*; Legal Supplement to the Gazette, No. 28 of 20 May 1967. Regulations made by the Governor under Section 8 of the Mauritius Constitution Order in Council as amended by the Mauritius Constitution (Amendment) Order 1967.

17. *The Guardian*, 26 April 1967; *M.E.F. Newsletter*, April 1967.

18. This was disproved shortly after the elections when the United Kingdom deported nine Mauritians who were emigrating. The Queen v. Secretary of State for Home Department and others, *ex parte* Bhurosah and others, *Le Mauricien*, 18 August 1967.

19. Meeting at Vacoas, 30 July 1967.

20. Central Statistical Office, *Bi-annual Digest of Statistics*, June 1968, Table 58, p. 44.

21. This account of events in Port Louis 3 is put together from the official police reports and the author's observation. One of the cars burned belonged to a friend and assistant of Duval and when the police searched the car 2,000 rupees were found under the seat.

22. Following the allocation of the best loser seats, the Independence party had forty-three seats and the *Parti Mauricien* had twenty-seven.

23. Bissoondoyal alleged that following the election the *Parti Mauricien* offered him the post of Prime Minister if the IFB members of the Assembly voted against independence (*Debates*, 22 August 1967).

24. *M.E.F. Newsletter*, September, October 1967, reporting a press conference given by Ramgoolam, gave the total number of relief workers in October 1967 as 32,000. The program was costing the government 35 million rupees per year. By March 1968, the number of relief workers had been cut to 17,768 (*Bi-Annual Digest of Statistics*, June 1968, Table 58, p. 44).

25. Donald P. Chesworth, "Crisis in Mauritius," in *Venture*, Vol. 20, No. 3, March 1968, p. 8.

26. *The Guardian*, 23 January 1968. One hundred and thirty-eight officers and men were sent from Singapore. *The Times*, 24 January 1968.

27. *Hansard*, House of Lords Debate, 13 February 1968, pp. 10-35.

Epilogue

1. Mauritius Chamber of Agriculture, *President's Report, 1973-1974* (Port Louis, 1974), p. 10. Approximately 37 percent of the crop was sold at the world price. Most of the remainder is sold to Great Britain at a negotiated price, under the terms of the Commonwealth Sugar Agreement.

2. "L'Ile Maurice et le MMM" (Port Louis, November 1973), p. 1.

3. J. M. Paturae, "L'Ile Maurice." *Annuaire des Pays de l'Ocean Indien*, Vol. IV, 1977, p. 588 (Marseilles, 1977).

4. J. M. Boisson and M. Louit, "Les Elections Legislatives du 20 Decembre 1979 à L'Ile Maurice: L'Enjeu Economique et Politique," *Annuaire des Pays de l'Ocean Indien*, Vol. IV, 1976.

5. Christian Lovit, "L'Ile Maurice." *Annuaire des Pays de l'Océan Indien*, Vol. IV, 1977, p. 380.

6. *Government of Mauritius Two Year Plan for Social and Economic Development* (Port Louis), 1980, p. 51.

7. Drummond Shiels, "Self-Government for Advanced Colonies," *Fabian Colonial Essays* (London, 1944), p. 109.

8. Blood, *Small Territories*; Burns, *Parliament as an Export*, p. 259.

9. Braithwaite, *Social Stratification*, p. 828; Max Gluckman, *Custom and Conflict in Africa* (Oxford, 1963), Chapter 1.

REFERENCES

Primary Sources

Public Records Office (London)

Of the Colonial Office materials, I used primarily the C.O. 882 series (Confidential Prints) and the C.O. 167 series (Correspondence). In several cases dispatches had been taken from the registers to be included in the confidential prints and were never returned. The documents that have become available since January 1968 have proved particularly useful. They shed light on the Retrocession Movement of 1921, and on the Colonial Office view of their rebel colony. They also include much correspondence about Dr. Maurice Curé and the Mauritius Labour Party, covering the period up to the date of the beginning of Donald MacKenzie-Kennedy's diaries, the Creech-Jones papers, and the Fabian papers.

C.O. 167/826-897. Correspondence between the Colonial Office and the Government of Mauritius.

C.O. 537/812. Supplementary Colonial Office correspondence. Police Security Reports of 1921.

C.O. 854/78 and 97. Circular dispatches regarding the introduction of labor legislation.

C.O. 882/4. No. 39. Papers relating to a Proposed Alteration of the Council of Government in Mauritius.

C.O. 882/4. No. 40. Further papers relating to a Proposed Alteration of the Council of Government in Mauritius.

C.O. 882/5. No. 45. Correspondence relating to an Inquiry held by the Right Honorable Sir Hercules Robinson, K.C.M.G., as Royal Commissioner, into the Condition of Affairs in Mauritius.

C.O. 882/6. No. 78. Indian Representation in Mauritius: Correspondence from 9, January 1900, to 27, January 1902.

C.O. 882/11. No. 148. Correspondence relating to the Constitution of Mauritius (1924–1928).

Documents in Mauritius

Anyone who has attempted to work in African archives will wonder at the Mauritian archives. Impeccably arranged, unbelievably complete, and well preserved (they undergo annual fumigation), they represent the life work of Dr. Auguste Toussaint. Dr. Toussaint is a professional archivist and has modeled the Mauritian archives on both the Public Records Office and the British Museum.

Mauritian newspapers, several government reports, most secondary sources, and some records of official correspondence were available in the archives. Other correspondence was in the Chief Secretary's office.

Archives of the Government of Mauritius
    Correspondence between the Colonial Office and the Government of
        Mauritius, 1890–1904.
Chief Secretary's Office
    Correspondence between the Colonial Office and the Government of
        Mauritius, 1904–1917.
    File regarding the Registration of the *Société de Bienfaisance des
        Travailleurs*.
    Minutes of the Consultative Committee Meetings, 1945.
Police Commissioner's Office
    Report on the Disturbances at Trois Boutiques, 1965.
    Report on Communism in the Chinese Community in Mauritius, 1966.

Parliamentary Papers (London)

Report of the Royal Commissioners Appointed to Enquire into the Treatment of Immigrants in Mauritius, C. 1115. London, 1875.
Report of the Mauritius Royal Commission 1909, Cd. 5185; *Minutes of Evidence*, Cd. 5186. London, 1910.
Report of the Committee on Immigration from India to the Crown Colonies and Protectorates, Cd. 5192; *Minutes of Evidence*, Cd. 5193; *Documents*, Cd. 5194. London, 1910.
Visit to the West Indies and British Guiana, December 1921–February 1922, Cmd. 1679. London, 1922.
Ceylon, Report of the Social Commission on the Constitution, Cmd. 3131. London, 1928.
Report on the Mauritian Sugar Industry, Cmd. 3518. London, 1930.
Financial Situation of Mauritius: Report of a Commission Appointed by the Secretary of State for the Colonies, Cmd. 4034. London, 1932.
Labour Conditions in Ceylon, Mauritius and Malaya, Cmd. 6423. London, 1943.
West Indian Royal Commission Report, Cmd. 6607. London, 1945.

Report on British Islands in the Southern Hemisphere, Cmd. 8230. London, 1951.

Government Reports

While a number of government reports on Mauritius were of assistance in the preparation of this study, I am listing only the most useful here.

Report of the Commission of Enquiry into the Riots in Mauritius in January, 1911. Port Louis, 1911.
Report by Kunwar Maharaj Singh on his Deputation to Mauritius. Delhi, 1925.
Hooper, C. A. *Report of the Commission of Enquiry into Unrest on Sugar Estates in Mauritius*. Port Louis, 1938.
Hooper, C. A. *Report on the Enquiry into the Conduct and Affairs of the Société de Bienfaisance des Travailleurs de l'Ile Maurice*. Port Louis, 1938.
Moody, Sidney. *Report of the Commission of Enquiry into the Disturbances which Occurred in North Mauritius in 1943*. Port Louis, 1944.
Baker, Kenneth. *Trade Unionism in Mauritius*. Port Louis, 1946.
Revision of the Constitution, Correspondence with the Secretary of State, Port Louis, 1947.
Gorvin, J. *Mauritius Economic Commission*, Vols. I, II. Port Louis, 1947–48.
On Constitution Development in Mauritius. Correspondence Between the Secretary of State and the Governor. Sessional Paper No. 5 of 1951.
Correspondence with the Secretary of State for the Colonies regarding the Presidency of the Legislative Council. Sessional Paper No. 5 of 1952.
Report of the Commission on the Conduct of Local Government Elections in Mauritius. Sessional Paper No. 1 of 1956.
Report of the Mauritius Electoral Boundary Commission. Sessional Paper No. 1 of 1956.
Constitutional Development in Mauritius. Sessional Paper No. 3 of 1956.
Correspondence on Proposals for Constitutional Change. Sessional Paper No. 3 of 1957.
The Luce Report: A Time for Decision. Sessional Paper No. 8 of 1958.
Titmuss, Richard M., and Brian Abel-Smith, assisted by T. Lynes. *Social Policies and Population Growth in Mauritius*. Sessional Paper No. 6 of 1960 (London, 1961).
Meade, J. E., et al. *The Social and Economic Structure of Mauritius*. London, 1961.
Constitutional Development in Mauritius. Sessional Paper No. 5 of 1961.
Report of the Constitutional Commissioner, Professor S. A. de Smith, November 1964. Sessional Paper No. 2 of 1965.
Constitutional Development in Mauritius. Sessional Paper No. 4 of 1965.
Report of the Banwell Commission on the Electoral System with Despatch from the Secretary of State. Sessional Paper No. 5 of 1966.
Agreement Reached in Mauritius on the Future Electoral System on the Oc-

*casion of the Visit of Mr. John Stonehouse, M.P., Parliamentary Under-
Secretary of State for the Colonies.* Sessional Paper No. 8 of 1966.
Electoral Registration in Mauritius. Sessional Paper No. 1 of 1967.

MISCELLANEOUS
1961 Constitutional Conference: Confidential Papers and Minutes of Pro-
    ceedings.
1965 Constitutional Conference: Confidential Papers and Minutes of Pro-
    ceedings.

ANNUAL SERIES
Debates of the Mauritius Council of Government: 1886–1947.
Minutes of the Mauritius Council of Government: 1930–1947.
Debates of the Mauritius Legislative Council: 1948–1961.
Debates of the Mauritius Legislative Assembly: 1961–1967.
Minutes of the Port Louis Municipal Council: 1924–1960.
Reports on the Colony of Mauritius: 1925–1966.
Mauritius Reports: Decisions of the Supreme Court: 1930–1966.
Poor Law Commissioners' Report: 1930–1938.
Reports of the Labour Department: 1939–1959.
Reports of the Department of Education: 1941–1959.
Reports on District Administration: 1948–1961.
Reports of the Ministry of Labour and Social Security: 1959–1963.
Reports of the Ministry of Education: 1959–1967.
Reports of the Ministry of Local Government: 1961–1968.
Census of Mauritius and its Dependencies: 1931, 1944, 1952, 1962.
Bi-annual Digest of Statistics: June 1968.

Private Papers

Atchia Papers. Correspondence and private papers of G. M. D. Atchia. In
    the possession of M. Atchia, Port Louis, Mauritius.
Banwell Commission Papers. In the possession of Colin Leys, University of
    East Africa, Nairobi.
Bissoondoyal Papers. Assorted documents and letters of Basdeo Bissoondoyal.
    In the possession of Basdeo Bissoondoyal, Port Louis, Mauritius.
Consultative Committee: 1946–1947. Complete minutes of the meetings of
    the committee. In the possession of Kher Jagatsingh, Port Louis,
    Mauritius.
Curé Papers. Correspondence relating to the founding of the Mauritius
    Labour Party and the activities of the party until 1941. In the possession of
    Dr. Maurice Curé, Curépipe, Mauritius.
Fabian Colonial Bureau Papers. Colonial Records Project, Rhodes House,
    Oxford.
Keith-Lucas Papers. Correspondence relating to the work of the commission

appointed to investigate the 1953 municipal election. In the possession of
Professor B. Keith-Lucas, Canterbury, England.

Mackenzie-Kennedy Papers. Diaries and scattered letters of Sir Donald
Mackenzie-Kennedy, in the possession of John Mackenzie-Kennedy, Port
Louis, Mauritius.

Mauritius Labour Party Papers. Minutes of the meetings of the Mauritius
Labour Party, 1936–1950. The minutes are detailed between 1936 and
1940. After 1940 they are sketchy.

Pope-Hennessy Papers. Correspondence relating to the Governorship of John
Pope-Hennessy. In the possession of James Pope-Hennessy, London.

Ramnarain Papers. Correspondence of Harrypersad Ramnarain, and the
complete minutes of meetings and correspondence of the North and Central Rivière de Rempart Industrial Association and the Mauritius Agricultural Labourers' Association, 1940–1947. In the possession of Harrypersad
Ramnarain, Port Louis, Mauritius.

Secondary Sources

Because of communal biases, few Mauritians have been able to write about
their island with objectivity, and few non-Mauritians have published anything
about the island. Secondary sources are, for the most part, memoirs or attempts to promote one point of view or another.

An anthropologist, Burton Benedict, is the only foreign social scientist to
have spent time in Mauritius. His first book, *Indians in a Plural Society*, is
based on his findings after living in two Mauritian villages, and is a very detailed account of Indian customs. His second book, *Mauritius, A Plural Society*, is a useful introduction to the island.

The two basic reference works for any student of Mauritius are Dr. Auguste Toussaint's bibliography, *Bibliographie de l'Ile Maurice*, and the *Dictionary of Mauritian Biography*. The former is a thorough list of all published
books, journal articles, newspapers, and government documents about or
pertaining to Mauritius, accumulated by Dr. Toussaint's assistant, P.
Adolphe. The second, based on the *Dictionary of National Biography*, includes the biographies of most leading Mauritians and colonial officials who
have served in Mauritius, with emphasis on the years before 1900 and therefore on the Franco-Mauritian population.

The following bibliography includes only those sources which were of particular use for the writing of this book. It does not include incidental references.

Mauritius

Babajee, Esnoo. *Banquet en l'Honneur de la France Victorieuse*. Port Louis,
1919.

Baker, Kenneth. *Trade Unionism in Mauritius*. Port Louis: J. E. Felix, Acting
Government Printer, 1946.

Barnwell, P. J. *Visits and Dispatches (Mauritius 1598–1948)*. Port Louis:
Standard Printing Establishment, 1948.

Barnwell, P. J., and A. Toussaint. *A Short History of Mauritius*. London: Longmans, Green for the Government of Mauritius, 1949.

Beejadhur, A. *Les Indiens à l'Ile Maurice*. Port Louis, 1935.

Benedict, Burton. "Factionalism in Mauritian Villages," *British Journal of Sociology*, Vol. 8, No. 4 (Dec. 1957), 328-341.

—. *Indians in a Plural Society: A Report on Mauritius*. London: H. M. Stationery Office, 1961.

—. "Stratification in Plural Societies," *American Anthropologist*, Vol. 64, No. 6 (Dec. 1962), 1235-1246.

—. Mauritius. *Problems of a Plural Society*. London: Pall Mall Press, 1965.

Bissoondoyal, Basdeo. *L'Histoire de l'Ile Maurice*. Port Louis, 1949.

—. *The Truth about the Sugar Industry and the Workers*. Port Louis, 1954.

—. *Professor Bissoondoyal and his Mauritian Movement*. Port Louis, n.d.

Blood, Sir Hilary. "Ethnic and Cultural Pluralism in Mauritius," pages 356-362 in *Ethnic and Cultural Pluralism in Inter-tropical Countries*. Brussels: International Institute of Differing Civilizations, 1957.

Boodhun, R. K. *Indian Centenary Book*. Port Louis, 1936.

Boucherville, de A. *Pour L'Autonomie La Patrie*. Port Louis, 1914.

Britter, A. D. *A Commentary on Facts. Being a Survey of the Principal Issues Raised by the Recent Unrest on Sugar Estates in Mauritius*. Port Louis, 1937.

Cabon, Marcel. *Biographie de Ramgoolam*. Port Louis: Éditions Mauriciennes, 1963.

—. *Laurent and Rivet*. Port Louis: Éditions Mauriciennes, 1966.

Chesworth, Donald. "Statutory Wage Fixing in the Sugar Industry of Mauritius," *International Labour Review*, Vol. 96, No. 3 (Sept. 1967).

Clifford, Bede. *Pro Consul*. London: Evans Bros., 1964.

Dictionary of Mauritian Biography. Port Louis: Société de L'histoire de l'île Maurice, 1941-1966.

Emrith, Moomtaz. *Muslims in Mauritius*. [Goodlands, Mauritius]: Emrith, 1967.

Fokeer, A. F. *The Reform Movement in Mauritius*. Port Louis, 1919.

—. *The Revision Movement and the Present State of Political Affairs in Mauritius*. Rose Hill, 1927.

Jeremie, John. *Recent Events at Mauritius*. London: S. Bagster, 1835.

Jugdambi, M. S. *Trade Union Movement in Mauritius*. Port Louis, 1962.

Lamusse, Roland. "Economic Development of the Mauritius Sugar Industry," *Revue Agricole et Sucrière de l'Ile Maurice*, Nos. 43, 44 (1964-65).

Laurent, Edouard. *L'Ile Maurice entre la France et L'Angleterre*. Port Louis, 1913.

Leblanc, Marie. *Le Retour de l'Ile Maurice à la France*. Merne Louise, 1919.

Macmillan, Allister (ed.). *Mauritius Illustrated*. London: W. H. and L. Collingridge, 1914.

Mookherji, S. B. *The Indenture System in Mauritius 1837-1915*. Calcutta: Firma K. L. Mukhopadhyay, 1962.

Napal, D. *Les Constitutions de l'Ile Maurice*. Port Louis: Mauritius Print Co., 1962.

—. *Manilal Maganlall Doctor*. Port Louis: Neo Press Service, 1963.

North-Coombes, F. *Mon Champs et Mon Moulin*. Port Louis, 1950.

Pope-Hennessy, James. *Verandah*. London: Allen and Unwin, 1964.

de Plevitz, Adolphe. *The Petition of the Old Immigrants of Mauritius 6 June 1871*. London, 1871.

Riviere, Joseph. *L'Ile de France à la France*. Paris, 1920.

[Stanmore, Arthur Hamilton Gordon, 1st Baron]. *Mauritius: Records of Private and Public Life 1871–1874*. 2 vols. Edinburgh: R. and R. Clark, 1894.

Swettenham, Sir Frank. *Also and Perhaps*. London: John Lane, 1912.

Toussaint, Auguste. *Bibliography of Mauritius, 1502-1924*. Port Louis: Printed by Esclapon, 1956.

—. *History of the Indian Ocean*. Chicago: University of Chicago Press, 1966.

—. *Une Cité Tropicale, Port Louis de l'île Maurice*. Paris, 1966.

The following list of general secondary sources includes only those books relating to British colonial history, decolonization, nation building, and the problems of plural societies which I found most relevant in writing this book.

Amery, L. S. *My Political Life*, Vol. II. London: Hutchinson, 1953.

Apter, David. *The Politics of Modernization*. Chicago: University of Chicago Press, 1965.

Bell, Wendell, and Ivor Oxaal. *Decisions of Nationhood: Political and Social Development in the British Caribbean*. Denver: University of Denver, 1964.

Binder, Leonard. *Politics in Lebanon*. New York: Wiley, 1956.

Blanshard, Paul. *Democracy and Empire in the Caribbean*. New York: Macmillan, 1947.

Braithwaite, L. "Social Stratification in Trinidad," *Social and Economic Studies*, Vol. 2, No. 2 (June 1952).

Bretton, Henry L. "Political Problems of Poly-ethnic Societies in West Africa." A paper presented at the Fifth World Congress of the International Political Science Association. Paris, 1961.

Burns, Alan. *Parliament as an Export*. London: Allen and Unwin, 1966.

Christian, William. *Divided Island: Faction and Unity on Saint Pierre*. Cambridge: Harvard University Press, 1969.

Coleman, James S. *The Politics of the Developing Areas*. Princeton: Princeton University Press, 1960.

Coleman, James S., and Carl Rosberg. *Political Parties and National Integration in Tropical Africa*. Berkeley: University of California Press, 1964.

Cumpston, I. M. *Indians Overseas in British Territories, 1834-1854*. London: Oxford University Press, 1953.

Davies, Ioan. *African Trade Unions*. Middlesex, Harmondsworth: Penguin, 1966.

Deutsch, Karl, and William Foltz. *Nation Building*. New York: Atherton Press, 1966.

Dotson, Floyd, and Lillian Dotson. *The Indian Minority of Zambia, Rhodesia and Malawi*. New Haven: Yale University Press, 1968.

Emerson, Rupert. *From Empire to Nation*. Cambridge: Harvard University Press, 1960.

Enloe, Cynthia. *Ethnic Conflict and Political Development*. Boston: Little, Brown, 1973.

Farmer, B. H. *Ceylon: A Divided Nation*. London: Oxford University Press, 1963.

Furnivall, J. S. *Colonial Policy and Practice*. New York: New York University Press, 1956.

Geertz, Clifford. *Old Societies and New States*. New York: Free Press of Glencoe, 1963.

Gillion, K. L. *Fiji's Indian Immigrants*. Melbourne: Oxford University Press, 1962.

Glazer, Nathan, and Daniel P. Moynihan. *Ethnicity*. Cambridge, Mass.: Harvard University Press, 1975.

Graham, Gerald. *Great Britain in the Indian Ocean, 1810-1850*. Oxford: Clarendon Press, 1967.

Hall, Douglas. *Free Jamaica*. New Haven: Yale University Press, 1959.

Hansard Society for Parliamentary Government. *Problems of Parliamentary Government in Colonies*. London: Hansard Society, 1953.

—. African Sechon. *What are the Problems of Parliamentary Government in West Africa?* London: Hansard Society, 1958.

Harlow, Vincent, and Frederick Madden. *British Colonial Developments, 1774-1885*. Oxford: Clarendon Press, 1953.

Heussler, Robert. *Yesterday's Rulers*. Syracuse, N.Y.: Syracuse University Press, 1963.

Hinden, Rita. *Empire and After*. London: Essential Books, 1949.

— (ed.). *Fabian Colonial Essays*. London: Allen and Unwin, 1945.

— (ed.). *Local Government and the Colonies*. London: Allen and Unwin, 1950.

Huntington, Samuel. *Political Order in Changing Societies*. New Haven: Yale University Press, 1968.

Jeffries, Charles. *Partners for Progress*. London: Harrap, 1949.

—. *The Colonial Office*. London: Allen and Unwin, 1956.

—. *Transfer of Power*. London: Pall Mall Press, 1960.

—. *Ceylon, Path to Independence*. London: Pall Mall Press, 1962.

Jennings, Sir W. Ivor. *The Approach to Self-Government*. Cambridge: Cambridge University Press, 1956.

Jones, Arthur C. *New Fabian Colonial Essays*. London: Hogarth Press, 1959.

Klass, Morton. *East Indians in Trinidad*. New York: Columbia University Press, 1961.

Kondapi, C. *Indians Overseas, 1838-1949*. New Delhi: Indian Council of World Affairs, 1951.

Kuper, Leo, and M. G. Smith. *Pluralism in Africa*. Berkeley: University of California Press, 1969.

Lee, J. M. *Colonial Development and Good Government*. Oxford: Clarendon Press, 1967.

Lofchie, Michael. *Zanzibar, Background to Revolution*. Princeton: Princeton University Press, 1965.

Lyttelton, Oliver. *The Memoirs of Lord Chandos*. London: Bodley Head, 1962.

McKenzie, H. I. "The Plural Society Debate: Some Comments on a Recent Contribution," *Social and Economic Studies*, Vol. 15, No. 1 (March 1966), 53-60.

Mackenzie, W. J. M. *Free Elections*. London: Allen and Unwin, 1957.

Mayer, Adrian. *Indians in Fiji*. London: Oxford University Press, 1963.

Morris, H. S. "Indians in East Africa: A Study in a Plural Society," *British Journal of Sociology*, Vol. 7, No. 3 (Oct. 1956), 194-211.

—. *The Indians in Uganda*. Chicago: University of Chicago Press, 1968.

Parkinson, Cosmo. *The Colonial Office from Within*. London: Faber and Faber, 1947.

Perham, Margery. *Colonial Reckoning*. London: Collins, 1963.

Porter, Arthur. *Creoledom*. London: Oxford University Press, 1963.

Purcell, H. D. *Cyprus*. London: Benn, 1969.

Pye, Lucien. *Aspects of Political Development*. Boston: Little, Brown, 1966.

Pye, Lucien, and Sidney Verba (eds.). *Political Culture and Political Development*. Princeton: Princeton University Press, 1965.

Rabushka, Alvin, and Kenneth Shepsle. *Politics in Plural Societies: A Theory of Democratic Instability*. Columbus, Ohio: Merrill, 1972.

Roberts, B. C. *Labour in the Tropical Territories of the Commonwealth*. Durham, N.C.: Duke University Press, 1964.

Rubin, Vera (ed.). *Social and Cultural Pluralism in the Caribbean*. Annals of the New York Academy of Sciences, Vol. 83 (Jan. 1960), 761-916.

— (ed.). "Culture, Politics and Race Relations," *Social and Economic Studies*, Vol. 11, No. 4 (Dec. 1962) 433-453.

Rudolph, Lloyd, and Suzanne Rudolph. *The Modernity of Tradition*. Chicago: University of Chicago Press, 1967.

Shils, Edward. *Political Development in the New States*. The Hague: Mouton, 1965.

Smith, M. G. *The Plural Society in the British West Indies*. Berkeley: University of California Press, 1965.

Smith, Raymond T. *British Guiana*. London: Oxford University Press, 1962.

Smith, T. E. *Elections in Developing Countries*. London: Macmillan, 1960.

Spackman, Ann. "Constitutional Development in Trinidad and Tobago," *Social and Economic Studies*, Vol. 14, No. 4 (Dec. 1965).

Tinker, Hugh. *A New System of Slavery*. London: Oxford University Press, 1974.

Verba, Sidney. *The Civic Culture: Political Attitudes and Democracy in Five Nations*. Boston: Little, Brown, 1965.

Weiner, Myron. *Party Politics in India*. Princeton: Princeton University Press, 1967.

Wight, Martin. *Development of the Legislative Council, 1606-1945*. London: Faber and Faber, 1946.

—. *British Colonial Constitutions*. Oxford: Clarendon Press, 1952.

Wiseman, H. V. *The Cabinet in the Commonwealth*. London: Stevens, 1958.

Wraith, Ronald, and Edgar Simpkins. *Corruption in Developing Countries*. London: Allen and Unwin, 1963.

Wriggins, W. Howard. *Ceylon, Dilemmas of a New Nation*. Princeton: Princeton University Press, 1960.

INDEX